ROUGH

ROUGH

*How violence has found its way
into the bedroom and what we
can do about it*

Rachel Thompson

◨ SQUARE PEG

1 3 5 7 9 10 8 6 4 2

Square Peg, an imprint of Vintage, is part of the
Penguin Random House group of companies whose addresses
can be found at global.penguinrandomhouse.com

Penguin
Random House
UK

First published by Square Peg in 2021
penguin.co.uk/vintage

A CIP catalogue record for this book is available from
the British Library

Trade Paperback ISBN 9781529110388

Typeset in 11.25/16.5 pt Epic
by Integra Software Services Pvt. Ltd, Pondicherry

Printed and bound in Great Britain by Clays Ltd, Elcograf S.p.A.

The authorised representative in the EEA is Penguin Random House
Ireland, Morrison Chambers, 32 Nassau Street, Dublin D02 YH68

Penguin Random House is committed to a sustainable future for
our business, our readers and our planet. This book is made from
Forest Stewardship Council® certified paper.

MIX
Paper from
responsible sources
FSC
www.fsc.org   FSC® C018179

For Annie and Elspeth, my grandmothers.
For Nancy, my mother.

Contents

Trigger warning

Dear reader – before we begin, I want to let you know this book explores sexual violence in detail and features first-hand accounts of violations, including rape and sexual assault. The book examines how systems of oppression manifest in our sexual culture and discusses racism, ableism, anti-fatness, transphobia, biphobia, homophobia and misogyny, which might be triggering for some readers. If, at any point, this book is triggering or upsetting, feel free to stop reading, take a break or skip a chapter – look after yourself.

Introduction

was 19 years old when it happened. It was my first year of university and the sum total of my limited sexual experience was a few intoxicated fumbles with men who didn't reply to my texts afterwards. I could count the number of times I'd had sex on one hand and I felt my inexperience keenly. I saw it as a deficit I needed to fill urgently, doing my utmost to hide that void from my peers, who all had an assured air of knowing exactly what they were doing. Or so I thought. Freshers week was my opportunity for reinvention, a chance to shake off the mantle of epithets that had defined my reputation in adolescence.

'Frigid' was the word that had followed me since age 12, when my school friend invited me to a sleepover at her house and proceeded to invite two much older boys over. As my friend took one of the boys upstairs to her bedroom,

I stayed downstairs with the boy who'd been designated as mine. I remember going into my friend's parents' kitchen in search of some orange squash, and the boy following me into the cupboard and grabbing my arse. 'You're a pervert,' I told him. 'Get off me.' He tried it again later on, groping me as I attempted to go upstairs to see if my friend was OK.

After the boys left, my friend asked me why I hadn't done anything with the boy I'd been left downstairs with. 'Because I didn't want to. Plus I don't fancy him,' I said. 'Doesn't matter. You should have done it,' she told me definitively. The next day my friend broke down and cried because she was worried she was pregnant after what had happened. She was the same age as me.

So here I was in my first year of uni, desperate to get rid of the reputation of inexperience that had followed me around my entire youth thus far. It was time to be a real young person, to do the things everyone else my age was doing. Because I didn't want to look back in my old age and think, 'Why didn't I have more sex?'

That's when I met Daniel. He was everything I was not: privately educated, obscenely wealthy, popular and cool. Daniel and I met on a night out with a bunch of friends. A nightclub in my university town was having a beach night, so I donned a bikini and a sarong. I was too drunk to stand for some of that evening, and I lost my keys after falling over into a bush and never found them again. There are huge swathes of the night that I cannot remember.

I woke up in Daniel's bed. From the moment I opened my eyes I knew something wasn't quite right. I hadn't taken my epilepsy medication the night before and now I was paying the price. My arms were twitching uncontrollably. My breath kept catching with every shock-like jerk. To the untrained ear it would have sounded like a dose of the hiccups. But I knew exactly what was coming.

I tried to go back to sleep in an attempt to ward off the impending loss of consciousness. I told him I wasn't feeling well. 'Let's go have sex in the shower,' he said to me. I didn't know how to tell him that if I stood up, I'd fall to the ground within minutes. But I did it anyway.

'I'll meet you in there,' he said, before bounding naked into the bathroom. In that moment, I betrayed my body and followed him willingly. The next thing I remember is waking up surrounded by paramedics and concerned faces. I'd had a seizure on the floor.

What stands out to me now is the distinct feeling of humiliation I felt as I sat in a bikini while the male paramedic told me, 'You can put some clothes on now.'

I asked Daniel to walk me back to my room because I couldn't remember where I lived. My 19-year-old self interpreted his actions in that moment as vaguely heroic. Perhaps because I hadn't yet known kindness from a man not related to me by blood. I went back to my room and slept all day, and when I woke up I texted Daniel. He replied one week later, asking 'you still awake?' at 2 a.m. 'Sorry, I was asleep. How's it going? X' I wrote the next morning. He texted me a week later, at around 10 p.m. this time. I was awake and, deciding I would like to see Daniel, I responded.

'Is your roommate home?' read his next message. I said that she was and he told me to come outside and meet him at the bottom of the drive outside my halls of residence. When I came face-to-face with him, we didn't kiss or hug or greet each other in any particular way. I recall looking at his eyes, which had a vacant look about them, but when he spoke he was lucid.

'Let's go explore the woods,' he said, grabbing my hand. We walked into the wooded area at the bottom of the lawn, where he told me to lie down on a mound of moss. We kissed and took off our clothes. That's when he got on top of me and did something I hadn't been expecting. In my inexperience, I had no clue that what he was doing wasn't just a 'normal' part of sex.

Daniel shifted his body up from his horizontal position so that he was sitting on my chest, his legs straddling me. Quickly, I realised I couldn't breathe.

I didn't say anything, I just froze.

There were multiple reasons I said nothing. 'Perhaps this is normal and I'm being weird,' I thought to myself. 'You're reacting this way because you have zero experience with blowjobs and you're probably just doing it wrong,' was another thing I convinced myself. 'It'll be over soon.'

I was silent, rigid, focused on trying to breathe. I couldn't expand my lungs fully because of his weight bearing down on me. All I could manage were tiny, shallow breaths. Panic seized my whole body. 'It'll be over soon,' I told myself.

Mercifully, it did end.

I breathed in air like someone who'd been underwater for too long.

He finished himself off and ejaculated on my chest without saying another word to me. We parted ways. When I got back to my room, I grabbed my toiletries and got in the shower. Inside its safe harbour, I turned the heat right up until my skin turned a shade of pink my grandmother would have called puce. I scrubbed my scalded skin with soap until it was painful to the touch.

It was over.

What stuck with me was the visceral fear I'd felt when I was lying underneath Daniel. For the first time in my existence, I'd had a genuine fear that I might die. That I might be starved of oxygen if I continued not breathing. I'd never felt my chest compressed in that way before. I didn't cry or scream or dig my nails into his flesh like I wished I had afterwards. I didn't even say, 'Hey, can we stop for a sec.' I just . . . lay there?

I couldn't shake the feeling that I'd got something that I hadn't signed up for. In my limited understanding of consent at the time, I characterised the encounter as consensual. I had consented to sex, but what had come next wasn't quite what I'd had in mind.

The next day, my roommate turned over in her bed and asked me how it had gone the night before. 'So fun,' I said to her without missing a beat. 'He's so good in bed,' I added, to make sure the narrative was believable.

'Do you think you'll see him again?' she asked me.

'I hope so,' I replied. The trouble is, I really meant it.

My experience was clouded by the fact that I really liked Daniel. Because he'd seen me have a seizure, because he'd walked me back to my halls of residence afterwards when my memory was still too foggy to recall where I actually lived, I thought he was a nice guy. I now try to look back on my past self with compassion, because I know that I was deeply inexperienced, living away from home for the first time in my life. I had never dated anyone, had never had a boyfriend at that point, and had only had sex three times before meeting Daniel. My experience was limited and my concept of what defined a 'good' experience was not fully formed.

I passed Daniel a few days later on the hill outside campus, and he looked at the ground to avoid my eye. I'd bump into him outside lecture halls and in nightclubs in town, and sometimes, depending on what mood he was in, he'd acknowledge my existence. My crush on him lived on for several torturous weeks, and I longed for another encounter with him.

This was not an isolated situation. Throughout my university years, I would bump into the men I'd slept with on campus; and each time, without fail, they'd look down at their phones or at the ground to pretend they hadn't seen me. I would always stare hard into their faces, jaw tightening with rage that I'd ever condescended to sleep with them to begin with. This was long before the word 'ghosting' had been coined. But ghosting was the order of the day at university. Ghosting was the punctuation mark at the end of each sexual sentence.

From then on, I pushed the memory of the night in the woods to the furthest reaches of my mind. It was as if I'd shoved it into an unused drawer, locked it and thrown away the key. It worked for a while, and I did not reopen that drawer for a decade. For years, I forgot that feeling of violation. The sense that the sanctity of my body had been desecrated.

When I was 29, the world changed. We began reflecting on our own personal pasts, the violations eked out on our bodies and minds. We tweeted them alongside two words: 'me too'. We talked about them, sometimes for the first time, with friends. We wrote down what we had endured. We tried to find the language to describe things that had happened to us that we'd never spoken about before.

When I was 19, I didn't see my experience as anything out of the ordinary. No words sprang to mind in the aftermath of the experience – I simply had no vocabulary to express it.

When I finally allowed myself to remember that night in the woods ten years after it happened, I struggled to find the words to characterise what had taken place. I had gone willingly into those woods, I had enthusiastically consented to having sex with Daniel, but he had done something that made me feel afraid. Scared for my own life.

Fear defined my early sexual experiences. During one encounter in my final year of university, this very same heart-pounding fear crept in when I withdrew consent and, in doing so, invoked the wrath of my partner.

'Yeah, you want this,' he'd yelled at me like an accusation. I looked up at him and I realised that I did not want this. His kiss felt unwanted, his tongue an invasion in my mouth. I didn't want him to touch me anywhere on my body. I wanted him to get off me. This had been a mistake of epic proportions. 'Is it good for you?' he asked with a smile.

'Actually . . . no,' I muttered hesitantly. 'I want to stop.' There was a brief silence, during which this man processed the words I'd uttered aloud.

His face twisted into an angry knot. 'What?' he spat through gritted teeth. 'What do you mean?'

'I'm sorry, I would like to stop,' I said.

He made a loud huffing sound to passive-aggressively convey his irritation. My withdrawal of consent was an insult to his fragile ego. I sat upright and pulled the covers around me to protect myself.

'I'm sorry,' I said to him, and straight away I wondered why I was even apologising. I'd changed my mind. I'm allowed to change my mind. We're allowed to change our minds.

I was quiet. I was trying to figure out if I'd done something really bad. I didn't – still don't – think I did. I wanted to stop, so we stopped. But he was angry. Really angry, actually. Acting as if I'd taken something that was his.

'You fucking bitch,' he snapped as he grabbed his wallet off the floor and put it in his jeans pocket.

'OK, time to go!' I said. I got up and threw my dressing gown around me, tying the cord around my middle as I rushed out of my room. My housemate Fran was standing in the hallway, alarmed.

'What the hell is going on?' she said.

'He's leaving,' I said.

She followed me down the stairs and I unlocked the front door. I stood to the side and gestured my arm towards the night air as if to say, 'Go forth, be gone.' He hovered for a moment, like he was formulating a thought.

'You're fucking fat, by the way,' were his parting words.

He stood in the driveway of our 1980s semi-detached and stared at us. His jaw tensed. He looked, for a split second, like he was thinking about coming back in. He began yelling incomprehensible things on the gravel outside the house.

I slammed the front door shut and locked it in a frenzied panic. I didn't want him to get back inside. My hands were shaking so much I permanently bent the door key out of shape. It never worked again.

When I went upstairs to my bedroom, a deep unease bubbled up inside me. My room no longer felt like it belonged to me. It had been sullied and besmirched. I asked Fran if I could sleep in her bed that night.

If you'd asked me in my twenties if I'd experienced sexual violence, I would have given you an unequivocal 'no'. I might have conceded that I'd had 'some bad sex' in my time. I might even have gone so far as to call them 'bad sexual experiences' or 'just a weird night'.

There is a very specific type of loneliness that comes with not being able to speak about these things. I didn't know that the women in my life were silently dealing with the very same thing.

But now that I've allowed myself the chance to sit with that experience a little, to mull it over, I'd call it sexual violence. When I described that night in the woods to my therapist, she told me, 'That's trauma.' As a 32-year-old woman, I ask myself the question 'Was that sexual assault?'

While writing this book, that moment of being unable to breathe kept coming back to me. It was as if I was being visited by my 19-year-old self and she was urging me to keep going.

She is the reason I wrote this book. But I wrote it for every woman, every femme, every non-binary person who's ever experienced something they didn't have the words to define. For those who've experienced something they'd rather forget. Who felt that what happened to them didn't match up to what they consented to. Who felt their experience was a 'grey area' or 'just bad sex' or 'not rape, but . . .' Who were harmed, but didn't believe they had the right to feel that way.

CHAPTER 1

What's in a name?

t's only in recent years that I've found words that aptly describe my early sexual experiences. Giving language to those moments has imbued them with a validity that underscores the fear and panic I felt. For a long time, I'd allude to 'bad sex' or 'not-so-great encounters' without proffering any more details, but in a way that hinted at something I couldn't quite bring myself to verbalise. This code was understood by the women in my life without the need for further probing – they understood it because they'd lived a similar reality.

I couldn't find the words because I didn't know any. In my teens and twenties, I pictured rape and sexual assault as the violent act of a faceless stranger in the dead of night, not something that could be perpetrated by someone I liked, let alone loved. I only came to understand my own experiences in retrospect, many years after they happened. Some of those events had been buried deep down inside. In 2017, around the emergence of the #MeToo movement – which was founded by Tarana Burke in 2006 – I began reading strangers' accounts of sexual violence and sensed glimmers of recognition at their words.

It was around this time that we began to talk more and more about the term 'grey areas' to describe nebulous experiences that don't necessarily fit traditional definitions of sexual assault and rape. As a society, we often talk about sexual violence as a binary – it's either rape or consensual sex. That dichotomy might benefit you if you're coming at it from the perspective of someone who's perpetrated a violation that sits outside the binary and so will evade consequences. But does this binary serve people who've experienced something that made them feel harmed?

When it comes to describing sexual violence, words really matter. Lena Gunnarsson, an academic specialising in gender studies, sexual consent and sexual violence at Örebro University in Sweden, believes that language is very important when tackling these experiences. 'In my forthcoming book, *Dynamics of Sexual Consent: Sex, Rape and the Grey Area In-Between*, I argue for the need for an intensified collective reflection on sex and consent, a reflection that allows room for ambiguity, grey areas and complexity,' she says. 'When we are asked to place all of our experiences in either the violence or the sex category, many experiences will at best be simplified and at worst not at all intelligible and heard.'

Within conversations about sexual violence, there is a great deal of disagreement over terminology. That is because too often language has been used to sanitise and minimise sexual violence, with terms like 'forced sex' or 'underage sex'. Just like sexual harassment and predation has been batted away and dismissed as 'boys will be boys' and 'he's just a ladies' man' and 'he's a skirt-chaser', downplaying violations through ambiguous, woolly language feeds into a culture of permissibility. When we sanitise sexual violence, we are saying 'it's OK, it's normal' instead of 'that was an unacceptable violation'.

An analysis of media reporting on sexual violence by Australian academics Sophie Hindes and Dr Bianca Fileborn looked at the terminology used by media outlets when reporting on the Aziz Ansari sexual misconduct allegations.[1] They found that publications positioned the allegations as 'non-violence' by using colloquial and ambiguous words 'that consistently downplayed and minimised the nature of the encounter as something other than sexual violence'.

This use of nebulous wording not only paints a false picture of the seriousness of a violation; it can have very real consequences for survivors of sexual violence. 'When language is used that minimises an act it can have significant impacts including people not taking victim/survivors seriously, certain behaviours being excused as "not a big deal", and consequently people may find sexual consent difficult to navigate in practice as non-consensual behaviours become minimised and normalised through language,' says Hindes, a doctoral candidate at the University of Melbourne whose research focuses on sexual consent in queer relationships.[2]

So, what is the justification for using minimising language in reporting? Following the publication of sexual abuse allegations against Harvey Weinstein, the *New York Times* received concerned emails and letters from readers about the language it used to describe sexual assault. In a letter to the editor, *New York Times* reader Diane Tider-Johansson criticised the use of the term 'non-consensual sex' in the newspaper's reporting. '"Nonconsensual sex" is the language of the accused, used to hijack the conversation and sugarcoat allegations of sexual assault,' she wrote. 'Bill O'Reilly, Harvey Weinstein, Roy Price, and others have all recently denied allegations of "nonconsensual sex" in this paper . . . It's time to stop allowing the perpetrators to frame the dialogue. Words matter, choose them wisely.'[3]

The *New York Times* defended its use of 'nonconsensual sex', but investigative editor Rebecca Corbett – who's been credited as the third woman to break the Weinstein story, alongside Jodi Kantor and Megan Twohey[4] – conceded that in hindsight 'rape' would have been a more accurate term to use. 'The easiest way to report claims of sexual harassment or assault without incurring legal liability is to cite the language contained in legal documents, such as complaints or police reports,' responded the *New York Times*' First Amendment Fellow, Christina Koningisor. In the absence of any such documents, Koningisor said, reporters aim to describe events as accurately as possible. 'This often

requires relying on information provided to us by those
involved in the incident or those who have some knowledge
of it. Using an evocative phrase or term to describe certain
behavior may make for more interesting reading, but it may
also suggest more than we know.'

The vast majority of sexual violence does not make headlines, and the overwhelming majority of survivors do not go
to the authorities to report what has happened. Legal language might best serve a newspaper that's trying to ensure
it doesn't get sued, but what about survivors who don't see
their experiences through the prism of the law and who
won't see themselves reflected in newspapers and magazines? What about survivors who aren't quite sure if what
happened to them counts as sexual assault or rape? And
what about those experiences that the law doesn't recognise as sexual violence?

If we isolate survivors and their experiences from cultural and legal ideas about sexual violence, how can language best serve their interests and the ways in which they
process trauma and grow to understand the reality of what's
happened to them? How do we characterise those experiences which don't neatly fit into definitions of 'assault' and
'rape'? How do we make room for ambiguity without feed-
ing into a culture that doesn't hold perpetrators to account?
And what about when a survivor characterises their experience as nebulous when it meets the definition of an assault
or rape?

This raises the question of who should be in charge of
choosing how to define experiences that fall anywhere on

the spectrum of sexual violence. Laina Bay-Cheng, professor of social work at the University at Buffalo School of Social Work, urges caution when it comes to foisting descriptors on other people's experiences. 'I think that we have to be really careful to be able to critique and interrogate circumstances without imposing words and definitions of a woman's experience on her experience. I think it's really important that women do get to call and say what they want about their experiences and that those things can change.'

The problem lies in that construction of a binary in defining our lived experiences. It's either rape or consensual, you're either consenting or a victim. Bay-Cheng believes these misconceptions are a problem. 'They're also temporal binaries. So there's this idea that you consent once and then anything that happens after that moment is fair game. And of course, that's not what any human interaction is like.'

This consensual versus non-consensual dichotomy is often weaponised in media discussions of high-profile sexual assault allegations. If a woman says she feels harmed after a sexual experience, we rush to ascertain 'was it consensual?' If she answers 'yes', the tendency is to close down those conversations, as if she doesn't have the right to feel violated. 'Yeah, but she consented, didn't she?' 'Didn't say no, though, did she?' 'Didn't get up and leave, did she?' Is the bar for sex so low that all we require is for it to be consensual? Consent is mandatory, but let's not forget, it's also the bare minimum. Time and time again I return to Rebecca Traister's 2015 essay on why consensual sex can still be bad, and I am always struck by the following line, a quote from Feministing editor Maya Dusenbery: 'Seriously, God help us if the best we can say about the sex we have is that it was consensual.'[5] Is consent the only metric when it comes to sex? What if that's the only thing you can say about it? What if you're not certain you can even call it consensual?

Societal preoccupations with the possible professional consequences of being falsely accused of rape mean we shut down conversations about sexual violence when we hear the word 'consensual'. It gives people permission not to care. In reality, men are actually more likely to be raped than be falsely accused of rape.[6] Only 4 per cent of reports of sexual violence reported to UK police are found or suspected to be false, according to Home Office research.[7] This prioritisation of perpetrators' careers comes at the expense of survivors, who exist in a culture where speaking up about sexual violence will undoubtedly be met with victim blaming, expressions of doubts, and attempts to undermine, invalidate and minimise their pain and trauma.

'We also create these binaries between sex and not sex,' says Bay-Cheng, 'as though these rules and ethics that dictate human relationships and human interactions on one side of the line somehow don't apply.' Just think of how you arrange plans when talking to a friend – there are negotiations of consent in our everyday conversations. 'Are you OK to come to mine before we head out?' 'What film do you want to watch?' 'Do you want to go out for dinner or get a takeaway?' 'What type of food do you want to eat?'

'Are you hungry now or do you want to wait?' 'Do you want a drink?' 'Do you want to try some of mine?' 'Can I taste yours?' But when it comes to sex, we consider consent complicated and unnatural.

The language we use to discuss consensual sex also conveys a hierarchy of sexual acts and feeds into the myth that some forms of sex are more valid than others. Take the term 'foreplay'; in the context of heterosexual sex, the word suggests that oral sex, fingering and hand jobs are mere appetisers to the main course – penis-in-vagina sex (PIV). But for people with vulvas, these sex acts are typically the ones that bring them the most sexual pleasure – not PIV. The word is also deeply heteronormative. By suggesting that oral sex, manual stimulation, mutual masturbation and other sex acts are mere warm-up acts – and not main-event sex – we invalidate LGBTQ people's sexual experiences and suggest that PIV sex is the most legitimate form of sex. This hierarchises sex acts, presenting certain sex acts as more acceptable forms of sex, and others as lesser versions. Another danger of this hierarchy lies in its ability to instil the belief that only certain acts require consent because they are more legitimate forms of sex.[8]

If you regard something as a lesser version of sex, do you understand that it requires consent? Then again, if you only believe that consent is required in sexual scenarios, how do you behave towards friends, colleagues and family members in everyday life? How is that different? After all, consent isn't just something we navigate in our sex lives. 'All the time, we are engaging in consensual interactions, and constantly checking in with each other. But somehow, when it comes to sex, we act as though those rules don't apply,' Bay-Cheng notes. 'That it's a special case, when, of course, it's not. So I think like this: these categories and these binaries, they always get us into trouble – and really, it gets women into trouble.'

In this book, I want to hold space for the ambiguous, for the interactions and experiences that feel nebulous, that are difficult to define, that you haven't quite found the right words for just yet. We'll explore the reasons why sometimes it's hard to categorise an experience and why we might struggle to do so. I believe only we have the power to describe what happens to us. We are the ones who decide what words best fit our lived experience.

So, how do you discuss the ambiguous without invalidating those experiences through poor or clumsy word choice? One term in current parlance is the 'grey area' or 'grey area experiences'. This is far from a perfect descriptor. Dr Fiona Vera-Gray – an assistant professor at Durham University specialising in violence against women and girls – tells me she's not sure the term 'grey area' is a helpful one. 'It feeds into that narrative of women being taught to doubt how something feels,' she says. 'Sexual experiences that are uncomfortable, painful or violating are just that. There's not a grey area there – they feel wrong.'

She adds: 'They may not fit a legal definition of sexual assault, but the law is just one way of establishing the norms of a society. It's not really the thing we should be using as the only arbitrator of what is or isn't acceptable. We need to encourage women, encourage ourselves, to believe our experience of a situation is valid, even when it is not legitimated by law.'

In 1987, feminist academic Liz Kelly published her 'Continuum of Sexual Violence', which put forth the idea that women's experience of sexual harm could not be restricted to that which falls within the legal definitions of sexual crimes.[9] In Kelly's research, she found that women experienced 'many unwanted sexual acts within what could be considered to be "consensual" relationships (e.g., marriage or long-established intimate relationships)'.[10]

Rejecting a hierarchisation of harms is crucial if we are to understand the grey area. No one story will be pitted as worse than, or more valid than, another. A lot of people favour absolute, rigid definitions of what constitutes sexual violence. But who benefits from such binary concepts? Kelly argues in *Surviving Sexual Violence* that men, both on an individual and a group level, 'benefit from limited definitions of sexual violence which function to distinguish a small group of "deviant" men from the "normal" majority'.[11]

What the law says

Deferring to legal language when discussing sexual assault is an imperfect and problematic strategy. That's because the language used in law does not account for the full scope of sexual violence – and, in the UK, it only defines rape as something carried out by men. Not only that, the laws in this country are not currently keeping pace with sexual violence and the evolving ways in which it is perpetrated.

In England and Wales, the Sexual Offences Act 2003 defines rape as something that occurs when a man penetrates the vagina, anus, or mouth of another person with his penis without consent:[12]

Rape
(1) A person (A) commits an offence if—
    (a) he intentionally penetrates the vagina, anus or mouth of another person (B) with his penis,
    (b) B does not consent to the penetration, and
    (c) A does not reasonably believe that B consents.
(2) Whether a belief is reasonable is to be determined having regard to all the circumstances, including any steps A has taken to ascertain whether B consents.
(3) Sections 75 and 76 apply to an offence under this section.
(4) A person guilty of an offence under this section is liable, on conviction on indictment, to imprisonment for life.

Layla, the anonymous sex educator and social worker behind the Instagram account @lalalaletmeexplain, doesn't think 'grey area' is a bad term, but with the caveat that we're not quite where we need to be in terms of language. Layla believes the difficulties we have with language comes from our laws on sexual assault and rape, which are not progressive.

'The terms around rape, or rather the law around rape, are non-progressive because it has to be a penis to be called rape,' she says. 'Basically the term "rape" is slightly non-inclusive at the moment because it talks about men and women rather than having any room for any other genders or non-binary people.'

While a penis has to be involved in order for the law to consider it rape, a woman can be guilty of rape if she assists someone in holding down the victim. 'I think it's section two and section six of the case, criminal act,' says Layla. 'She can still get as high a sentence as rape. So it's not like she can only be done for sexual assault. She can be done for, I think, GBH, and a woman can still receive the same sentence basically.'

Assault by penetration is another form of sexual offence. This occurs when the perpetrator penetrates a person's vagina or anus, but not their mouth, using something other than a penis. This happens with intention, and without the consent of the victim. Objects include a finger, a sex toy, a tongue or any other item. A person of any gender can be the perpetrator of this offence, and the victim can also be of any gender.[13]

Causing someone to engage in sexual activity is also classed as a sexual offence. This happens when a perpetrator of any gender makes the victim (also of any gender) touch themselves sexually without consent. This sexual touching includes masturbating as well as using a vibrator.[14]

Sexual assault is legally defined in England and Wales as sexual touching that is non-consensual and intentional.

The perpetrator and victim can be of any gender. But what exactly constitutes 'sexual touching'? Per Rights of Women, a women's charity working in a number of ways to help women navigate the law, the legislation says touching is sexual in two contexts. The first is when the touching is 'sexual by its very nature; this is likely to be only where a penis has entered a person's vagina, anus or mouth, or a vibrator is used'. The second context is when the touching could be sexual but 'it depends on where and how it happens, what the perpetrator thinks, what the victim thinks and what a reasonable person looking at the touching would think'.[15]

In the UK, legal definitions of sexual assault and consent differ in Scotland, Northern Ireland, and England and Wales. This means that there are technically three different legal definitions of consent in the UK, depending on which country you live in. In England and Wales, the Sexual Offences Act 2003 stipulates that consent takes place when that person 'agrees by choice, and has the freedom and capacity to make that choice'. In Northern Ireland, consent is characterised by a person having the capacity to make a choice.[16]

In Scotland, the Sexual Offences Act 2009 gave new wording to how consent is defined. According to the Law Society of Scotland, 'Consent means free agreement provided the person is not incapable due to drink or drugs. A person has not consented if violence is used, or threats of violence, or they are being unlawfully detained. Consent cannot be given when the person is incapable, while asleep or unconscious. Consent to some sexual conduct does not imply consent to other conduct, and consent may be withdrawn.'[17] This withdrawal of consent, the law stipulates, can occur at any point before or during the conduct.

What's really refreshing about the Scottish law is that it makes clear the circumstances under which consent cannot be given, including being incapable of giving consent because 'of the effect of alcohol or any other substance'. It also includes specific reference to instances where person A consents to sexual conduct because person B is impersonating a person known to A.[18] And it stipulates that it is impossible to consent to sexual activity when a person is asleep: 'A person is incapable, while asleep or unconscious, of consenting to any conduct.'[19] Reading through the legislation, I was struck by the following line: 'Consent to conduct does not of itself imply consent to any other conduct.'[20]

In order to examine the root cause of the misconceptions our society holds about sexual violence, we should acknowledge that many people in this country look to the law as a moral barometer. This impact is referred to as the law's 'expressive value', according to Clare McGlynn, professor of law at Durham University and an expert in violence against women. 'The law plays a really significant role in setting out what society's views are,' she says. 'We would talk about it in terms of the kind of expressive value of the law. It says "this is wrong" at one basic level.'

McGlynn uses the example of cyberflashing, which is not yet criminalised under English and Welsh law. The Law Commission – the body tasked with reviewing the law in certain areas and coming up with proposals – has published proposals recommending cyberflashing be included as a sexual offence under the Sexual Offences Act 2003. 'I would make an argument to criminalise cyberflashing because it sends this clear message, but is that going to stop cyberflashing? No, of course it's not. It's just a first, but it's an important first step,' she says. When it comes to digital sexual violations, the law is not keeping pace.

McGlynn argues that significant changes need to be made to English law to adequately cover the gaps. We'll be exploring this in more detail in chapter 14.

What's clear from recent campaigns such as activist Gina Martin's fight to make upskirting illegal, or journalist Sophie Gallagher's campaign to make cyberflashing illegal, is that it often takes a while for our laws to catch up to what's happening in society. Therefore, I do not believe we can rely on the law to provide clarity when we define what does and does not constitute sexual violence.

Reading through the myriad legal definitions of sexual offences and what legally constitutes consent, you'd be forgiven for being a little bit confused. This is because our culture puts a higher price on the consequences of being accused of sexual violence than it does on the aftermath of surviving sexual violence. Placing our faith in definitions constructed by the justice system is also highly problematic, particularly for people from marginalised communities who have experienced systemic abuse and discrimination at the hands of this system.[21] With the rise of abolitionism, carceral feminism – which relies on policing, prosecution and imprisonment as a solution to sexual violence – is becoming increasingly questioned.[22] For some people in this country, changes to the law can bring about a paradigm shift in attitudes towards sexual violence. But for many, placing trust and faith in an institution that routinely fails survivors of sexual violence, and disproportionately targets Black people, is not an option.[23] Sex workers say they've held back from reporting abusive clients to the police because they're worried about getting arrested themselves.[24] Our solutions to tackle sexual violence must look beyond the law, and instead focus on societal change.

It's pretty commonly accepted that the criminal justice system is failing sexual violence survivors: 99 per cent of rapes reported to police in England and Wales in the year ending March 2020 ended in no legal proceedings.[25] But despite the inaction from the criminal justice system, sexual violence is hugely prevalent. In the UK, one in five women will experience sexual assault during her lifetime.[26] And 3.4 million women in England and Wales have experienced some form of sexual assault since they were 16, according to the Crime Survey for England and Wales.[27] Of the victims, 83 per cent did not report their assault to the police.[28] Meanwhile 631,000 men have experienced sexual assault. Only around 15 per cent of people who experience sexual violence report it to the police, according to a Ministry of Justice report.[29]

But those figures tell us just one part of the story. What they don't account for are the unacknowledged rapes and sexual assaults. They don't account for sexual violence that isn't defined by the survivor as assault or rape or all the experiences that feel nebulous.

A few notes on my use of language in the book

When I refer to 'women', that definition of course includes trans women. In an ideal world, this should go without saying, but all too often conversations about sexual violence erase and exclude the experiences of trans people, who experience the highest rates of sexual violence.

Names of interviewees have been changed throughout this book. Additionally, I have not imposed definitions onto interviewees' experiences and have tried to keep the language as close to the terminology used when they were described to me. That is a deliberate choice, because I believe it's important to honour the words people use when describing sexual violence and more nebulous sexual experiences. As we grow, and as our life experiences shape and evolve our thought processes, how we categorise past experiences may also change. That process is a deeply personal one.

References to laws and the criminal justice system throughout this book are intended to demonstrate how a lack of legal clarity creates societal confusion about what constitutes sexual violence. These discussions also detail the very specific ways the law fails survivors of sexual violence. The references do not advocate carceral solutions to gendered violence, but instead encourage looking beyond a legal prism in defining sexual violence.

The term 'non-consensual' is used in this book when referring to specific sexual acts, like non-consensual choking, non-consensual ejaculation or non-consensual spitting. 'Non-consensual' is not a perfect term, as demonstrated earlier in this chapter. The use of it as a qualifier in this book is to describe specific acts using precise language. By naming the exact act, we can discuss violations that exist on a spectrum of sexual violence without using vague language that might sanitise the act, or obfuscate understanding of what sexual violence looks like in real life.

CHAPTER 2

Stealth

Daisy's friends had been having fun, no-strings encounters, so she decided to have one too. What happened next, though, was far from fun. Nor was it devoid of consequences. She didn't want to sleep with a stranger, so she picked someone she already knew – albeit vaguely. He was a mutual acquaintance that she'd hung out with a few times with her friends. She chose him because he was, in her words, 'nice, clean, and fairly respectful'.

'He seemed a safe pair of hands,' she says. 'I decided that I was going to have my first one-night stand with this boy.' Daisy uses the word 'boy' to describe him – but he was no more a boy than she is a girl. At the time, she was 21 years old and a university student. The 'boy' was about 23 or 24 and had graduated already.

Daisy cut right to the chase and messaged the guy, asking him out. 'I'm quite a forthright person,' she says. He agreed straight away and they met up for a drink. There was a connection and they seemed to get on really well. Daisy describes the evening as 'incredibly romantic'. After three or four drinks, he asked her if she wanted to come back to his and 'watch a film'. Daisy jokes that this was before the days of Netflix and chill. They went back to his place, put on a film, but did not watch it.

Until this point, Daisy had primarily been in relationships with women. She had hooked up with a few guys, but hadn't dated any of them. She wasn't on the pill or using any form of contraceptive. That night, when things heated up, Daisy asked him if he had a condom. His reply was uttered in a strange cadence. He said, 'Yeah, I've got a condom' – except there was a prolonged emphasis on the 'yeah'. Nevertheless, he put on the condom.

Daisy says she was having a lovely time. She was on top and she felt in control. Until, that is, she became aware that the condom had come off. The man she was having sex with kept going, however, as if nothing had happened. Daisy says as she wasn't very experienced, she didn't feel she could assert herself in the situation.

'I remember thinking, well I'm on top so I must be in control of this. This must be fine as well, because it's not like he was pinning me down or anything. But I just did not feel able to say, "Hang on, I think the condom has come off."' Daisy felt him come. 'Then he finished and he was hanging on to my hips,' she says. 'And I just said: "Did you just come inside me without a condom?"'

He smiled at her in a way she describes as an 'aw, shucks' expression before saying, 'Oh whoops, sorry.' It was his next act that fully revealed the non-accidental nature of the violation. 'He did this really hokey thing,' Daisy says. 'He kind of looked to one side where he'd clearly taken it off and tossed it, and he was like, "Oh, there it is!"'

Daisy has thought about that exchange a good deal since it happened. But in that moment, she chose to believe that he genuinely hadn't realised it had come off. She reiterates her lack of experience as a reason why she gave him the benefit of the doubt. 'I was like, maybe this was an honest mistake. Because at this point I was like, I think I do like this boy. He's never given me any reason to believe that he would do something that was so disrespectful after I had very explicitly said, "I'm not on any contraception and here's why."'

That was the first time Daisy ever had to take the morning-after pill. She didn't have to pay for it, thankfully, but she did have to order it from a girl in her university debate society who happened to be behind the counter at the pharmacy that day.

That would-be one-night stand turned into a three-and-a-half-year relationship. The first serious relationship she'd had. Daisy says she decided to believe that what had happened was an innocent mistake. That was just what sex was like, she thought. And she continued to believe that for another four years.

It was only in 2017 that anyone disabused her of that idea. Around this time, clickbaity headlines began appearing about a 'disturbing new sex trend' that went by the name 'stealthing'.[1] That word had been given to the practice by its perpetrators, who wrote about it in online subcultures.

The framing by online media outlets was troubling. The cynical journalist in me knew from experience that headlines that include the word 'trend' are more likely to get clicks. Stealthing was different, though. We weren't talking about a newly coined term for innovative methods for dumping one another. It was alarming to see it blithely labelled as a 'sex trend'.[2] To me, this was patently rape.

Daisy read the articles about stealthing back then and talked to her new boyfriend about it. 'He was just like, "that's a heinous thing for a guy to do".' And I said, "Wait a minute, this happened to me."' She told her boyfriend how her ex had done this to her on their first date. Daisy asked him if there was any chance this could have been a mistake, that perhaps he hadn't realised the condom had come off. 'My boyfriend was like, "absolutely fucking not",' she says. He told her it could only have been a 'very deliberate thing'. 'I just remember thinking, oh he's a piece of shit,' she says.

Non-consensual condom removal didn't happen again during her earlier relationship, but Daisy says she started taking the contraceptive pill soon after that first encounter. 'I was just like, well, if stuff like that happens, I guess that's what I've got to do.' She says her experience did not affect her in a long-term way, but other iterations of uncomfortable acts appeared in the sex they had as a couple. Eventually, they broke up.

Daisy wrote to me recently and told me she feels fortunate that the violation didn't affect her more. 'I am often reminded these days how lucky I am to have made it this far with so little mistreatment and consequently so little fear and pain when it comes to the men in my life.' Daisy's use of the word 'lucky' after describing her own experience of sexual violence speaks volumes about the level of mistreatment and abuse that women and marginalised genders have come to expect from men. We internalise the idea that whatever has happened to us could have been a lot worse, we put it down to 'experience' or a 'learning curve', and we count ourselves 'lucky' because we view it as 'normal'.

Daisy isn't alone in her experience. Catherine had a drunken one-night stand where she experienced something she described as related to stealthing. She and the man were about to have sex for a second time. 'The guy said he didn't have another condom and I said I didn't have one either,' she recalls. He reacted with surprise at first, and then got up and said he had a condom in the bathroom.

'In hindsight, he clearly picked our used condom out of the bin, rinsed it and reused it,' she says. 'I vaguely noticed something was up at the time but dismissed the suspicion/ was too drunk to care, but thinking back that's obviously what he did. Thinking back on the night it's also clear that he was sober while I, although consenting, was very drunk.'

Daisy describes what happened to her as a 'grey area experience', while Catherine describes it as something that made her uncomfortable during sex.

What do we mean by 'grey area experience'?

As previously discussed, the 'grey area' is a term that refers to a nebulous middle ground in consensual sex that is seldom talked about. Into this middle ground fall experiences that are non-criminal, but that leave us feeling harmed and violated. Experiences that are 'at the murky interface of consent and coercion', as Swedish academic Lena Gunnarsson defines it in an article.[3]

This is where things get a little bit complicated. Within this grey area, I believe there are two things going on. The first are sexual experiences which fall outside of a legal definition of rape or sexual assault, which nonetheless feel violating, degrading, painful or traumatic. The second is something psychologists call unacknowledged rape – an experience that meets the hallmarks of rape or assault but is not labelled as such by the victim. Instead, terms like 'misunderstanding', a 'hookup gone wrong' and 'grey area' are used.

You may have read Daisy's account and felt it wasn't a grey area at all, however. For many, her story will read unequivocally as rape. She did not consent to sex without a condom and therefore it breached her consent, simple as. But broader cultural attitudes towards acts like stealthing are not as black and white as they should be. In 2018, 40 per cent of people surveyed by the End Violence Against Women coalition said it's never or usually not rape to remove a condom without a partner's consent. Broken down, it amounts to 19 per cent of people thinking stealthing is 'never rape' and 21 per cent thinking it wouldn't normally be rape.[4]

A 2017 study by Alexandra Brodsky found stealthing was alarmingly prevalent, and explored the harm this practice inflicts on women's lives.[5] During her research, Brodsky spoke to Rebecca, a doctoral student living in a university town in the US who worked for a local rape crisis hotline. Rebecca would receive calls from students at the state college. 'Of these callers, a significant number describe upsetting sexual contact that they struggle to name,' Brodsky writes. 'Their partners have, during sex, removed a condom without their knowledge. Their stories often start the same way: "I'm not sure this is rape, but . . ."' This harm that students didn't know the name of was something Rebecca had also experienced at the hands of a boyfriend when she was in her first year of undergraduate study.

Brodsky began researching the phenomenon of stealthing when she started law school in 2013 because she realised many of her women friends were 'struggling with forms of mistreatment by sexual partners that weren't considered part of the recognised repertoire of gender based violence – but that seemed rooted in the same misogyny and lack of respect'.[6] Brodsky found that US law is 'largely silent' in the face of this widespread act of violence.

Non-consensual condom removal puts victims at risk of pregnancy and STIs. Brodsky's research also showed that the practice harms its victims in other ways. Survivors she interviewed described non-consensual condom removal as 'a threat to their bodily agency' and as 'a dignitary harm'. One survivor said that, for her: 'The harm mostly had to do with trust. He saw the risk as zero for himself and took no interest in what it might be for me, and that hurt.'[7] In addition to causing trust issues, the act of stealthing can have far-reaching consequences for women, including the feeling that they have no agency over their own body.

The lack of acknowledgement of the risks for the other person came up during an interview I conducted while researching this violation. Anna had gone to visit a man she'd previously had a holiday romance with. During sex, he removed the condom without her consent. 'I only realised afterwards, when he was done,' she says. It likely happened when they were changing positions.

She was about 21 years old. 'I was young and was just out having a good time, so I just didn't make a big thing of it. But the thing was I don't even think I was taking the pill, at the time I was also a bit like, oh I'm sure it'll be fine. And then I was like, "Stop trying to be the cool girl. Like, it's not fine."'

The next day they went to the beach with friends and she turned to him and said, 'Look, I've been thinking about it and actually, to be safe, I should go to the pharmacy.'

'Yeah, you're right, absolutely. I'll take you,' he replied.

'He was always super nice about everything. He never made me feel shit,' she told me. She got the morning-after pill. But that pharmacy trip wasn't the end of it. What she later realised was that she had contracted chlamydia. Antibiotics did their work in the short term, but Anna's trust wasn't as quickly remedied.

Stealthing perpetrators have been known to brag about this practice online. 'I developed my own little tricks and techniques at achieving my main objective ANY time I had sex, making sure I shot my load deep inside the girls unsuspecting ****,' one perpetrator's account reads. 'I did this over and over with so many girls i can't even begin to count them.'[8] Brodsky suggests one possible motivation behind stealthing: 'One can note that proponents of "stealthing" root their support in an ideology of male supremacy in which violence is a man's natural right.'

While rape campaigners are in agreement that stealthing constitutes sexual assault, we're only just beginning to see a very small number of stealthing convictions in a handful of countries. In 2019, a man in England was convicted of raping a sex worker after removing the condom, after the woman clearly stated that condom use was a condition of her agreement to have sex with clients. The prosecuting lawyer, Jodie Mitchell, told the court: 'She repeatedly protested, "I don't do that – please, no." She tried to wriggle away but he told her to stop. He told her he had beaten people up and robbed people.'[9]

This landmark case has been hailed by lawyers as a 'paradigm example of the developing legal concept of "conditional consent".' According to Nick Dent, a criminal defence lawyer at Kingsley Napley, conditional consent cases involve 'ostensible consent to sexual intercourse being vitiated, in circumstances where the conditions of the consent have been broken, or withdrawn'. Previously, police and prosecutors had considered conditional consent cases 'legally and evidentially difficult to prosecute'.[10] In light of the rise in cases pertaining to conditional consent, the Crown Prosecution Service has updated its Rape and Sexual Offences guidance to include more detailed information on conditional consent.[11] The 2019 case could set a legal precedent for future stealthing survivors seeking justice, whose cases could fall under 'conditional consent'.

So far, courts in the United States have not legally addressed or named the practice. But one landmark trial in Germany in 2018 saw a man convicted for stealthing.[12] The defendant was tried for rape but found guilty of sexual assault at a local court in Berlin. He received an eight-month suspended jail sentence from the court and was fined 3,000 euros and ordered to pay an additional 96 euros for a sexual health test for the victim.

'It wasn't rape but . . . '

Shortly after Olivia turned 22, she started dating a man she fell wildly in love with. One night, they had dinner and drinks and spent the night together. They had sex and then went to sleep. In the middle of the night Olivia woke up face down, aware of a man on top of her body just as he began to penetrate her.

'His hands were around my wrists, his body weight hold-ing me down, it was over quick,' she says. 'We immediately went back to sleep.'

She describes the sex they'd been having up to this point as 'aggressive and rough and very consensual. It had a "take me" kind of vibe and I was into it. So when I was woken up with a man somewhat forcefully having sex with me, I didn't actually mind. It didn't feel good, but it didn't hurt, aside from him pulling my hair accidentally,' she says.

'The next morning I said something about being woken up in the middle of the night and he said something along the lines of, "Oh, yeah. I wasn't really awake. I just couldn't help myself with a beautiful naked woman lying next to me and snake brain was yelling FUCK HER NOW."'

Olivia thought about it and assumed the reason he felt OK being so forward was because of the nature of the sex they'd been having up to this point. 'I thought that since I had said yes every time before, it made sense to him that I was down no matter what for some quick, sleepy, middle-of-the-night sex,' she says. 'I let it go and the event was never spoken of again.'

Olivia went on to have a three-year relationship with the man in question. Towards the end of the relationship, when things started to get difficult between the two of them, she kept thinking back to that night. Olivia's inter-est in having sex had dropped significantly and she never wanted to have sex, which caused an issue between them. She'd say no three out of four times and her partner would ask her if there was someone else, or he'd 'mope around the house'. She would occasionally say yes every once in a while because she 'felt bad for him'. But those occasions made her feel regretful and resentful afterwards. And his anger when she rejected him made her, in turn, feel angry that her partner felt so entitled to her body.

'Once I started to realise about his attitude towards sex and his shitty entitlement to my body, I kept thinking back to that one time years ago when he had fucked my sleeping body. I see that now as a red flag. That was a warning sign of how he thought of sex and acted on his desires. I never said anything to him about that because it felt futile to bring something up that had happened so long ago, and that he probably didn't even remember,' she says.

'After a lot of consent panels and readings at my university, after hearing #MeToo stories, I've gained a better understanding of what good and truly consensual sex looks like, and I believe that night could easily be seen as rape, at least by women. He would absolutely not see it that way.'

Olivia is now shocked that she ended up in a serious relationship with someone who raped her at the start of the relationship. She says she would absolutely not tolerate anything like that now. 'I don't know that it has affected me long-term, but if it has, then it's just given me a list of bullet points of what not to do. However, every failed relationship gives people a map of what not to do.'

Alarmingly, research suggests it's not uncommon for victims of sexual assault to realise years after – or even much later in life – that something that happened to them constituted sexual assault or rape. A 2016 meta-analysis of 28 studies of 5,917 women and girls aged 14 and over who experienced sexual violence found that 60 per cent of survivors didn't label their experience as 'rape'. The research found that many sexual violence survivors use more benign descriptors, like 'bad sex' or 'miscommunication'.[13]

The fact that the majority of women who experience forced sex don't call it rape is shocking – and we should absolutely be concerned about the psychological, physiological and societal impact that comes with that. Unacknowledged rape has not been extensively studied, but research estimates that around 60 per cent of female university students have experienced unacknowledged rape.[14] Other estimates suggest that between 30 and 88 per cent of all sexual assaults are unacknowledged by the victim.[15]

So, why is this happening? Professor Heather L. Littleton, a psychologist who specialises in social-cognitive factors in sexual assault and trauma, explained it to me over email: 'Many women who have an experience that legally would be rape, instead label what happened to them as something that is not a crime, such as a miscommunication.'

The way our culture talks about and defines rape can have a significant impact on a person's ability to recognise when it has happened to them. 'Rape scripts' are mental scenarios constructed from ideas and stereotypes about how rape is typically supposed to play out.[16] 'The more someone's experience with rape differs from their script – or stereotyped ideas they have about rape – the less likely they are to label it as such,' says Littleton. 'In other words, their experience does not "match" what they think rape looks like – maybe they trusted the assailant, the assault was not violent, they did not resist strongly, or the perpetrator was a woman.'

These scripts stem from media reporting and on-screen depictions of rape – which typically are violent 'stranger danger' rapes. For some survivors, their script may evolve over time. A person's perception of rape could change as a result of sexual assault awareness education, or through more accurate media coverage, more varied fictional depictions of rape, or even by hearing another rape survivor's experience, Littleton says. It could take someone years to realise that their experience was actually rape.

Research by the End Violence Against Women coalition has suggested an alarming confusion about what rape is and the harm it causes. It shows that 33 per cent of people in Britain think it isn't rape if a woman is pressured into having sex but there's no physical violence. And one in ten people are 'unsure or think it's usually not rape to have sex with a woman who is asleep or too drunk to consent'. Furthermore, research by the sexual health charity FPA found that only 47 per cent of people think it's OK to withdraw consent if they're already naked.[17]

It's easy to look at these results and despair. They signal something deeply wrong with how our culture views sex. And they show worrying misconceptions about how consent works and what sexual violence looks like. But what we really need to do is to start having bigger conversations that challenge these pervasive ideas. Our silence on the topic is harming women and marginalised genders.

Situational ambiguity also plays a role. Dr Veronica Lamarche, a psychology lecturer at the University of Essex, tells me there's a number of issues contributing to this phenomenon. 'Our rape scripts have traditionally focused on violent assaults by strangers,' she says. 'However, the majority of assaults do not happen in that context, but rather in the "grey areas" of sexual intimacy. This situational ambiguity makes it hard for victims to clearly say "I was assaulted" because their experiences don't perfectly map onto the model scenario.'

The stigma attached to rape and cultural ideas about the consequences of accusing someone of sexual violence also present obstacles in acknowledging the reality of a violation. 'Some examples could be that the assailant is in their social circle and they worry people might not believe them or will take the side of the perpetrator, or they are in an ongoing relationship with the assailant, or they do not want to take on the stigma of being a rape victim,' Heather Littleton explains. She adds that her research has shown that people regard being labelled a 'rape victim' as a 'highly stigmatised status'.

This stigma makes it difficult for survivors to come forward. As Lamarche says, this stigma 'encourages people to second-guess whether their experience "counts" as an assault (e.g. "you don't want to ruin someone's life over nothing". . .). These barriers make people reluctant to come forward and talk about their experiences out of fear of being stigmatised, victim-blamed, and generally not helped or supported.'

Is it a problem if someone doesn't realise they've been raped or assaulted? Littleton says that there might be short-term advantages for not acknowledging rape. 'It may enable you to avoid the stigma of being a rape survivor, allow you to maintain relationships with your social group – this could be especially important if the perpetrator is a member of the survivor's social group. It also may make it seem more manageable to cope with.'

So, what are the consequences of survivors not realising that they've been raped or assaulted? Laura Wilson – associate professor of psychology at University of Mary Washington – tells me that research suggests unacknowledged rape survivors are 'less likely to report the crime to police, less likely to seek services – e.g., medical, mental health – and more likely to be victimised again in the future.' Some studies show that unacknowledged rape may be associated with lower symptoms of PTSD compared to acknowledged rape, but there may be longer-term negative consequences.

'The survivor may not engage in any proactive behaviors to prevent another assault or change any risk behaviours they are engaging in,' says Heather Littleton. She conducted a study of college students in the US and found that 'unacknowledged rape survivors were more likely than acknowledged ones to experience a new sexual assault over a two month follow-up'.[18] The unacknowledged rape survivors also drank more heavily than acknowledged survivors. 'For survivors who continue to be distressed, not acknowledging the rape can become more challenging over time and could erode one's sense of efficacy – essentially a survivor may view herself more negatively for not "getting over" the incident if she views it as a more benign event like bad sex,' Littleton says.

Both Wilson and Littleton believe more rigorous research is needed on the complexities of the impact of rape acknowledgement. I asked Littleton about the societal consequences of unacknowledged rape, and she urged caution in putting the onus on survivors to do something about the problem of sexual assault. 'I think the bigger problem is that we as a society continue to view rape as not a serious problem and continue to believe that survivors are somehow at least partially at fault for their assaults,' she says. 'Individuals who commit rape are unlikely to face legal or even social sanctions for doing so. A survivor who does not acknowledge his or her rape is in many cases responding to these societal attitudes.'

This culture of seeing the victim as somehow at fault can result in survivors not telling anyone what happened to them out of fear of being victim-blamed. Take the experience of Jane's – one that she describes as a 'grey area'.

'There was an ex who finished inside me when I told him not to. His excuse was that he was enjoying it too much to stop.' After it happened, Jane said to her then-partner, 'What the hell? I told you not to.' He seemed surprised she was even bothered. 'He said sorry and that's when he said he didn't stop because he was enjoying himself too much,' she says.

She felt that if she confided in anyone about it, they'd have just told her she should have made him wear a condom.

'I felt really violated and weird afterwards. I felt disgusted that he'd done something to my body that I'd asked him not to and then I was the one left having to deal with it.'

He often complained about using condoms during the course of their relationship. 'Once when we were having sex with a condom, he suddenly stopped, rolled off me and said he was going to sleep because it didn't feel good enough,' she says. Jane wasn't with him very long, but now she feels she should have dumped him the first time he started complaining about condoms.

Stories like this form a bigger picture of violence against women that is getting worse. Experiences of stealthing and unacknowledged rape go largely undiscussed in the media and society at large. But both have the power to cause significant damage and trauma to the women who experience them.

These are the stories we don't hear about. Perhaps they weren't violent stranger rapes, so they didn't make the news. Perhaps a celebrity wasn't involved, so it didn't make the news. Perhaps it didn't fit the 'rape narrative', so it didn't make the news.

If we look at social attitudes and legal viewpoints, stealthing is only just beginning to be recognised as sexual violence. And the years-long lack of clarity has real-life consequences for survivors who've been violated and yet live with the belief that what they experienced wasn't a valid form of assault or rape.

CHAPTER 3

A hand around your throat

A bigail went on a Bumble date with a guy she'd been messaging who seemed lovely, charming and good-looking. She still considers him the most attractive man she's ever slept with. They'd been chatting over WhatsApp for a few weeks before meeting up at a bar near his flat. At this point, she'd been on dating apps for a few years and had become good at vetting matches, so she didn't have any qualms about meeting him. In fact, she felt comfortable and safe doing so.

'I went back to his afterwards with the intention of having sex, and during sex he choked me without my consent, was extremely rough and hit parts of my body,' Abigail says. She was more shocked than frightened when it was happening. 'When he was choking me I didn't have the breath to tell him to stop and he seemed to be enjoying it so I didn't want to make a fuss,' she adds.

The next day she had bruises all over her body – on her neck and breasts – and she had marks on her bum where he had slapped her. 'This was really unusual for me as I'm dark-skinned. I don't bruise easily.' She showed her friend the bruises, partly 'as a joke', she says, and partly because she was unsure what had happened and how she was supposed to feel about it. Her friend was really shocked and took it very seriously. Abigail felt confused by this at the time. 'I've been sexually assaulted before and I was once dragged into a dark driveway by a man trying to rape me, so in my head I didn't feel like the two experiences – stranger in an alleyway and attractive man on Bumble who texted me the next morning telling me how nice a time he had – were the same,' she says. Over time, though, she did grow to feel uncomfortable with what had happened.

Abigail agreed to go on a second date with him a week or two later – this time at her flat. She was really nervous about the second date and decided to tell him that she didn't want to be choked. But in the end, he didn't attempt to choke her again. 'We lost touch after that, but it took me a few months to realise what had happened to me was sexual assault,' she says.

Abigail knows the difference between consensual rough sex and what happened to her that night. 'I had a boyfriend who was into being dominated and we had really long, honest conversations about what he wanted me to do to him and vice versa, long before we actually tried anything,' she says. 'Rough/aggressive sex is great if you have had a conversation about it beforehand and have safe words that allow you to stop.' Abigail and her then-boyfriend used safe words and she never felt uncomfortable or that she was being taken advantage of.

When I first started interviewing people about their sexual experiences for this book, I was inundated with emails and messages from women who'd been choked without consent. As 28-year-old Morgan told me, 'being choked or having your hair pulled feels like the default move for many men during sex'. Morgan doesn't like being choked, so she will flag that now with sexual partners. But in the past, she let it happen because she thought it was the norm. 'Most of my female friends experience this as well – it's incredibly prevalent.'

More and more women are reporting experiences of non-consensual choking during sex, research shows. Over a third of UK women under 40 have endured non-consensual choking, slapping, gagging or spitting during sex. Sexual violence campaigners say there is burgeoning pressure on young women to consent to 'violent, dangerous and demeaning acts'. Relationship counsellors are calling this a 'silent epidemic', the effects of which they are dealing with on a daily basis.[1]

This belief that non-consensual choking is 'the norm' in sex means that some women feel they can't say anything through fear of being perceived in a negative light by sexual partners.

Take Kara's experience. She laughed it off the first time it happened. 'Ha ha, heat of the moment,' she reassured the guy. But after a few days she could still feel his hands around her neck. Kara had been choked during sex unexpectedly and without her consent. Four years later, she's no longer laughing it off. 'It took me a long time to realise how not okay it had been and how violating it actually was.' She was 19 at the time. Kara is 23 now and her relationship to sex is 'not the best it could be'.

'Until very recently, I felt like my body was no longer mine,' she says. 'A lot of times when I gave someone access to my body, they took advantage of it.' Looking back, that moment made her feel 'small and very unsure', and over the years there have been more microaggressions, acts she describes as 'little things'. But those little things have added up over time to become something bigger, making her feel increasingly detached from her own body.

Kara feels that, without those microaggressions, she might have a healthier relationship with sex and her body. 'Though I'm getting there, I think it would've made things easier had I realised sooner that I can be vulnerable with someone without them taking it too far; and more importantly, that it's OK to say no if it does happen.' At 19, Kara didn't know that an unspoken no didn't equate to a yes. She also didn't know that she had the right to say no after saying yes – and that the no should be respected. Kara now knows that there are people who will understand that her silence isn't an automatic yes. And that her yes can be revoked at any time.

Under English and Welsh law, it is legally impossible to consent to certain injuries or your own death. There are exceptions to this common law principle – in instances of surgery and injuries within a sport context, for example – but sexual activity is not included in those exceptions. That means there are some sex acts exceeding a certain threshold of violence that legally can't be consented to. 'You can't consent to them if they're over a certain level,' says Professor Clare McGlynn.

This principle has been underscored by the Court of Appeal in a number of big cases, notably in R v Brown in 1993. In this case, a group of gay men who inflicted injuries on each other in consensual sado-masochistic sex were prosecuted for unlawful malicious wounding and actual bodily harm (ABH) – contrary to the Offences Against the Person Act 1861. 'The law at the moment says you can't consent to certain types of BDSM because they'll be above this threshold of violence that you literally can't consent to,' McGlynn explains. 'So, there is an argument that some forms of consensual sexual activity are criminalised, even though they're consensual. Outside of that, you cannot consent to your own death, you cannot consent to certain levels of physical violence, even when you consent in sexual relations.'

How that principle came to be established in law is problematic, however, and the R v Brown case is a guiding principle on the relationship between consent and harm in British culture. During the 1980s, a three-year investigation resulted in police questioning around 100 gay and

bisexual men who were engaging in consensual sadomasochistic sex acts (S&M). Despite the fact that everything
that took place was consensual, five men were convicted
and given significant prison sentences.

The case set a legal precedent which governs the relationship between consent and harm, and the extent
to which we can consent to harm. In an episode of the
RightsCast podcast, academics at the University of Essex
Human Rights Centre discussed the bearing this case has
over this country's legal system and the problems stemming from it.[2] On the episode, Dr Matt Lodder, a histor-
ian of tattooing and senior lecturer in art history at the
University of Essex, says that R v Brown 'is really foun-
dational to the way the entire British legal establishment
understands consent', adding that it's often the first thing
British law students learn about consent in textbooks.
Dr Emily Jones, a feminist international legal theorist,
echoes this: 'When I did my law degree, this was the case
that you learn about what is consent in criminal law.'
Jones adds that R v Brown is presented as beyond the limit
of consent, establishing what you can legally consent to by
way of physical harm. 'We're training all of these lawyers
to go out into the world and start thinking, like, BDSM
that reaches the levels of grievous bodily harm, so breaks
two layers of skin – this is the general definition in the
Offences Against the Person Act – is not OK. And that's
really problematic.'

The R v Brown case was appealed at the European Court
of Human Rights, where questions over the case being a

matter of the right to privacy were explored, but the conviction was upheld.

The context of the case is also relevant. This happened in 1990s Britain, during a time of moral panic and widespread, deep-rooted homophobia. During the House of Lords judgement, Lord Lowry referred to sadomasochism as a 'perverted and depraved sexual desire . . . Sadomasochistic homosexual activity cannot be regarded as conducive to the enhancement or enjoyment of family life or conducive to the welfare of society.'[3]

And not only does this legal principle mean that consensual BDSM and kink acts are criminalised and conflated with violence under the law; it also means body modification and certain piercings are in breach of this principle. In 2019, a body modification artist was jailed for carrying out consensual procedures, such as tongue splitting, on customers.[4] So, given that the R v Brown ruling is an example of institutional homophobia, not to mention kinkphobia, we really need to ask: is this case really what we should be using to define the legal limit of consent?

One result of this principle is that the law is very clear on the act of non-consensual choking. 'If you consent to sex but you don't consent to choking and if someone then chokes you or tries to choke you, then they are committing the offence of assault because you're not consenting to that,' says Clare McGlynn.

'So, in some ways with that, the law is quite clear,' she adds. 'You don't need a change of law there to deal with people [non-consensually] choking you during sex. The problem there is: a) that people are wanting to do it, and b) that people think they can do it without getting consent, and c) that many women feel coerced into having to say yes to it. Those are the problems, and the law can't really deal with those problems.'

Under the Sexual Offences Act 2003, sexual assault is committed when someone touches another person sexually without consent.[5]

Sexual assault

(1)   A person (A) commits an offence if—

(a) he intentionally touches another person (B),

(b) the touching is sexual,

(c) B does not consent to the touching, and

(d) A does not reasonably believe that B consents.

(2)   Whether a belief is reasonable is to be determined having regard to all the circumstances, including any steps A has taken to ascertain whether B consents.

(3)   Sections 75 and 76 apply to an offence under this section.

(4)   A person guilty of an offence under this section is liable—

(a) on summary conviction, to imprisonment for a term not exceeding 6 months or a fine not exceeding the statutory maximum or both;

(b) on conviction on indictment, to imprisonment for a term not exceeding 10 years.

Non-consensual choking has become increasingly reported, particularly among young women. Recent media coverage has focused on the heavy presence of choking in mainstream pornography. But discussions of non-consensual choking – which is sexual assault – and pornography require a level of nuance that's not always present in some of the reporting on this topic.

When porn is talked about in relation to sexual violence in the UK media, there is a worrying flattening of discourse that takes place. Headlines blaming porn as the sole driving force behind sexual violence and the main cause of rape culture are not only inaccurate, they also feed into a broader effort to ban or restrict access to porn. They also fail to recognise the real culprits behind sexual aggression: systems of oppression.

Porn's relationship to sexual violence has been extensively researched over the course of several decades since the 1970s, but academics have not reached a consensus. A 2020 meta-analysis of research found that evidence did not suggest that non-violent porn was associated with sexual aggression. The research also highlighted a number of methodological weaknesses in previous research on the topic.[6] If you look closely at much of the research on this topic, you'll find that researchers have found associations between porn consumption and certain behaviours but, crucially, they have not proven that a causal link exists. Some studies, and subsequent media reporting on the findings, conflate an association with causality, which are two different things.[7] As sex educator Justin Hancock explains, 'an association does not mean something causes another.' He continues: 'People may have these attitudes in order to be drawn to watching porn, so there could be a change in attitudes as a result of watching porn, or it could be that there isn't. Or someone who is interested in porn may have some of these attitudes in the first place.'[8]

Nonetheless, it is important to interrogate the sexual misinformation and tropes that mainstream porn disseminates, particularly among young people who use it as a tool to learn about sex. We should take care not to promote false narratives about porn, but at the very same time, we should be able to dissect mainstream porn's stereotypes and misinformation without it being misconstrued as a rallying cry to legislate porn or to blame it for the evils of society.

It is a problem that mainstream porn has become a primary resource for young people wanting to learn about sex. Alarmingly, many young people aren't learning about the crucial tenets of consensual, safe sex through robust sex education. Research by the UK's Sex Education Forum found that half of young people hadn't learned about real-life scenarios concerning sexual consent, and over a third had been taught nothing at all regarding sexual consent.[9] Given that vast numbers of young people are not learning about what consensual sex should look and feel like, they are filling in the huge gaps in their knowledge through any resources they can get their hands on. The most readily available resource is free porn sites like Pornhub and YouPorn; it comes, therefore, as no surprise that we have widespread misconceptions about what real-life sex is like, and what our partners might want and expect during sex.

Erika Lust, one of the few female porn directors, says that 'face slapping, choking, gagging and spitting has become the alpha and omega of any porn scene and not within a BDSM context. These are presented as standard ways to have sex when, in fact, they are niches.'[10] 'Breath play' or erotic asphyxiation – a niche BDSM act – has been co-opted by mainstream pornography, crucially without showing the consent protocols that are central to the BDSM community.

I want to clear up a common misconception here: referring to non-consensual choking as rough sex or BDSM is misleading and incorrect. First and foremost, the absence of consent means this act isn't taking place in the context of consensual rough sex. By conflating BDSM and sexual violence, we do two egregious things: we excuse sexual violence and normalise it as just 'part of sex'; and we demonise the BDSM community and fuel pre-existing negative stereotypes surrounding it.

In recent years, I've noticed that as we begin to talk more about these types of violations, the language we use is becoming increasingly murky. In British tabloids, headlines about 'rough sex' are often used in articles about women who've been murdered. On social media, discourse stemming from high-profile allegations of abuse and sexual violence become muddied when the accused has previously stated an interest in kink or BDSM. Non-consensual choking is not rough sex – it is sexual violence.

TV and movie depictions of BDSM acts also fail to show consent, and misrepresent the activities of a community with consent at its very core. When sex acts like choking are presented as mainstream in porn and entertainment with no discussion of safety, consent or boundaries, it disseminates dangerous misinformation that suggest choking does not require consent and underplays the risk carried by the act. As my colleague, Mashable journalist Jess Joho notes, 'the miseducation spread by such narrow and irresponsible media depictions of kink lead the public to not even realize that some more "mainstream" acts – like choking, spanking, or even certain types of dirty talk – are, in fact, BDSM, and should always be practiced with the safety measures established by the BDSM community to ensure everyone's consent and well-being.'[11]

Annie Lord, British *Vogue*'s dating columnist, says the release of *Fifty Shades of Grey* brought BDSM acts into mainstream consciousness. 'I remember thinking that unless you were into getting hit/spanked/gagged/choked etc., you were "bad in bed" or boring and conservative, which obviously when you're a teenager is the most horrifying idea.' She adds that it's taken her a long time to realise she only likes the semblance of pain – she'd enjoy it if someone were to pretend to choke her, but if she felt she couldn't breathe or if it hurt, she wouldn't enjoy that.

'I feel like so much of the time, women are terrified of saying something which might hurt or embarrass men. In sex, I regularly choose to go through things I don't enjoy because the thought of correcting them is worse.' Lord thinks that, rather than just 'doing this stuff', she should have played around with her sexual partners and built up to it, and it shouldn't have been embarrassing if she said she wasn't into it. 'If it wasn't embarrassing to be wrong, or it was accepted that when you first sleep with each other there's going to be a discussion, I think bad experiences would be less common.'

When I speak to people who've experienced non-consensual choking, it's clear that consent and safety measures are not being practised. In a conversation with Anya, she tells me she's noticed this act creeping into the sex she's having with men. 'On a couple of recent occasions, men have begun to choke me during our first time having sex.' The first time it happened, she pulled the man's hands off her neck, continued having sex, and never got in touch with him after the encounter. The second time it happened, however, she told the man to stop and asked him why he was doing it. 'He said other girls seemed to like it,' she says. 'I asked him if he liked it and he said he didn't have a preference. He didn't do it again during later sexual encounters.'

I ask Anya how she felt after those two incidents. 'Mad,' she replies. 'If people enjoy that as a sexual preference that's fine, but each person is different and you should ask their permission before bringing violence into the bedroom.' Anya tells me those experiences changed things for her. 'I won't not talk about it if it happens again. I don't want any further grey areas in my sex life.'

Choking is a high-risk act that can lead to death. It results in near misses, the momentary loss of consciousness and passing out. It requires careful consideration about safety implications. Crucially, it requires consent to the specific act itself. Consenting to penis-in-vagina sex, for instance, isn't the same as consenting to choking or any other sexual acts. There should also be a safe word or a physical gesture to alert a partner if you're in physical or mental distress. And those partaking in choking acts should consider after-care – a hug, a conversation or even a cup of tea.

Violations like forced choking are making women and femmes feel afraid during sex. Recent research by the Indiana University School of Public Health found that nearly a quarter of adult women in the United States have felt scared during sex.[12] Choking was one of the most common causes of this fear, with 23 out of 347 respondents describing feeling scared because their partner had tried to choke them without warning and without consent. One 44-year-old woman who participated in the study said her partner 'put his hands on my throat to where I almost couldn't breathe'.[13]

'Most of the choking instances described appear to have not been discussed by partners in advance; the other person just started choking the respondent,' writes Debby Herbenick, the professor and sex researcher who authored the report. 'Consequently, some worried they were being strangled: a common form of intimate partner violence, especially committed against women who partner with men.' Given that strangling and choking are a major cause of death for women who are killed as a result of domestic abuse, it's not surprising these women were afraid.

According to Herbenick's research, 13 per cent of sexually active girls between ages 14 and 17 have already been choked.

'Scary' is a word used by another woman I talked to about her experience of non-consensual choking. Describing a sexual encounter with a man she'd been seeing when she was at university, Laura recalls, 'He had a thing about choking and tried to initiate it on our first night together without any kind of verbal cue. Just felt his hands around my throat all of a sudden. Luckily, I felt able to tell him to cut it out, but it was scary seeing as he was probably about twice my weight and size. Nasty thing to do to someone. I think he genuinely thought he was being sexy.'

That wasn't the last time Laura felt scared while in bed with him. One night, he was playing with her nipples when he became a little bit too rough, and it started to hurt. She told him to go easy. 'He immediately grabbed my nipples and twisted them roughly 180 degrees. In intense pain, I asked him why he did it and he responded: "Sometimes girls say no when they mean yes."'

That fear can last years, even decades. Rosie was in an abusive relationship many years ago, and last year a flashback of a traumatic event occurred while she was drying her hair. 'I was getting ready for work and I experienced a terrifying flashback to when the ex-boyfriend in question had started strangling me in my sleep – a memory that I had completely forgotten. Or maybe buried,' she says. 'He would do it during sex too, but this time he was experimenting or something. I don't know.' Fifteen years later,

Rosie was standing with her hairdryer in her hand, and her blood ran cold because she was suddenly, out of nowhere, recalling this past event. Rosie describes it as a surreal moment. 'I swayed on the spot and kind of felt like I was having an out-of-body experience. Then of course came the panic as my heart started racing and I started shaking uncontrollably.' Rosie had experienced intrusive memories and thoughts before, but had never had a flashback like this. Whenever she reads about domestic abuse, the thing she finds is often missed out is the long-term impact it can have on survivors.

For their *Guardian* piece on the 'the fatal, hateful rise of choking during sex', journalists Anna Moore and Coco Khan spoke to a young man who choked his girlfriend – and had been doing so for several years – 'because she likes it,' he said. Days after speaking to Moore and Khan, the man got back in touch: 'I thought about our conversation and asked her about it. She said she doesn't actually like it; she thought I liked it. But the thing is, I don't: I thought it's what she wanted.'[14]

In a BBC piece on the rise in violent acts, a woman identified as 'Emma' said she felt 'terrified' when she had a one-night stand with a man who started choking her. In her thirties, she had just come out of a long-term relationship. 'We ended up in bed and during sex – without warning – he started choking me. I was really shocked and felt terrified. I didn't say anything at the time because at the back of my head, I felt vulnerable, like this man could overpower me.' She added: 'It felt like this was stuff he had seen online and wanted to play out in real life.'[15]

Non-consensual choking is sexual violence, end of story. It's not synonymous with rough sex, it's not BDSM. Confusing those entities only downplays the fear and trauma that non-consensual choking causes.

CHAPTER 4

'This went too far'

Allie met a guy through a fetish dating app that her friend had recommended to her. She wasn't anticipating actually meeting anyone, but as it turned out, she did get chatting to someone. He was attractive, she says, and he seemed nice. So they arranged to meet up for a drink.

'I had a grand total of two sips before he suggested we go back to his as he lived two minutes away. And having not had any "fun" for a few weeks, I thought why not and went for it.' Allie bitterly regrets that decision. 'It's the only time and the only partner I've ever felt unsafe with, and I've slept with more than a hundred men,' she tells me. The guy was clearly into BDSM and humiliation, but what she experienced at his hands crossed a line.

Before penetration, Allie felt hesitant. 'He was calling me a whore, and while I have no problem with these types of phrases with a boyfriend during sex or someone I trust and who knows my limits, this went too far. He then proceeded to start slapping me during sex.' He slapped her so hard she blacked out for a second – but he didn't even realise she'd lost consciousness. 'He then decided to push my head down into a pillow as he fucked me, and I felt it had gone a bit too far but didn't say anything. In hindsight, I wish I had and not sure why I didn't as I'm usually quite vocal about what I do and don't like in bed,' she says.

'He then came all over my face. Again, it felt humiliating and only something I'd normally allow a boyfriend to do. I went home after. I walked away feeling as if I'd been forced into what we'd done, but that's not true as I didn't disagree – but my body didn't like it and I felt like crying the moment I left his flat.' Allie never slept with him or spoke to him again.

'Afterwards, I felt like I'd let myself down,' she recalls. 'Partly because I hadn't respected myself, and because I hadn't said no when I felt uncomfortable. I take pride in being confident, but in this instance I felt small and a tad worthless, like the "whore" he had imagined me to be. I don't condone sex- or slut-shaming for myself or others, but that's how I felt. Like an object that he'd played with, as opposed to a sexual partner.'

The experience affected her for a few weeks afterwards and she felt hesitant the next time she had sex. 'To be honest, it's taught me a valuable lesson – because these days, if I ever feel uncomfortable, I'll say no. Regardless of the situation and who it is.'

Experiences like Allie's are alarmingly common. A third of British women under the age of 40 have been subjected to unwanted slapping and other violent acts. Hitting during sex comes with real risks. It can leave very visible marks on a person's face, and there's the chance of a broken nose, cheekbone or jaw. If someone has previously had a head injury, a sudden slap or punch can provoke a headache or migraine. If non-consensual hitting is repeated on a long-term basis, there is a risk of PTSD and psychological trauma.

Sarah was 16 when she got a partner for the first time. 'She used to do whatever she wanted to me, whenever she wanted,' she explains. That 'whatever she wanted' involved non-consensual hitting and roughness. 'I had bruises and all, and I really did not enjoy being submissive and the pain. But at the time I thought that was just part of a relationship.' That relationship lasted eight months. It wasn't the last time Sarah experienced non-consensual hitting during sex, either. 'It's also happened a few times where a person I was sleeping with slapped my ass without consent.'

I asked Professor Clare McGlynn where the law stands on acts of non-consensual hitting or spitting. Under English and Welsh law, the individual act of hitting or spitting would not be regarded as a sexual assault in itself – rather, the entire experience would be seen as an assault. 'Technically, a sexual assault has to have a "sexual element" to it; it's got to be something that's obviously sexual or that reasonable people would deem to be sexual,' McGlynn says. 'So if you thought about spitting, for example, I think you'd probably struggle to identify the act of spitting as a sexual assault.' But while spitting on its own wouldn't qualify as a sexual assault, it would render the entire sexual experience an assault if introduced without consent. 'Say you agree to sexual activity, and then they start spitting on you. The whole thing then becomes a sexual assault – that's how I would see it,' McGlynn explains.

'If you look at it as the whole thing then yes, clearly it can be a sexual assault. If you really wanted to get technical, you'd have to try to prove that spitting on someone was a sexual act.' She adds the caveat that you might be able to do so by arguing that the spitting occurred in the context of sexual intercourse, and that something about that act must feel sexual for the perpetrator. But legal points aside, McGlynn says what it ultimately boils down to is: 'You've got to have affirmative consent and active discussions like, "Oh, can I hit you?" "Can I spit on you?" – and not just assume that that's what people can do.'

Kara, who shared an experience about choking in chapter 3, was in a relationship with a man for six months, and recalls, 'The first time we had sex, he gave me a little slap on the butt. I didn't say no then. When a little slap grew into serious bruising, and eventually "roughness" resulting in more extreme things, I still didn't know how to say no.'

Kara and her ex never asked or discussed each other's 'rough preferences' in bed. Her reasons for not saying no were because she felt the violence was 'tame', and because she was the one who occasionally initiated sexual activity with him. The fact that she sometimes instigated things made her wonder whether, deep down, she liked it – but back then she was very unsure of how she felt.

Beth Ashley, a journalist specialising in sex, queerness and body positivity, believes non-consensual slapping, spanking and hitting stem from consent miseducation and learning about sex from mainstream porn. The reality is that mainstream porn is not designed to provide proper sex education. It is a profit-driven industry that portrays sexual fantasies rather than realism. It is entertainment, not education. 'I had a conversation with a friend a while back, who had been reading up on sex-positive articles online. This is the first time he'd ever engaged with any of that kind of content and he was really shocked to find out that you're supposed to get consent for every individual act that happens in sex, and not just permission to have sex,' she says.

'He told me, "I've spanked people without asking them." He'd switched to new positions without consent. And while they didn't respond to it badly, he was just suddenly hit with the idea that he could have really upset someone.' She emphasises that the person who told her this is 'not a bad person', but someone who grew up watching porn from age 12 and who hadn't had an open conversation about sex with any friends, family or trusted adults.

This misconception about how consent actually works is not unique to Ashley's friend. There are big knowledge gaps among huge swathes of the population when it comes to consent. One major gap is the principle that consent is an ongoing negotiation, that it can be withdrawn at any time, that each individual sexual act – be it fingering, oral, anal, a change in position, a hand job – requires consent. Alarmingly, just 39 per cent of young people aged 14–17 think it's OK to withdraw consent if you're already undressed. That same survey found that 9 per cent of people don't think it's OK to withdraw consent if they've been bought dinner or drinks, if they've already kissed the other person, if they are in a bedroom, if they've previously had sex with that person or if they're already naked. Just 13 per cent said they'd be likely to discuss issues of consent with a partner.[1]

'I talked about consent to a lot of different guys who told me that they wouldn't have thought to get individual consent for moving positions or spanking or touching someone's hair, which a lot of women actually really don't like, but which happens a lot,' Beth Ashley says. 'They were under the impression that consent stops after you've got the yes, that the consent negotiation is finished once you've decided to have sex with one another, and that was so normalised to them.' She says she's also had this same conversation with her female friends, who've told her they wouldn't question it if someone spanked them without consent because 'it's just normal to them, even if they don't like it'.

The reality is, though, many young people first learn about sex through pornography. A British Board of Film Classification survey found that children as young as nine years old had watched mainstream porn in the UK – unbeknown to their parents.[2] It can be an avenue of exploration when young people become curious about sex, perhaps after overhearing conversations at school. 'I'm Generation Z and so are my friends. We all looked at porn to see how sex worked,' says Ashley. 'I can remember being fifteen and I was going to be having sex with my boyfriend that weekend and I watched loads of porn because I didn't know how to do a blowjob.'

A 2016 report by the University of Middlesex found that, by age 16, 65 per cent of boys and girls had seen online porn, and 28 per cent of children aged between 11 and 12 had viewed it. More than half the boys surveyed said they believed the sex they'd seen in porn was realistic. Despite these findings, 87 per cent of boys and 77 per cent of girls surveyed said the pornography did not help them understand consent.[3]

In a National Union of Students survey, 60 per cent of university students said they use porn to find out more about sex and 40 per cent said porn had helped their understanding of sex, but almost three-quarters thought it provided unrealistic expectations.[4]

That lack of realism is at its most damaging when it fails to reinforce the need for consent when introducing any new sex acts into an encounter – particularly when those acts carry a certain degree of physical risk. Layla, who is behind the Instagram account @lalalaletmeexplain, says she's constantly having to correct misconceptions about consent being an ongoing negotiation. 'I am constantly having to drill in the message that consent is fluid, and that your boundaries can change at any point, and that someone can be inside you and you've consented to them being inside you and if you say stop, and they don't, then it immediately becomes rape.'

Layla is well known for running something called 'poll time' on her Instagram account, during which followers submit questions about sex and Layla converts them into polls for followers to answer. 'In poll time, I often get questions like, "Is it OK if my boyfriend had sex with me while I'm sleeping?" There shouldn't be this idea that because I have consented, because he's my boyfriend, that means he can just fuck me anytime he wants,' she says. 'There's this total weird lack of bodily autonomy that women feel, and I think it comes from social conditioning, just this notion that to be a good woman you have to people-please, and we raise our daughters and our sons so differently.'

Layla often hears about the effects of sexual misinformation on people's real-life sex lives through DMs and comments on her Instagram. One was from a man who said he'd been choking his girlfriend during sex for the entirety of their sexual relationship, but that he didn't actually enjoy it. The only reason he did it was because he'd seen it in porn and he assumed all women loved it because of the way that women respond to it in porn.

'He said to his girlfriend, "Why do you love choking so much? You seem really into it,"' says Layla. 'She says, "I'm going to be honest, I absolutely hate it. I just do it because you love it."' Both people in that relationship were doing something they'd seen in porn because they 'thought they had to', explains Layla, and there had been no communication or discussion.

When Layla writes about consent or boundary-setting in bed, the reactions can be quite telling. 'I always get comments from men who are like, "this is all great and everything, but now you're turning sex into something completely robotic" and "this is not fun anymore, we'll have to get people to sign forms before we try anything out". There's this weird inability to imagine sexy communication around consent. Why couldn't you go, "It'd be really cool if I could put my hand around your throat, would you enjoy that?" That's not necessarily robotic or unsexy.'

This idea of consent being a mood killer, a buzzkill, something that ruins the moment, is a common misconception. In an episode of NPR's *This American Life*, reporter Chana Joffe-Walt went into a US college classroom where first-year students were learning about enthusiastic consent in a workshop. When the instructor described consent as a 'continuous process of checking up, or checking in, either/ or', students fixated on how that would affect 'the mood'. 'You keep asking her? That's weird,' said one. 'That kind of messes up the mood,' another first-year chimed in. 'I'm not trying to be funny, but if she says yes, and you know, she keeps saying, yeah, I've got to be like, hey, you sure? Are you really sure? We're about to do this.' This conversation about whether it would be ruining the mood continues for an hour. 'There is genuine panic behind that question,' says Joffe-Walt.[5] But where is the genuine panic about hurting someone?

When I ask Layla if she has any advice for someone whose sexual partner is choking or spanking them without their consent in a relationship setting, she says, 'Communication, that's it. I always say to people that if you don't feel that you can communicate this stuff to your partner, then you really have to look at whether this is the right relationship.'

She continues: 'If you can allow somebody to do something so intimate as put their penis inside you, but you don't feel you can have a conversation with them, then already we have a massive red flag.' If you communicate this information to your partner and they do not change their behaviour, this is a major red flag. If you don't feel you're able to have a conversation with that person, then 'you do need to start thinking about where to seek support, maybe trying to leave the relationship,' Layla says. 'You have to be able to feel like you can say "I really enjoy this" and "I really don't enjoy this".'

A note on kink shaming

When we discuss non-consensual choking, spitting, hitting and other non-consensual rough sex acts, I've noticed a few troubling things that happen. If we are discussing allegations against a high-profile person who has previously expressed an interest in BDSM or kink, some people dismiss those allegations because 'it was just BDSM'. An interest in BDSM does not cancel out sexual violence, and nor does it mean that a person is 'fair game' for abuse.

Another problem is that many people fear that calling out non-consensual choking, spitting and hitting as sexual violence could be perceived as kink shaming or sex negativity. This stems from a lack of education and positive on-screen portrayals of what BDSM actually involves when it's practised correctly. I've spotted that some people tend to use the umbrella term 'choking' to describe both consensual and non-consensual choking, conflating consensual sexual activity with an act of sexual violence.

This conflation crops up often in conversations surrounding non-consensual choking, which is sexual assault. @lalalaletmeexplain addressed this in an Instagram post after she was accused of kink shaming when she began to discuss problematic TikTok videos that were normalising non-consensual choking and non-consensual spitting.

One of the TikToks in question featured a 20-year-old man with hundreds of thousands of followers describing choking a woman during sex and spitting in her mouth. There is no mention of consent during the video. 'OK, I know I'm not alone with this one, but spitting kink, OK, hear me out. I used to joke about it a lot in college, right? And be like "come here and let me spit in your mouth" really straight up and really blunt, but it'd be a joke. Then I was with this girl, and I was on top, hand around her throat, and I looked down and I said "open your fucking mouth" and she did. And I spat in her mouth, and oh my god, running my thumb around her lips afterwards as she swallowed.'[6]

'Jumping into a conversation about the dangers of non-consensual choking or violent sex to say that it is kink shaming is the same as men jumping into conversations about rape to shout "Not all men",' Layla wrote in her response. 'I face backlash from people everytime I post about this subject. Never have I once stated that there is anything wrong with rough sex between consenting adults who are both having a good time. If I said that nobody should have rough sex because it's harmful, that would be kink shaming.'

She added: 'BDSM is a niche practice and it is all about trust, respect, honesty, consent, and a mutual exchange of power. This is not what is being promoted on TikTok by misogynistic men, boys and pick me girls. The derailing of these conversations allows abusers to pass off their behaviour as a kink.'[7]

Writer Nicole Froio – who holds a PhD on sexual violence and masculinity – unpacked the history behind the 'rhetoric of sexual freedom being used by men to excuse their ill-treatment of women' in an article for Bitch Media. 'This conversation isn't new: It hearkens to the feminist debates of the 1980s where theories of sexuality and sexual citizenship caused an ideological split between "dominance feminists" and "sex positive" feminists.' Dominance feminists viewed sex as 'inherently oppressive', explains Froio, while '"sex radicals" (a split from feminism that later became known as queer theory) viewed sexuality as a possible site of liberation, often framing queerness and women's sexuality as liberatory'. Both camps of feminism were critiqued for different reasons.

During what's been termed the 'feminist sex wars' of the 1980s, dominance feminism positioned men's 'sexual domination' of women as the main driver behind women's subordination. 'While dominance feminism was critiqued for being totalising and uncreative about the possibilities of women's resistance and negotiated agency in sexual exchanges, sex-positive theorizations of sexuality were critiqued for defining sex as inherently positive,' Froio writes.[8]

The overarching point here is that abusers can exploit the work of the sex positivity movement, co-opting the language of consensual sexual practices like BDSM or kink in a bid to defend sexual violence. Shutting down conversations about sexual violence through fear of kink shaming benefits abusers.

What can we learn from the BDSM community?

In the BDSM community, spanking and hitting fall under the umbrella term 'impact play'. That term refers to any impact on the body that's specifically for the purpose of sexual gratification and can involve toys like whips, paddles and floggers. Consent and communication are really important when engaging in this practice.

Impact play, when practised correctly, requires both communication and safety considerations. Conversations about trying spanking or slapping should ideally happen long before you even enter the bedroom together. 'For my clients who want to be slapped, or spanked with a paddle, I prefer they start the conversation days before the actual event itself,' explains somatic psychologist and sex therapist Dr Holly Richmond in *Allure* magazine's comprehensive beginner's guide to impact play.[9]

Those conversations should involve what sexual partners want and what is off limits. BDSM practitioners will discuss hard limits and soft limits with sexual partners. Hard limits, as the name suggests, are acts that are strictly off limits. These need to be communicated clearly to a sex partner prior to engaging in any impact play. Soft limits, meanwhile, are things you're hesitant to try right now, but you might change your mind in the future about them.

During impact play, safe words – which have been agreed beforehand by everyone involved in the act – communicate when it's time to stop, with immediate effect. And aftercare, as Sophie Saint Thomas writes in *Allure*'s guide, 'is post-play etiquette in which all parties check in on one another to ensure the scene was enjoyable, tend to any bruises as well as emotional needs, and communicate how all parties feel.'

As well as respecting safe words and sexual boundaries, impact play also requires knowing where it's safe to be hit. These areas are called 'safe zones', and essentially they are the areas of the body that are well protected by fat or muscle – it's best to avoid hitting unprotected body parts which might damage vital organs. 'You want to hit areas on the body that are fleshier and fattier,' dominatrix Goddess Aviva tells *Allure*. 'The ass, thighs, and front of the legs. You want to avoid hitting someone on their spine. You want to avoid hitting someone on the lower back where the kidneys are. You want to avoid basically any area in which you could damage organs.' When it comes to slapping or hitting, avoid the eyes, nose, ears and mouth. Other areas to be avoided are the kidneys, tailbone, spine, hips and neck.

It's also important to have a conversation about marks beforehand. 'If you don't want marks, the dominant is going to have to be extra careful,' writes Alice Little in her 'Impact Play 101' guide. 'Some people find being marked by their partner during a scene a big turn-on. Think it over before going full speed ahead.'[10]

There are reasons why rules like the above exist – these are risky acts that can cause people internal and external physical damage. It's worrying, therefore, to see impact play being brought into mainstream porn without a portrayal of any of the consent and safety practices that usually go hand in hand with it.

It would be too generous to place the entire blame for non-consensual spanking, slapping and hitting on a lack of consent education. But it's certainly true that the longer misinformation about BDSM practices persists, the longer the assumption that these acts don't require consent will live on. Nonetheless, misogyny absolutely underpins the assumption that all women 'want' to be treated violently and that these acts don't require consent.

CHAPTER 5

The money shot

When Sarah first slept with a man, she was 17. She had slept with women before she slept with men. 'During the penetration doggy-style he changed holes without discussing it with me,' she recalls. He kept going, saying 'Try it! Try it! If you really can't, I'll stop!' On another occasion, this man ejaculated on her face without warning her or talking to her.

'Once, I was giving a blowjob to a sexual partner and asked him many times to let me know before he came, and he came in my mouth without warning me and I was so surprised that I swallowed,' she says.

'Facial ejaculation' is not the term that's used in common parlance to discuss the events just described. This act is more commonly referred to as a 'facial', the 'money shot', the 'cum shot' or, if on the neck, a 'pearl necklace'.

Language aside, what Sarah's encounter lacked first and foremost is consent. She had no prior knowledge and nor was there any communication as to what was about to happen. Some people enjoy consensual facial ejaculation as part of their sex lives – but the emphasis is on the consensual aspect here. As with all elements of sex, introducing this act requires consent and communication.

The prevalence of this act is well documented. Almost 45 per cent of young men said they'd ejaculated on a partner's face, per a 2013 study of young French people aged between 15 and 24.[1] So, how exactly did the 'facial' get normalised?

Facial ejaculation started out as a cinematic device for closing the narrative in porn in the 1970s. With the rise of online pornography, facial ejaculation became part of mainstream sexual culture. That's not to say that facial ejaculation wasn't carried out until the 1970s, however. The Marquis de Sade wrote about it in his novel *The 120 Days of Sodom*: 'I show them my prick, then what do you suppose I do? I squirt the fuck in their face . . . that's my passion.'[2]

One movie in particular played a rather huge role in bringing facial ejaculation to the forefront of mainstream imaginations: *Deep Throat*. As Linda Williams, a film studies professor at UC Berkeley, writes in *Hard Core: Power, Pleasure and the Frenzy of the Visible*, the film 'introduced narrativity in the genre and coined the cum shot as its defining figure'. Of course, this movie was certainly not the first to feature scenes of bodily ejaculation, but the 1970s were the era that introduced this leitmotif that signalled the close of the narrative – the porn equivalent of a full stop at the end of a sentence. 'Where the earlier short, silent stag films occasionally included spectacles of external ejaculation (in some cases inadvertently), it was not until the early seventies, with the rise of the hard-core feature, that the money shot assumed the narrative function of signaling the climax of a genital event.' (Stag films, referenced in the above quotation, were the predecessor of modern pornography.)

A cursory Google search of 'facial ejaculation' will throw up articles pertaining to the practice in relation to feminist discourse. One article, published in *Cosmopolitan* and entitled 'I'm a Feminist, but I Like When He Comes on My Face', argues that being a feminist and liking facials shouldn't be diametrically opposed stances. The author expresses her hesitation in sharing this, 'for fear it would detract from my feminist identity'.[3] Of course, there's nothing unfeminist about liking consensual rough sex, or consensual dom/sub dynamics, or consensual ejaculation. Frankly, I find the very suggestion that there's a feminist binary when it comes to sex acts pretty disingenuous, lacking in nuance and oversimplistic. And this next point should be obvious – but after speaking to scores of women, it's patently not getting through to a lot of people. Just as we make a big distinction between consensual sex and rape, I think we need to make it clear that facial ejaculation is not exempt from the rule that each sex act in any encounter requires consent. When something is positioned as the standard way to end a sexual interlude, you can see how someone might wrongly assume that it doesn't require consent. Obviously, that is not correct. As world-renowned psychosexual therapist Dr Ruth Westheimer writes, 'Explaining to teens that "facials" are not the norm is as important as telling them how babies are born.'[4]

It's important to mention that this chapter is by no means an attempt to kink shame or pathologise anyone who enjoys giving and receiving a consensual money shot. Nor do I want to generalise by suggesting that all women find this act humiliating – that's categorically not true. As journalist Rebecca Reid writes in an article for *Metro*: 'It's old fashioned and disrespectful to assume that no woman would want to have come on her face – that it's the kind of hideous shame which women put up with in order to please a man.' For the piece she spoke to two women who said they enjoy facials, and who described the act as 'the mark of a job well done' and 'really hot'. But Reid concludes that she herself finds facials deeply unpleasant. And one 27-year-old woman she spoke to said: 'I find it disrespectful. It's not arousing to lie there waiting for him to finish, and of course I don't get any sexual pleasure from it – there are no pleasure receptors in my face. It's boring, and it makes me feel stupid. And then I have to clean up.'[5]

Angela has had two men ejaculate in her mouth without her consent. 'One of them knew this,' she says. Both experiences made her feel extremely uncomfortable. 'Another pressured me into letting him ejaculate onto my body which I didn't and don't enjoy but didn't have the confidence to say no when I was younger.' Angela, who's now 33, has slept with four men in her life. 'The first two were entirely selfish but I never experienced anything negative – we'd just do the deed with very little foreplay and it was totally focused on them and their pleasure. The next two slightly better, more equal but interestingly very porn-performance focused, and although both cared about my pleasure, they seemed quite stunted by pornography.'

What drives the desire to ejaculate on a person's face without consent? Is it marking one's territory, staking a claim of ownership? Is it a desire to debase, demean, and assert dominance? Chyng-Feng Sun – clinical professor of Media Studies at NYU, whose research looks into this specific area of sexual aggression – interviewed over fifty heterosexual men and women both in individual interviews and in focus group discussions. She found that men who have watched facial ejaculation in pornography found it desirable; and while some found it strange or repulsive at first, after repeated viewing they came to expect such scenes. 'Most who liked watching it also wanted to do it to a real person,' she says. 'Some did it to their girlfriends with or without their consent; some would not want to do it to their girlfriends because they "respect them", but had no problem doing it to hook-ups or "scumbags"; and some strategically "season" their sexual partners for such an act by ejaculating on other body parts and moving on to the ultimate goal.'

If someone 'respects' their partner too much to not want to ejaculate on their face without their consent, then it seems like that person might associate that act with an absence of respect. It's not flattering, by the way, to say you respect your girlfriend, wife or partner 'too much' to violate her in this way – but that it's fine for it to happen to women you regard as less respectable. That's misogyny, plain as day.

The female participants in Sun's research expressed how the act made them feel. 'The vast majority of the female subjects found the act humiliating but had been requested to do it by male sexual partners or hook-ups,' says Sun. 'Some refused, and those who relented did so out of a sense of obligation for long-term partners or to please their partners. A woman said, "The reason to have sex was to improve the relationship. Why would I tell him I was not happy and make the relationship tense?"'

Sun asked the participants why they didn't seek consent before ejaculating on their partners' faces. 'Some subjects felt that there was no need to ask for consent because they could tell that some women, who had a certain sexual energy, might be OK with whatever you are doing to them. Some felt that women wanted to be manhandled, overpowered or humiliated, but they did not yet know that themselves, or they did not want to say so – so you should just do it and they will like it anyway.'

During her research, Sun talked to a university instructor who she describes as 'steeped in feminist theory', who told her that he liked dating 'professional women who are strong and nurturing' and then sexually dominating them. 'He said they eventually submitted to him (beyond just sexually) and he lost interest. From the interviews, I do see a broad sense of misogyny regarding these subjects' views about women's nature.'

Sun thinks the relationship between pornography consumption and this behaviour isn't as simple as direct causation. This is because media doesn't affect people in the same way, and other factors like someone's upbringing, attitude and experience also play a role. Nonetheless, one can trace this act's origins to the porn industry.

'This is what I think,' she concludes. 'Some men really want to engage in this act, and instead of asking and getting rejected, they just do it, and usually there are no serious consequences.'

Similar to choking, the act of facial ejaculation is positioned by women's magazines as 'hot', but it is not without consequences or health risks. Sex educator Alix Fox told me it's possible to get chlamydia of the eye if contaminated fluids make contact: 'You don't have to have sex for that to happen. It can happen if you touch your face around the eye area and you've got infected fluids on your hands.' (It's important here to note that chlamydia can be quickly and easily treated with antibiotics.)

How can we change porn culture?

It's really troubling to learn that children and teenagers are watching porn and believing it's realistic. You might have heard about the UK government's plans to introduce robust age verification checks in a bid to prevent minors accessing pornography. These plans were due to be implemented in July 2019, but were later shelved. If they'd gone through, the UK would have become the first country in the world to introduce age checks. The age verification methods proposed involved uploading a passport or driving licence to prove your age, or buying a 'porn pass' from a newsagent. While laudable in its aims, anyone who's ever been a teenager can attest to the fact that young people will likely find a way to circumnavigate age restrictions such as these. Not only that: the plans raised serious questions about how creating a porn block would harm sex workers' livelihoods.[6]

Pornography is playing a role in presenting BDSM acts like spanking, choking and the like as mainstream elements of our sexual culture. But, at the same time, it is not including the consent protocols that typically go hand in hand with these acts when practised by the BDSM community. This omission of the consent and safety elements of these acts means that mainstream porn sites are disseminating sexual misinformation.

So, how do we bridge that knowledge gap? Educational porn is one option, according to Beth Ashley. 'I don't think porn is going anywhere,' she says. 'And a lot of people argue that it shouldn't because of the jobs it provides the sex workers and the avenue it does provide for those who want to explore their sexuality and different kinks.'

In an article for Restless Network, Ashley spoke to young people about how they turned to pornography when they wanted to learn how to do something sexual. She spoke to a 22-year-old woman who used porn at age 16 to try to learn about lesbian sex. 'When I knew I was going to have sex for the first time, I watched porn to learn how to finger a girl "properly",' she told Ashley. 'I struggled to find anything that helped and ended up watching a You-Tube video instead. I thought mainstream porn probably just wasn't my cup of tea, but nowadays I know I just don't like porn that's for the male gaze.'[7]

Ashley believes change has to come from porn, because mainstream porn presents such unrealistic ideas about sex. 'The woman is positioned in ways that wouldn't even necessarily engage in orgasm but it looks good to the male masturbator watching; the orgasms are fake and violence happens so casually in mainstream porn,' she says. 'We don't get to see any sort of consent exchange for that, or a discussion of boundaries between the performers.'

Erika Lust is one of the creators of instructional porn, providing tutorials titled *Tips n' Tricks for Lickin' Clits* and *Tips n' Tricks for Suckin' Dicks* via one of her brands, XConfessions. As Ashley notes in her article: 'The films begin how any mainstream porn would; kissing and fumbling towards the bed before one performer says "Hang on. How do I give an amazing blowjob/cunnilingus?"' They then cut away to interviews with members of the public talking about what they enjoy about these sex acts. Narrators also comment on the technique employed by the stars of the oral sex tutorial.

Florence Barkway and Reed Amber of Come Curious produce tutorial-style porn films. 'We know that many people come to porn to learn how to be better in bed, so it made sense to make something specifically for that,' they told Ashley. 'There's a huge gap in the market for ethical educational porn, and we wanted to fill it.' Barkway and Amber recognise that mainstream porn isn't going anywhere – and nor is young people's curiosity. 'It's always going to be there, and curious kids will always deep dive on the internet. Instead of trying to shut down sites, the best avenue would be to start educating on what's real and fake in porn. They should be taught about consent and appropriate behaviour.'

Ashley was reminded of her own teenage self while researching educational pornography. 'I just immediately thought back to me googling blowjobs at fifteen and thought, if I'd have seen this, I'd have probably had more fun having sex for the first time,' she says. 'I wouldn't have been thinking about how I looked, I wouldn't have been worried about what a fool I looked like, I wouldn't have been worrying if I was doing it properly.'

The crucial difference for Ashley is that the educational pornography felt safe while not losing the 'sexiness' that you'd typically be looking for in porn. 'You could masturbate and learn at the same time.' Ashley ran the educational porn past some of her friends, who admitted they'd watched pornography when they were younger to figure out how to do things, and they all agreed that they'd have loved to have had access to instructional porn like this.

Switch to ethical porn

We should also be mindful of the sources of the pornography we're watching. If you watch porn on an open-access free website like Pornhub, I'd strongly consider switching to ethical porn.

In December 2020, the *New York Times* published an op-ed entitled 'The Children of Pornhub', which revealed how the website overlooked the fact that it was hosting videos of rape – both of children and of adults – and other abuses.[8] The piece prompted an enormous reaction online, and Pornhub took action, banning downloads and unverified uploads.[9]

Following the report, Mastercard and Visa cut ties with Pornhub due to the illegal content being hosted on the site.[10] After the loss of this credit card support, Pornhub deleted 10 million unverified videos.[11]

For years, Pornhub was criticised for hosting abusive and illegal content. Prior to the publication of the *New York Times* piece, journalists had been covering Pornhub's repeated abuses. Earlier that year, the BBC's gender and identity reporter Megha Mohan had interviewed Rose Kalemba, who was raped as a 14-year-old girl and the video of the attack ended up on Pornhub.[12] Over a period of six months, Kalemba emailed Pornhub countless times asking for the video to be removed. 'I sent Pornhub begging emails,' Kalemba told Mohan. 'I pleaded with them. I wrote, "Please, I'm a minor, this was assault, please take it down."' She received no response and the videos remained on the site. Kalemba told me over email: 'I actually emailed Pornhub every single day for over six months, not just several times and they ignored every single one until I impersonated a lawyer. I would do it at the same time every day after school.' It was only when Kalemba changed tack by setting up this new email address and posing as a lawyer, sending Pornhub an email threatening legal action, that she managed to gain any headway. The videos were removed within forty-eight hours.

In another case, Pornhub removed a channel called GirlsDoPorn, which tricked women into having sex on video. Twenty-two women sued GirlsDoPorn and the owners and employees of the channel were charged with sex trafficking.[13] Pornhub only removed the videos following the federal indictment, however.[14] The videos had a devastating impact on the lives of the women who'd been tricked, and several attempted suicide.[15]

Scores of other victims have reported problems trying to get illegal content removed from Pornhub and other popular aggregator sites. But the takeaway message from many of these stories is: these sites will only do something about rape content and illegal content when faced with a lawsuit or a huge loss of earnings.

As Mashable's Jess Joho writes: 'Free porn sites (aka "tube" sites) often rely on profiting off of widespread piracy, making it near impossible for performers to earn a living.'[16] These tube sites – which include MindGeek, Pornhub and Xvideos – haven't just been accused of monopoly and piracy, they've also been linked with some disturbing legal allegations involving coercion.[17]

Ethical porn is centred on performers' rights, safety and consent. As Joho points out, 'there's really no such thing as guaranteed ethical free porn in the way that tube sites provide it'. If you're into porn and you want to ensure you're consuming porn that's been made ethically, there are a number of free and paid sites you can frequent, like Bellesa.

co – a popular ethical porn provider which categorises itself as a feminist porn site.

Banning porn isn't the answer. And crossing your fingers and hoping your kid doesn't access porn isn't realistic either. Changing our relationship with porn is what really needs to happen. At some point, young people will see porn. Our priority should be on educating young people that what they see in porn isn't reflective of real-life sexual interactions and emphasising that porn is entertainment, not education. We should also highlight the omissions in mainstream porn, drawing their attention to the absence of consent and boundaries, and the lack of protection. As adults, accessing free porn can happen at the touch of a button. But knowing what we know about Pornhub and its competitors, it's time to consider more ethical alternatives that put sex workers' rights, safety and consent first.

CHAPTER 6

'Lie there and let him do it'

You had sex with them, but you didn't really feel like it. They wanted it more than you did, perhaps. They were in the mood for it, but you weren't. Maybe neither of you really wanted it, but you felt like it was what you were supposed to do. Perhaps you had sex with them because you wanted to feel close to them. Because you wanted them to know you love them. I'm talking about something called unwanted sex – sex that's consensual, but not wanted or desired.[1]

As humans, we have sex for all kinds of different reasons. One study actually identified 237 different expressed reasons people engage in sex. Those reasons ranged from altruistic – like wanting the person to feel good about themselves – to vengeful – 'I wanted to get back at my partner for having cheated on me' – to the basic human feeling of wanting to experience physical pleasure.[2]

Unwanted sex can occur in the context of a healthy relationship. But unwanted sex can also happen as part of wider sociocultural factors, including class, socioeconomic status, gender and race, leading to sexual boundaries being violated. One in twenty women have had an unwanted consensual experience, according to one study.[3]

Strategic consent

Philippa was in an abusive relationship with a man when she was 21 years old. She would have sex with her boyfriend in order to make him stop verbally abusing her and physically attacking her. 'He never raped me, and he didn't try to make me have sex when I'd told him I didn't want to,' she explains. 'However, I did have a fair amount of sex that I fucking hated, and I did it because he'd fall asleep after coming. I worked out after a while that just to make him shut the fuck up and fuck off and to escape this horrific situation I was in with an angry violent man screaming in my face and standing over me, hitting me and waving knives at me for the rest of the night, that if I could get him to fuck then he'd go AWAY (at least temporarily) and I'd get a break. So lil 21-year-old me is having to try "seduce" this guy I hate, while he is calling me a slut and pushing me or whatever the drama is about this time, and lie there and let him do it, then I get to have a break.'

Philippa managed to escape the relationship by causing the man to break up with her. 'One night he beat me up pretty bad, more than just the odd punch here or there like usual, and I had the thought "wow, I think he is going to kill me one day", so I was so horrible and cold to him over the next couple of months that eventually he wanted to break up with me. I knew it would be easier that way than if I left him; once it was over it would be properly done instead of five years of being stalked or whatever.'

Her plan worked, and he broke up with her. Two of her girlfriends moved in with her and her life turned around dramatically. 'I suddenly went from having a horrific, shit life to a really fun, nurturing, happy one,' she says.

Reflecting on her experience, Philippa doesn't think the experience has scarred her too much when it comes to sex. 'Obviously I had nightmares for years about the whole relationship, and even now I still get freaked out when movie characters are like him, or if drunk men start yelling in my vicinity, but at least he didn't destroy my sexuality or ruin it for me, which I can totally imagine happening to people in similar situations.' If anything, Philippa needed to reclaim her sexuality as her own. 'I really treasure my sexuality/sensuality/sexiness now as golden. In fact, I did at the time, which made me so additionally angry and hate him so much for taking that and turning it into something gross.'

Philippa has read a lot about PTSD in the years following her experience, but has not tried therapy yet. Overall, she feels she has done really well on her own, but thinks she might go to therapy one day. Philippa's experience is not an isolated one. More than four in ten women live in fear of refusing a partner's sexual demands, and feel they have no choice but to agree, according to a UN global study of 52 countries.[4]

A question that is often asked when women talk about bad sexual experiences and grey areas is: 'Did she say yes?' Once we've had our answer – which in this case is yes – the conversation will end. We feel satisfied with that yes and ask no further questions. Laina Bay-Cheng says this focus on the yes/no consent binary misses the full context of the experience. 'If we're only using "yes" as the metric for whether sex was OK or not, we are missing the fact that many women are saying yes for reasons that have to do with poverty and violence and a lack of adequate resources,' she explains. 'I think it's a problem if we just want to know "Did she say yes or not?" so that we can then walk away and clean our hands and be like, "Great, we have nothing to worry about." I find that simplistic and really objection-able.' Bay-Cheng, who is an expert on the impact of social injustice on girls' and women's sexual lives, says the question instead needs to be 'Sure, she consented, but why?'

There's another problem in how we interpret stories like Philippa's. Some may read her account and think, 'If only she knew she didn't have to consent to that.' But, in our misguided instinct to problematise Philippa's behaviour, we would be overlooking the context of the situation. 'When people talk about unwanted sex, they sometimes say "what can we do to help her understand she doesn't need to con-sent" or "she doesn't have to say yes to these older guys",' says Bay-Cheng. 'Well, actually, if that's the safest place she has to stay for the night, then actually, she's not wrong.'

Rather than criticising the choices that women make, we need to focus instead on the context in which those decisions were made. 'It's a real problem when you tell a woman that she made the wrong choice, when in fact she made absolutely the savviest, most strategic choice she could. Really what we should be dissatisfied with is that she didn't have better choices in the first place. That's where our interventions should be – not in correcting her.'

'Strategic consent' is a term coined by Bay-Cheng to broaden our understanding that sexual consent is not just about sex, 'and that for many girls and women, sex is a necessary – and sometimes the only – way to access resources and pursue other goals'. In strategic consent, a woman may have consented to have a roof over her head for the night, or for safety, stability, and perhaps even the promise of a better life.

'The reality is that for young women who contend with some combination of misogyny, racism, economic injustice and age-based restrictions, sex is often not about what or whom they find attractive or exciting or pleasurable,' says Bay-Cheng in her definition of the term emailed to me. 'Instead, sex and consent are based on what's necessary, called for, expedient or safest (even if just in the moment). In other words, disadvantaged young women often don't have the luxury of consent that is only about sex; their consent has to be strategic.'

We talk often about women's sexual agency, and the unspoken assumption is that women are all in possession of that commodity in equal measure – but we rarely discuss how race and class intersect with sexual agency.[5] There is a lot of debate about what the term 'sexual agency' actually means, but a widely accepted definition is that it is the freedom and power to express and control your own sexuality, without being coerced or exploited.[6]

'Whenever we talk about agency, almost inevitably it reverts into some sort of measurement of a woman. "How agentic is she?" "How assertive is she?" "And what can we do to get her more of those things?"' Bay-Cheng finds this a problematic and simplistic way of thinking. 'Moving away from agency is important, and understanding instead that all women have agency but our agency is shaped by our social conditions.'

Sex as 'paying them back'

'Lie back and think of England.' That's the phrase Abigail, who shared another of her experiences in chapter 2, uses to characterise some of her sexual experiences with men. She didn't want to have sex with these partners, but she didn't feel comfortable enough to say no.

'I went on one date where the guy took me to a really fancy restaurant and bought me loads of posh wine and I got really drunk,' she recalls. 'I felt really guilty that he had paid for everything, so went back to his after to "pay him back". Mid-blowjob, I threw up on his penis. After I had cleaned myself up, he asked to have sex and I was so out of it I just said no and passed out.' Abigail now realises that she didn't need to 'pay him back' and that she didn't owe him anything just because he took her out.

In a very unscientific poll of my Instagram followers, I asked if they had felt they owed someone sex after that person paid for a date, or if their date had expected sex after paying. Eighty per cent of respondents answered 'yes'. Laina Bay-Cheng refers to this as a 'transaction script': 'That script of like, "well, he's been really nice to me" and "oh, maybe I led him on" or "oh, he probably paid for that and now he thinks . . ."' But there's also an idea of not wanting to seem awkward by saying no to sex we don't want, and not wishing to be talked about by our peers as difficult or 'frigid'.

'As there's more attention given to this idea of women as sexually empowered – and especially young women are supposed to seem so sexual, and together, and cool and hip – that being awkward and seeming awkward may feel like a much worse thing than going along with sex that isn't violent and physically damaging,' says Bay-Cheng. 'I think the social penalty for being awkward can feel greater than the penalty of being like, "I didn't really want to do that but whatever."'

We're often aware of these scripts or ideas, and the pressure to follow them and our own desires to resist those scripts. 'Women are constantly using energy either resisting scripts or following them,' Bay-Cheng explains. 'So, even when women are resisting that script, it's still in your head.'

Layla, the sex educator behind @lalalaletmeexplain, often addresses topics like this with her community of 150k followers. 'I think this is all tied into women being socially conditioned to be people pleasers, but also not being taught that sex is for us,' she says.

As Gabrielle Jackson writes in *Pain and Prejudice*: 'From the moment she's old enough to understand, almost every girl is taught that it's her role to be a pleasure giver—after all, what does pleasure have to do with herself?'[7] Women are socialised to believe that they exist to provide pleasure, not to experience it themselves; they're also conditioned to be the gatekeepers to sex, the ones who sex is done to, rather than being seen as sexual participants with needs and desires.

Layla tells me she has had lots of unwanted sex. 'I have been in situations where a guy picked me up and it's taken him two hours to get to me and then, I'll be at his house and I'll really not want to, but I'll feel like, oh, it'd be really rude, he's taken all this time and I've got no way of going home.' When Layla was much younger, she would dissociate during unwanted sex and would instead focus her mind on road maps and calculating a route during the sex. When people dissociate, they feel disconnected from themselves and the world that surrounds them. People experience dissociation in many different ways, but it is known to be a way that the mind copes with stressful and traumatic situations.[8] 'I don't even remember the sex, I just remember, I would try and plan journeys from one place to another and I'd imagine every road that you'd have to go down to get to there, until the sex was over,' Layla explains. 'And if you asked me what happened during the sex, how did it go, I wouldn't even be able to tell you. But I could tell you a really good route of how to get to a certain place.'

This idea of feeling you owe someone sex is not an uncommon experience. On the internet, you will find scores of Reddit posts, blogs, and articles about this aspect of our dating culture. In a post on r/relationships, one woman asks fellow Redditors whether she owes her male date sex after he paid for their $350 dinner.[9] The Redditor explains that her date insisted on taking her out and he chose a 'super fancy restaurant' where he ordered an extravagantly expensive bottle of wine. He proceeded to take her all over town for pricy drinks and dessert, spending a total of more than $350 in one evening.

'Neither of us is in a position to live extravagantly, so, to me, his doing this signals that he really likes me,' she writes. 'I like him a lot, too, but I don't feel able to reciprocate the way (I think) he thinks I should. We haven't had sex yet, but we've made out, gotten naked and I give him BJs every time we are together.'

This idea doesn't come out of women's imaginations. It's uncomfortable to think about, but this is an ingrained aspect of sexual culture that sometimes rears its ugly head. This expectation to pay someone back after they've bought dinner or drinks isn't just an implicit expectation, it explicitly manifests itself through requests for reimbursement, as if one end of the bargain has not been held up. In heterosexual dating culture, women report being asked to reimburse male dates for dinner or drinks if they don't have sex with them after the guy has paid. Chloe Matthews, a student paramedic who lives in Hull, went viral after receiving a text from a guy named Danny she met on a night out. The text read: 'Could you transfer me for those drinks I bought you last nite since we didn't go home togeva wasn't really worth my time was it lol x.'[10] When she tweeted a screenshot of the text, it gained 67k likes and 10k retweets.

Matthews isn't the only woman to have received text messages like this though. Biomedicine student Abby Fenton was on a night out in a club in Sheffield when a guy offered to pay for the drink she'd ordered. The pair exchanged numbers and parted ways. Two weeks later she received a text asking her to transfer £6.50 for the vodka and coke he'd bought her. 'Hi hope u don't mind love but can you transfer me back £6.50?' wrote Liam. Abby didn't recognise the name at first and replied asking 'who's this'. 'Liam from the viper rooms a few weeks ago,' the response began. 'I bought yer a drink? Can I have money back for it? Will give u sort code and account no.'[11]

After a flurry of other viral text screenshots showing men asking women to refund the drinks they'd bought, journalist Sophie Gallagher interviewed a man who believed paying for a date entitled him to sex. 'If she doesn't want to sleep with me after I've paid a lot for a first date, I'll weigh up the likelihood of that being the case next time,' Ali, 29, told her. 'If she's simply ungrateful or disrespectful, I need to cut my losses and find another prospect.'[12]

This entitlement to women's bodies isn't exclusive to dating culture and apps. Male sexual entitlement can also manifest in long-term heterosexual relationships. Victoria used to be married to a man who felt he was entitled to sex with her. 'He treated me like sex was his right. He would make me feel guilty if I didn't want to have sex with him. He'd coerce me with guilt, in fact.'

Sex with her husband was always about him. He would get bored if she asked him to satisfy her. 'Once, I asked to have my nipples stimulated and he hurt me – like, pinched them so hard that they were bruised and the skin was abraded for days,' she says. 'He even told me directly once that having sex with me was his right. I told him that was rape and he got very angry.' When I ask Victoria how her ex-husband's behaviour made her feel, she replies: 'Like a person who did not deserve sexual feelings. I didn't like my body around him and I lost all attraction to him whatsoever. I am still working on the emotional damage from this relationship.'

Unwanted sex and anxious attachment

Our attachment style can influence the ways in which we have sex, sometimes resulting in unwanted sex. One study showed that attachment styles had an effect on women's likelihood to consent to unwanted sex with someone they were dating. Anxiously attached women were the most willing to consent to unwanted sex, citing 'fears that their partner would lose interest in them as reasons for their compliance'.[13]

Attachment theory, developed by British psychiatrist John Bowlby, explores how an infant's earliest relationship with their primary caregiver shapes the way they form relationships when they're grown up. The theory was later expanded on by Canadian-American psychologist Mary Ainsworth, who came up with three distinct attachment styles based on how infants reacted in unfamiliar situations away from their parents: secure attachment, anxious-resistant attachment and avoidant attachment.

Secure attachment in infants manifested itself in babies showing distress at being separated, but finding comfort. When reunited with their parents, they were easily soothed. Anxious-resistant attachment – aka anxious attachment – showed itself in infants who were more distressed when their parents departed, who sought comfort and also appeared to punish the parents for leaving. Infants in the avoidant attachment category were unfazed when separated from their parents and showed no or little stress. When their parents came back, they ignored them or actively avoided them.[14]

We all have an attachment style based on our earliest relationship with our primary caregiver, according to the theory. 'So what?' you may well be wondering. Well, research has shown that our attachment style goes on to affect the quality of the relationships we have as adults, the type of sex we have, and even how we communicate about sex.[15] Secure attachers are comfortable with their romantic partners – they have no difficulty giving and receiving love, and they rarely worry about their partners leaving them.

Anxious types are afraid their partner will leave them and they worry their partners don't match the love they feel for them. Avoidant attachers prefer not to show how they feel to their partner, and don't feel comfortable getting vulnerable. In short, they don't like to get too close.

Sex educator Dr Emily Nagoski's book *Come As You Are* delves into the science of attachment theory and its impact on the sex we have. 'People with anxious attachment styles are most likely to engage in anxiety-driven "solace sex" – that is, using sex as an attachment behaviour – which can make sex intense without making it pleasurable.'[16]

The term 'solace sex' was coined by therapist and author Sue Johnson to describe sex that aims to prove you are liked or loved by a partner. 'Solace sex can feel like a relief, because you're easing fear. But let's not mistake relief for pleasure,' writes Nagoski. Anxious attachers are more likely to consider sex a barometer of the quality of a relationship, and they're also more inclined to worry about sex, according to Nagoski. 'They're less likely to use condoms, more likely to use alcohol or other drugs before sex and, unsurprisingly, have higher rates of STIs and unwanted pregnancy. Anxious attachers experience more pain, anxiety, and health risks.'

Researchers have also found sex to be beneficial to anxiously attached people in long-term relationships, however. Sex can help anxious attachers satisfy their need for 'intimacy, closeness, reassurance' and relieve their relationship-focused worries. That same research showed that anxious types have a tendency to use sex as a gauge for how their partner feels about them and a way of gaining security.[17]

Maintenance sex

Researchers Sara Kern and Zoë Peterson of the Kinsey Institute conducted research into coercive sex and unwanted sex and identified two types of consensual, non-coerced unwanted sex.[18] The first type is called 'non-coerced sex with avoidance motives'. What that means is: sex that is agreed to in order to avoid a negative consequence, be it perceived or real. That could mean consenting to sex with someone because you don't want to hurt their feelings, or having sex with someone to prevent a fight or a confrontation.

The second type of unwanted sex is called 'non-coerced sex with approach motives', which refers to sex that is consented to in order to elicit a positive outcome. That could mean to improve the partner's mood (without the existence of coercion, nagging or pressuring) or to improve the overall relationship.

Maggie told me the following experience of unwanted sex in her relationship: 'I sometimes just do it [sex] because I know they want it – even if I don't – because I know it's important to make our relationship work. I pretty much always enjoy it once I get into it but I guess sometimes not.' This type of sex is called 'maintenance sex' and can be defined as 'not really in the mood but let's do it anyway'.[19]

Take Eleanor's experience. When she was younger, she experienced a dip in her interest in sex. Her male partner would give her the cold shoulder and stop talking to her when she didn't want to have sex. He'd tell her there was something wrong with her. 'He'd insist I didn't find him attractive and refused to listen to me when I told him it was known that women could have periods where they have a lower sex drive. When we were in the stages of breaking up, he finally bothered to google and admitted I was right.'

She's now in a relationship with someone who wants sex more often than she does. 'I did go through a period of having sex that I consented to but didn't really want – not because he was pressuring me but because I wanted to make him happy.' When she eventually admitted that to him, her partner was incredibly upset. 'It made him feel like a monster,' she says. Since then, they've managed to achieve excellent communication in their relationship and 'balance out want and need' very well.

Within the context of a healthy relationship, one partner might consent to undesired sex to keep their partner happy, because they want to keep the passion alive, or because their partner desires sex more often than they do. Some asexual people have reported engaging in this type of unwanted sex – non-coerced sex with approach motives – in relationships with non-asexual people.[20] As social psychologist and sex researcher Dr Justin Lehmiller notes: 'It's important to recognize that being asexual does not necessarily mean that one is aromantic – many asexual persons still want romantic relationships, and sometimes they partner with someone who is sexual. In these cases, some asexuals report a willingness to have sex because they want to please their partner.'[21]

How should we feel about unwanted sex?

Reading these accounts of the various types of unwanted sex, you might have seen parallels to yourself or something that happened to you. You might have read this chapter and felt that these experiences are normal, just part of growing up. Conversely, you might have read these stories and felt alarmed.

In the more than ten years I've been reporting on sex and gender, I've seen very little coverage – if any – on the topic of unwanted sex. I wanted to include the topic in this book because I believe that women's experience of unwanted sex within the context of the patriarchy merits discussion. Scholars are divided on the topic – some normalise it, while others problematise it. But unwanted sex is not a synonym for rape or coercion.

'Where I come down on unwanted sex is that it is normal insofar as you're talking about statistical norms,' explains Laina Bay-Cheng. 'So there are three ways of defining normal – there's healthy normal, there's socially acceptable normal, and then there's statistical normal. So unwanted sex, it's statistically normal for men and it's especially prevalent among women.'

As for whether unwanted sex is healthy normal and socially acceptable normal, Bay-Cheng says that's up for debate. 'What I would say is that consenting to something even if it's normal to consent to it statistically speaking, in the midst of power differences, either within the relationship or surrounding the relationship, that is not a good thing.'

Beyond the context of sexual scenarios, we often consent to things we don't want to do. At work, we might say yes to a project because we want our boss to think we're amenable. You might also say yes to eating at a restaurant you don't like because your friend wants to go there. The problem with unwanted sex lies in a wider context of systemic power imbalances. 'It's the larger context of gender, racial and class inequalities that get in the way and that make it dangerous,' Bay-Cheng concludes.

One might be tempted to ask the somewhat patronising question 'How do we tell women they don't have to consent to sex they don't want or desire?' But women's behaviour isn't the problem here – the real issue actually lies in the misogynistic, racist, unequal culture we all live in.

CHAPTER 7

All agony, no ecstasy

Olivia Funnell first experienced vaginismus when she was 17 years old. Now aged 28, she says the condition has had a big impact on her sex life and her relationships. When she was younger, she would burst into tears from the pain she experienced during sex. Her sexual partners were not very understanding.

Vaginismus is a chronic pain condition that causes the vagina to suddenly tighten when you attempt to penetrate it with something. According to the NHS, the condition is 'the body's automatic reaction to the fear of some or all types of vaginal penetration'. It's treatable, but the condition causes serious pain and discomfort. I got in touch with Funnell after reading an article she'd written for the *Guardian* about the impact of vaginismus on her sex life. In that article, she describes the agony she felt during sex as a 'tearing, burning pain that felt like I was being ripped in half'.[1]

Sometimes, she would fight back tears during sex out of a fear of being perceived as uptight, and she kept trying and trying. 'For me, sex became something I had to do to have a boyfriend. Not a mutually enjoyable way of displaying affection for another human being. It was, sadly, a transaction.' Describing sex with a former long-term partner who knew she had vaginismus, Olivia writes that she was nearly winded from the pain. 'He was mean and I cried. A lot.'

While Funnell's current boyfriend is kind, patient and supportive, as was the boyfriend before that, the vast majority of her sexual experiences have been distressing. 'Almost every other person that I have slept with over the last eleven years or so were rude, made me feel bad about myself as though I was ruining their sexual experience, or pressured me somewhat to continue when I said that I didn't want to,' she says. 'One guy told me that having sex with me was like "fucking a corpse" as I was trying to remain still so that I could focus on keeping my pelvic floor relaxed.'

Funnell says that her younger self was not very assertive and she feels that she allowed the people she had sex with to make her feel bad about herself. 'I really should have stood up for myself and left the room.' Living with vaginismus made Funnell feel like a 'prude', and it made her feel uncomfortable in her own body. She believes that her inability to have penis-in-vagina sex – or rather, to have pain-free vaginal sex – deterred potential boyfriends and girlfriends. 'But then again, perhaps having vaginismus was a blessing in disguise and kept the people who only wanted me for my body at bay.'

Funnell has received treatment for vaginismus and, as she's grown older, she's become more comfortable with sex. 'Whilst I no longer experience excruciating pain, I do sometimes have complications such as not being able to have penetrative sex because my pubococcygeus muscle will not relax and a penis cannot get through, almost as if there is a wall.' All in all, Funnell has come a long way with the kind of sex positions she can now engage in, and she feels her attitudes towards sex have become healthier, but she feels there's still a long road ahead of her. Vaginismus has had a big impact on her confidence and has caused a fear of physical intimacy. 'I still struggle to relax with my partner even though I know there is nothing to be afraid of, and I would classify myself as having an incredibly low sex drive which I attribute partly to vaginismus and partly to a conservative upbringing.'

When Funnell wrote that article back in 2016, vaginismus wasn't a condition that had been talked about much. But with recent portrayals on TV in Netflix's *Sex Education* and *Unorthodox*, the condition has been brought into mainstream consciousness and the conversation is beginning to change. Funnell thinks historically 'many women with this condition did grin and bear it' to get through sex. 'Sadly, I'm sure there are still women out there who don't realise that they have vaginismus and are probably suffering in silence because they do feel some sort of pressure, whether it's from themselves, society or their partners,' she says.

'My heart goes out to them because no one should ever feel like they have to engage in sex, particularly if doing so will cause them pain.'

About one in ten British women experiences pain during sex, according to a study published in *BJOG: An International Journal of Obstetrics and Gynaecology*.[2] Research using nationally representative data in the US found that 30 per cent of women experience pain during vaginal sex, and 72 per cent experience pain during anal sex.[3] A large proportion of women do not tell their partners when sex is causing them pain.

Take Tara Langdale-Schmidt's ordeal of living with vulvodynia – a condition that caused her to feel a burning pain at the opening to her vagina during sex – and her years-long journey to get a diagnosis and treatment. In a *Bustle* article, Tara describes the impact her condition had on her sex life.[4] Her partner Jason was supportive and told her they didn't need to have sex if it hurt her. For four years, doctors minimised Tara's pain and recommended wine and ibuprofen for the pain, failing to diagnose her condition. It was only through her own research that she found out she was suffering from vulvar vestibulitis, a type of vulvodynia. In the end, Tara got so fed up with doctors prescribing treatments that didn't work, she invented a magnetic dilator. The first time she had pain-free sex, she cried.

Pain and sex are inextricably intertwined in many women's sexual realities. Consider for a moment our willingness to accept this as a society. 'The world is disturbingly comfortable with the fact that women sometimes leave a sexual encounter in tears,' says Lili Loofbourow in an essay published in *The Week* entitled 'The Female Price of Male Pleasure', which was written in response to a disturbing debate that occurred in 2018.[5]

A relatively unknown website called Babe.net published a story in January 2018 detailing allegations of sexual misconduct against comedian Aziz Ansari. In the days and weeks that followed, it became clear this story was one of the most polarising and hotly debated accounts to emerge during this era. In the article, a woman identified only as 'Grace' describes a date with Ansari and alleges he ignored her verbal and non-verbal cues showing how uncomfortable and distressed she was. She left the encounter – which she described as 'the worst night of my life' – feeling violated.[6]

The story prompted an outpouring of opinion pieces questioning Grace's actions (not Ansari's alleged behaviour, of course) – why didn't she leave, why didn't she make her discomfort known? But perhaps the real question being asked was: 'Why are you bothering us with a concern as trifling as women's discomfort during sex?'

Loofbourow's essay, however, cuts through these ill-informed takes and paints an accurate and affecting portrait of the reality of women's sex lives and what constitutes 'bad sex' to them. 'A casual survey of forums where people discuss "bad sex" suggests that men tend to use the term to describe a passive partner or a boring experience,' writes Loofbourow. 'But when most women talk about "bad sex", they tend to mean coercion, or emotional discomfort or, even more commonly, physical pain.' Debby Herbenick, an academic specialising in human sexuality, echoes this assessment, telling Loofbourow: 'When it comes to "good sex", women often mean without pain, men often mean they had orgasms.'

Sara McClelland, associate professor of women's studies and psychology at the University of Michigan, has conducted extensive research into the role gender plays in determining the meaning of sexual satisfaction. 'Female participants described the low end of the scale in extremely negative terms, using terms like "depressed", "emotionally sad", "pain", and "degradation",' reads one of her papers on the matter. 'No male participants used terms with this degree of negative affect.' Instead, men described low sexual satisfaction associated with reasons like loneliness, having an unattractive sexual partner, and not enough sexual stimulation.[7]

It's worth noting that women's experiences of living with pain conditions vary greatly. This chapter explores the pressure – be it societal or from a sexual partner – women with such conditions feel to have sex, even when it causes them excruciating agony. But certain gynaecological conditions mean that some women are not able to participate in certain sex acts. During my research, I spoke to women living with endometriosis who cannot have vaginal sex with their partners, despite desperately wanting to. With palpable frustration and anger, they described the devastating impact their condition had wreaked on their relationships and mental health.

If we take a look at the scientific community's attention to the issue of female dyspareunia – the medical term for painful sex – it's very telling. In her essay, Loofbourow compares the number of clinical trials researching dyspareunia and erectile dysfunction: '*PubMed* has 393 clinical trials studying dyspareunia. Vaginismus? 10. Vulvodynia? 43. Erectile dysfunction? 1,954.' The difference between those figures is staggering. There are five times as many studies on male pleasure than there are on female sexual pain. How can this be? As Loofbourow puts it: 'Because we live in a culture that sees female pain as normal and male pleasure as a right.'

Women's pain is normalised in our culture. But for Black women, pain isn't just normalised – their pain isn't believed and it isn't taken seriously.[8] Preliminary findings from the not-yet published Pain and Pleasure study by Dr Shemeka Thorpe, postdoctoral research fellow at the University of Kentucky, found that 60.9 per cent of Black women reported experiencing unwanted sexual pain during consensual sex. And racial bias in the reproductive healthcare field has devastating consequences. Black women are five times more likely than white women to die because of complications in their pregnancy.[9]

The lack of research extends to more common gynaecological conditions. One in ten British women and people with uteruses of reproductive age has endometriosis, according to Endometriosis UK. But, despite its prevalence, doctors still don't know what causes endometriosis, and on average it takes 7.5 years to get a diagnosis.[10] Black women are about half as likely to be diagnosed with endometriosis compared to white women.[11] As Lucia Osborne-Crowley notes in a Refinery29 report: 'Because the condition is under-researched and misunderstood, treatment options are extremely limited and there is no known cure. As if that's not enough, we still don't know what causes endometriosis in the first place.'[12]

Delve further into what little scientific research exists on dyspareunia and you'll find academic acknowledgement of this normalisation of women's sexual pain. In a scientific paper on the current state of dyspareunia and its management, one researcher wrote that 'everyone who regularly encounters the complaint of dyspareunia knows that women are inclined to continue with coitus, if necessary, with their teeth tightly clenched'.[13] In the very same paper, it's noted that around 15 per cent of women have chronic dyspareunia that is 'poorly understood, infrequently cured, often highly problematic, and distressing'.

That visceral image of women enduring sex with teeth clenched is not easily erased from one's mind. Author Soraya Chemaly reflected on this quote in particular in her book *Rage Becomes Her: The Power of Women's Anger*, stating: 'Gritting teeth is something people do when they are in pain. But it also happens to be something they do when they are filled with rage.'

This act of gritting one's teeth through the pain is something journalist Hannah Van-de-Peer knows all too well. She hadn't heard of the condition until she was 19 years old, when a medical student she was seeing brought it up with her 'jokingly'. Up until then, she had struggled with the very idea of penetrative sex. 'Every time a man had attempted to penetrate me – with anything; a finger, a penis, or a sex toy – I'd ended up doubling over in pain. Before properly looking into vaginismus and each symptom, I thought the pain I'd experience during penetration was simply due to the fact that I was a virgin.'

Van-de-Peer says the entire reason she didn't have sex until she was 21 was because she'd pictured first-time penis-in-vagina sex as painful. She expected to bleed profusely. The idea that it could be an enjoyable experience was not something she was able to envisage. At the age of 20, Van-de-Peer talked about how she was feeling with another person for the first time. 'I'd previously informed my then-boyfriend that penetration was painful for me, that I was a virgin and I didn't think I was "ready" to have penetrative sex just yet,' she says. 'After a few months of trying – again, not just penis-in-vagina, we were also trying with fingers and a vibrator – we realised it wasn't working out.'

Her boyfriend at the time, who didn't know anything about vaginismus, told her that attempting penetration was like 'hitting a brick wall over and over again'. That description rang a bell for Van-de-Peer – she remembered reading a similar phrase in an article on vaginismus. That's when she and her boyfriend discussed the possibility that she could have the condition. Six months later, this possibility was confirmed through a medical diagnosis.

In the sexual experiences she'd had prior to getting into a relationship, Van-de-Peer tried to grin and bear it through the pain. 'Whenever I had casual, non-penetrative sex with other people, I felt as if it was "unsexy" to point out when certain things were hurting,' she says. She found it hard to explain why she didn't want that person to 'take her virginity' when they offered to. She tried to make herself as small as possible in her reactions to things during sexual encounters with strangers. 'I was uncomplaining, quiet and compliant, even when I didn't want to be.'

When Van-de-Peer was first diagnosed with vaginismus, she felt overwhelmed and found it 'almost too much to deal with'. She hadn't learned about the condition in sex education at school and she didn't know anyone else who was suffering from the condition. Thoughts about not being able to have children, of never being able to undergo a smear test, of having to tell future sex partners that she was 'impaired in some way' played in her mind on a constant loop. Those thoughts frightened her so much, they prevented her from going back to the doctor. During that in-between phase, she felt down whenever her boyfriend started to talk about sex. 'Often I'd beg him to try penetrating me even though we both knew it would cause me emotional/psychological turmoil, and when it inevitably failed to work I'd get into the shower and privately break down,' she says. 'I felt like a broken woman; a failure as a girlfriend and a future mother.' She felt like her femininity had been stripped away from her. 'These are all hetero- and cisnormative views which I now find embarrassing to talk about, but this, I feel, is how a lack of proper sex education can impact people.'

When she finally saw a GP and overcame those debilitating fears, she found the experience to be positive and productive. The doctor she saw was sensitive and thorough, and she reassured Van-de-Peer that her condition was not rare. 'She asked me a series of questions based on my sexual history – including anything that may have caused physical or emotional trauma, such as sexual assault (this is not something I've personally experienced).' Van-de-Peer was tested for a variety of STIs and other conditions which can cause painful sex, like chlamydia, gonorrhoea and vulvar cancer. The GP also talked to her about some breathing exercises she could do while inserting a small dilator into her vagina. 'To my surprise, I was able to painlessly insert the full length of the dilator, and even size up in my next appointment,' she says. 'At the end of the appointment, my GP commended my bravery for speaking up about my ordeal and reassured me that all types of sex are meant to be *fun* – even first-time penetrative sex!'

Once she'd received the all-clear for vulvar cancer and STIs, she began the treatment process. Van-de-Peer discovered that the type of vaginismus she was suffering from was a mild version, which she found surprising, given just how much she'd been struggling in the years running up to seeking help. 'I responded to my various forms of treatment very quickly, such as Kegel exercises (90+ reps a day!), a course of hydrocortisone cream, and dilators,' she explains. 'Within three months, I was able to use tampons during my monthly periods. Within six months, I was comfortably using penetrative sex toys for the first time. In late September 2019, I had full, enjoyable penetrative sex for the first time.'

Even though she's since broken up with her then-boyfriend, Van-de-Peer is able to have sex with as many people as she wants to without worrying about the pain. And she's rediscovered her own relationship with pleasure by experimenting with penetration on her own. She also no longer worries about how she's going to get through future smear tests. Van-de-Peer says the stigma of the condition felt just as detrimental to her development as the physical symptoms of it. 'I now echo my doctor's sentiments that sex, in every form, as long as it's consensual, is meant to be a fun experience,' she says. 'There isn't anything fun in telling a sex partner that you have a disorder which prevents you from being penetrated, just as there isn't any fun in lying back and taking unwanted pain for the sake of the other person's pleasure.'

Van-de-Peer has written about her experience for platforms like HuffPost UK and the BBC, and as a result she hears from young women in their late teens and early twenties who are experiencing vaginismus symptoms. These young women frequently ask Van-de-Peer how to tell their (usually male) partners that they can't be penetrated. 'Often, these women feel that their boyfriends will laugh at them, ignore them or lose all sexual desire for them,' she says. 'In this sense, vaginismus sufferers' earliest sexual experiences will hold a lot of pain and embarrassment, which leads them to believe that this is how sex should be, and steers them away from it altogether.' She also hears from women who experience pain during sex due to a variety of other causes, and who refuse to speak to their partners about it because of a fear they'll be 'ruining the moment'.

Keeping quiet about your own pain through fear of ruining the moment is alarmingly common. Very little research has been dedicated to the reasons why women experiencing pain during sex don't tell their partners, but one 2019 study co-authored by Allison Carter, research fellow with the Kirby Institute, UNSW Sydney, explored the complex reasons why women avoid telling partners.[14] Using nationally representative data from the 2018 US National Survey of Sexual Health and Behavior, the study found that only half of women told their partner they were in pain during sex; one in five women who reported painful sex said they wanted the sexual experience 'a little bit or didn't want to have sex but said yes anyway'; and one in five said the sexual encounter was 'a little or not at all pleasurable'. One of the key factors in women not disclosing pain to their partners was because of the normalisation of sexual pain.

The paper states that 'the decision by some participants in our study to have or continue sex despite experiencing pain and not to engage in pain-related discussions was oftentimes situated as normal, inconsequential, and unproblematic'. While some respondents reported adjusting positions or trying to go a little slower to minimise pain, others saw their pain as 'inevitable' and downplayed the existence of any issues because it had already been discussed or because it was a long-standing problem. 'The normalization of pain played out in a number of different ways, with the pain always being present, ordinary and routine, or unimportant, and sometimes this normalization was specific (e.g., it's normal to be dry and not excited).'

In addition to the normalisation of pain, it was apparent to the researchers that internalised gender roles and cultural scripts were at play in heterosexual relationships. Those included women not wanting to be 'rude or demanding', women being expected to adopt 'a docile or submissive sexual persona', and men being in control of sex. 'Consequently, some women chose to prioritize their partner's enjoyment, and, ultimately, go along with painful sex without discussing it. Others did so in order to avoid a situation that might become awkward or uncomfortable or to protect their partners' ego or feelings . . . the emotional labor some women are expending in their relationships was quite evident, such that women were responsible for satisfying men's sexual urges, managing their feelings, and keeping the relationship intact.'

Other studies have shown that communicating about painful sex with a partner can result in greater sexual pleasure. But speaking up isn't always an option. As the above study points out, 'there may be social costs or emotional ramifications to stopping sex in the middle. Physical excitement may decline, partners may get angry or upset, or women may be seen (or see themselves) as abnormal or inadequate.'

Women who did communicate their pain and discomfort to their partners reported reduced levels of discomfort and pain. 'This may be through enhanced emotional closeness and intimacy, changes to physical positions and movements, or an interaction of both increased intimacy and physical responsiveness,' the researchers explain. 'Just as pleasure is not always physical, the experience of pain may be influenced by how much women feel their partner is attentive, communicative, and loving.'

Not all partners respond well to being informed that their sexual partner is in pain, or that they need time to warm up or to alter the pace. Julie, who has recently been diagnosed with endometriosis, has been called a 'mood killer' by sexual partners for asking for time to ease into things. Prior to her diagnosis, she had always known something was wrong, because of how difficult her sex life has been. Julie, who's only had male sexual partners, says that sex becomes a massive stressor in relationships because she's not able to participate fully. 'Penetration is impossible without severe pain, and no matter how hard I try to relax or relieve friction it doesn't go away. I've been told that I'm a mood killer or a tease because in my mind I want to have that connection with my partner but my body refuses to allow that.'

With previous sexual partners, Julie would avoid situations involving sex because she knew the pain would show up, and the thought of having sex would make her tense up and stress out. 'If I would visit a partner for the weekend they would ask to have sex and I would always say "ehhh, maybe not tonight" or "I'm just not feeling it" – my way out of it,' she says. 'But if I did agree to having sex, it's a difficult process to get started. I required a significant amount of warm-up time.'

This process of warming up to sex is crucial for Julie. She's tried deep breathing and muscle relaxation techniques to no avail. 'Which is why I describe sex as "hitting a wall", and sometimes I will try to warm up but it just hurts too much so I have to stop. That, specifically, is why I've been called a tease, but I've also been called a mood killer because the whole process of warming up can really kill the mood.'

Julie's current partner is very understanding, however. Even prior to her diagnosis, he was very patient with her and asked if he could do anything to make sex more comfortable. 'So far, I think my current partner is the only one with the maturity to understand what I mean when I say my brain really wants to but my body is saying no. He's happy to take the time to do his best to avoid pain for me, and he understands when I just can't relax and have to stop.' Julie feels a weight has been lifted now that she has a diagnosis. She is seeking treatment through surgery so she can have a healthy sex life.

Women who experience chronic gynaecological pain conditions have a range of experiences when it comes to sex and relationships. It's important to note that many women living with conditions like endometriosis want to have sex with their partners, but are physically unable to. Amelia has endometriosis and first had sex when she was 20, after experiencing painful periods and other endo-related pain for a decade. At that point, she hadn't yet been diagnosed with the condition. 'My first experiences were uncomfortable, but I expected the discomfort to go away. Over the years, however, the discomfort turned into throbbing, searing pain,' she says. Her husband has been her only sexual partner – that's something she didn't plan, but it worked out that way. 'He's very compassionate, and lets me initiate, since he doesn't always know when I'm having a bad pain day. I do think he can be too cautious, sometimes, because he tends to avoid sexual situations completely, so that I never feel pressured. His heart is in the right place, though.'

She adds, 'I've tried a couple of treatments, and the most successful was physical therapy. However, after COVID-19 limited my access to physical therapists, my husband and I are now completely unable to have penetrative sex. So, I guess it impacted my sex life by getting rid of it.'

Having a compassionate partner who won't prioritise their pleasure at the expense of someone else's pain should be the bare minimum. But, sadly, that is patently not the reality of everyone's lived experience. It's easy to make a sweeping assertion that women should communicate more when they're in pain, and that, in turn, their partners should be more willing to accommodate their needs. But the problem runs deeper than that – it's clear we have significant issues on a cultural level.

Many of the experiences in this chapter really shine a light on the harm that gender roles have on heterosexual culture. Dr Fiona Vera-Gray says that existing sexual and gender norms position women as those sex is 'done to' and men as those who 'do' sex. 'Women's sexual pleasure and sexual desire is rarely seen as as important as men's – resulting in many men prioritising their own sexual needs over women's or seeing women's sexual pleasure as an "achievement" that proves their own sexual prowess,' she says. 'These norms combine with gender norms that teach men both that they need to prove their heterosexuality and that they have an entitlement to women; and teach women that we need to be polite, that women who assert themselves sexually are bad women, that sexually and emotionally we need to prioritise the feelings of men.'

This combination of norms provides a conducive context for some men to treat women in ways that are violating, uncomfortable, degrading or painful. 'But the key here is that though that context exists for all men, only some men choose to take it up in this way,' says Vera-Gray. It's not just the culture to blame – we need to look at the actions and decisions of individual men, because otherwise these norms can become an excuse.

We should also look to our sex-ed curricula. Hannah Van-de-Peer feels failed by the sex education she received during her primary and secondary schooling. 'Female pleasure was not spoken about whatsoever,' she says. Aside from never hearing about how women and people with vaginas masturbate, pain was normalised in conversations about first-time sex for women. 'Male sexual issues – such as erectile dysfunction – were taught at length, but female sexual issues like vaginismus were not. It was insinuated that losing your virginity as a woman would be a painful and messy experience. We were told to prepare for blood and discomfort.' Nothing was said about the different kinds of discomfort that can occur in sex, and their causes – such as dryness, lack of lube, and vaginismus. 'The girls' sex education was incredibly deterring, as we were never taught that pain during sex is *not* normal and that sex should be an enjoyable experience.'

Justin Hancock, sex and relationships educator at Bish UK, also believes that sex education often reinforces the idea that sex is painful for women. 'People with vaginas are taught that first time sex will probably hurt, let alone not be enjoyable,' he says. 'According to Natsal [the National Survey of Sexual Attitudes and Lifestyles], around 10 per cent of young women regularly experience pain during sex, and I think that this comes from a lack of teaching about how sex might be pleasurable, this idea that penis-in-vagina sex is the only game in town, and a lack of teaching (and understanding) about vulvas.' Hancock thinks patriarchal assumptions about what sex is and who it's for still run very deep. 'The idea that women only want love and men only want sex is still one of the underlying "truisms" that we hear all the time, but yet is patently untrue.'[15]

If you received sex education at school, consider how sex was described to you – and how your expectations were shaped by those descriptors. In my experience, I was told to expect pain the first time I had penis-in-vagina sex (the only kind of sex our curriculum acknowledged). I never learned about female pleasure. The only time I ever heard the word 'clitoris' was during a period hygiene seminar, when one of my classmates called out the word and was instantly rebuffed by a visibly embarrassed instructor. The picture of sex I formed during my formative years was that pain was the default experience. *Pleasure? What's that?* Those teachings have, it seems, been disseminated far and wide.

As Carter and her co-authors conclude in the aforementioned study on sexual pain: 'This should go without saying: Pain is not a sexual affliction that women should have to endure.' Women should not have to grit their teeth in silence to endure painful sex. Our culture needs to be less willing to accept women's sexual pain as a fact of life. Or as collateral damage for the sake of someone else's pleasure.

CHAPTER 8

'If you want to fuck me, fuck all of me'

Carolina describes herself as a curvy woman. 'Looking at me, you can tell I enjoy cake and carbs. It has taken me years and years, but I am finally genuinely learning to love my body.' She identifies as bisexual and enjoys BDSM. Over our email conversation, Carolina recalls a particular fatphobic microaggression she's experienced multiple times: 'I've been with people who were very handsy and literally "skipped" over the industry-standard "ugly" bits of me.' Carolina's past treatment has affected the way she interprets men's advances towards her. 'I have become so conditioned and jaded that I am convinced men approach me because they just want to "stick it in my ass" and not because they saw me dancing, or liked my smile.'

Carolina says she's experienced untold instances of boundaries being crossed during her sexual experiences with men. During BDSM encounters, sexual partners have ignored safe words. 'In the BDSM community, you create safe words to try and regain control if things get too intense for you. I've been in the situation where I didn't say it loud enough and it "wasn't heard".'

She's also had sexual acts demanded of her. 'I've been with men who only cared about themselves finishing and demanded I use my mouth, offering empty promises for my turn and never fulfilling those promises.' Overall, she feels her needs have been ignored during encounters: 'There are men who think sex is over after they orgasm. All. The. Time.'

The microaggression through omission of touch is something several women who identify as plus-size, curvy or fat have identified. As Carolina describes, this microaggression means partners deliberately avoiding touching parts of the body that are fleshier. Several women I've spoken to report sexual partners deliberately avoiding touching their tummy or FUPA – an acronym that stands for 'fat upper pubic (or pussy) area'. Marie Southard Ospina, a writer and editor who writes about fat liberation and body positivity, tells me this microaggression by avoidance of touch occurred in the vast majority of her experiences for the first five years she was experimenting with her sexuality. 'The very first person I hooked up with, for example, deliberately seemed to avoid the softest parts of my body: tummy, thighs, chubby arms, and bum. It was so obvious that he didn't want to touch me where I was visibly the fattest, which led to a constant awkwardness because, really, those parts of the body make up most of my body. What's left to touch? Shoulders and boobs, I guess.' This behaviour continued with several partners of all genders, she says.

Writer Gina Tonic wrote a piece for *Vice* entitled 'How to Have Sex With a Fat Girl' – which is essential reading – addressing this specific microaggression. Her advice? Touch the FUPA. 'It's a universal truth known by fat girls that the FUPA is the most intimidating part of our body. I know this because my FUPA has been touched so little that I'm surprised she hasn't shrivelled up and fallen off,' she writes. 'If you want to fuck me, fuck *all* of me . . . You'll be surprised how hot holding on to soft flesh feels when you get over yourself, get a grip, and get into the actual body of the fat girl you're shagging.'[1]

Omission of touch is just one of the many forms of microaggressions faced by fat women and non-binary people. Southard Ospina explains some of the other violations that occur: 'Fat womxn face countless forms of microaggressions in the bedroom. Partners who insist on turning the lights off because they think we'll "feel more confident" that way. Partners who won't take our tops off so as not to be disgusted by our stomachs. Partners who are nervous about making us feel self-conscious by touching our softest bits, and ultimately make us feel self-conscious by assuming we should be ashamed of those bits.'

She continues: 'The microaggressions can quickly become macro as well. I know so many fat womxn who've been abused and manipulated in the bedroom, only to be told they should feel lucky because no one else would ever touch us. I know fat womxn who've been raped by people who tell them they should be grateful for the atrocity. Our bodies are culturally believed to be repulsive and unlovable, and this seems to give a lot of people the fuel they need to dehumanise us completely.'

Fiona, another plus-size woman I spoke to in my research, recalls a sexual experience where her flesh was grasped roughly, causing her pain. 'One guy grabbed my stomach – I'm overweight so it is a little pouch – and used it to move me up and down. It hurt and made me so insecure.' This wasn't the only time Fiona felt mistreated during sex. 'I was under the influence of alcohol at the time but one casual sex partner kept moving me to different parts of the house and outside. Thinking back, I'm now pretty sure there were other guys watching without my consent.'

Gina Tonic tells me that the nature of the microaggressions depends on the person you're having sex with. 'A thinner person might comment they've never been with someone so big before; a fat person might comment on you both being unattractive. The worst I experienced was when a guy wanted me to go on top and I didn't want to, and he tried to encourage me by promising I wouldn't "crush him" when the idea of my body crushing anyone had never crossed my mind before.'

Alice was in a relationship for two and a half years with a male partner who had 'very prescriptive sexual inclinations'. 'It started with fetishes: on our first night together he got a watch out of his bag and asked me to wear it,' she says. 'Half-drunk and full of desire, I went along with it. This soon became normal, along with a whole litany of other things: positions he liked me to lie in so he could see my rolls – he had a fat fetish – as well as ways I had to wax myself, and routines based on his sexual desire, and not mine.'

Alice got used to these demands and went along with them because she had low self-esteem. 'By the end of our relationship, I was experiencing pain during sex so he made me see a doctor, who basically told me my vagina was rejecting him and his aggressive sex; this was pretty much the beginning of the end.'

When asked how these experiences made her feel, Alice uses one word: 'objectified'. 'Nothing he demanded during sex had anything to do with me, and was all about him. I was a prop for his enjoyment and not a person with needs. Overall, I suppose it made me feel cheap. That's not to say that I think all fetishes are like that, but for me it felt very much like his arousal had nothing to do with me and everything to do with his fetishes, and so I suppose it depersonalised the whole experience.'

Alice left her partner and sought therapy. Had she not got help, she feels, the impact of this experience would have been disastrous on her. 'I still struggle with intimacy, and am quick to assume that if anything goes wrong with a relationship it's because men only want me for my body, or as a vehicle for their own sexual desire,' she says. Alice is slowly shedding these ideas, but it's a process that takes a great deal of work and self-awareness.

When it comes to fetishes and kinks, consent isn't just a considerate thing to do or an added bonus: it's compulsory. Marie Southard Ospina tells me that 'as with any fetish or kink, the keyword when it comes to fat fetishism in my opinion is *consent*. No one should be made to feel fetishised if they don't personally want that. Certainly, no one should be manipulated into gainer, feeder or feedee dynamics unless that's a sexuality they personally find affirming.' Gina Tonic echoes this and says honesty is the best policy: 'Honesty is wholly necessary when dealing with fetishes, especially in this case, where the fetishisation is of another person.'

Language matters. And the words we use have consequences. Labelling attraction to fat people as a 'fetish' speaks volumes about the deep-rooted anti-fat bias in our culture. By calling it a fetish, sexually desiring a fat person is positioned as a niche sexual interest consigned to a realm beyond what might be deemed mainstream. 'Nobody calls people who exclusively date or sleep with thin partners "thin fetishists", because thinness is valued and normalised in our culture,' Southard Ospina says. 'We only perceive fat admirers as deviant because we perceive fatness as deviant.'

Desiring a thin or slim person = normal, mainstream. Desiring a plus-size person = fetish, atypical. Let's be honest here, the fact our culture cannot conceive of sexual interest in fat people as conventional reeks of fatphobia – also known as anti-fat bias.

Your Fat Friend is an anonymous essayist writing about the reality of life as a fat queer white cis woman. In a powerful Medium post titled 'Is Fat a Fetish?' she rejects the idea that attraction to plus-size bodies is necessarily a fetish. 'Fat people are so categorically undesirable, we're told, that any attraction to us must speak to a darker urge or some unchecked appetite.'[2] Comedian Sofie Hagen echoed these thoughts in an Instagram post on the topic: 'Why is it even considered a fetish to love fat people? I've seen MILLIONS of men worship thin women – and solely see them as bodies to fuck. Yet that's never described as a fetish.'[3]

If you've ever watched a TV show or movie depiction of fat fetishism, chances are it'll have been portrayed as deeply sinister or a deviant act. Marie Southard Ospina disagrees with this vilification and pathologisation of the fat fetish community. 'Are there "bad eggs" within this sexuality? Of course. There are "bad eggs" across all sexualities, kinks, fetishes, and even the most "vanilla" of sexual encounters,' she says. But there's also a tendency to assume that fat people who sleep with fat admirers, chasers or feeders are being disempowered. As Gina Tonic tells me, 'There's the misconception that the people who are being fetishised don't like it. There's a whole community of plus-size people whose own sexual preference is being adored, worshipped, and even fed more in the bedroom in order to get bigger.'

Through fat advocacy, we tell people to 'love their bodies' – why shouldn't that include loving those bodies in a sexual

way, Southard Ospina asks. 'I have a lot to thank the fat fetish community for, particularly BBW [Big Beautiful Women]
and SSBBW [Super-Sized Big Beautiful Women] models
within it. Through these womxn, I learned so much about my
sexuality. I learned to see the beauty in my softness. I learned
about turning myself on. I learned how to appreciate my rolls
and let them be appreciated.'

Her advice for fat women wanting to feel more
empowered is 'don't immediately discount fat admirers as
potential partners'. Southard Ospina herself only dates and
sleeps with fat admirers. 'I never want to experience the
microaggressions that characterised the earlier portion of
my sexual awakening, ever again.' She has come far in her
journey towards appreciating her body, and she wants anyone she's with romantically and sexually to feel exactly the
same. 'I do not wish to be wanted "in spite" of my body; but
to get off on everything my body is and for my partners to
feel the same.'

While it's clear that we should not mischaracterise fat
fetishism, it's really important to remember that not every
plus-size person wants to be fetishised. Beth Ashley, who
as a journalist often writes about sex, queerness and body
positivity, says she's experienced fetishism during sex. 'I'm
a size 16. Because of the way my body is, I am plus-size. I
have very, very big boobs and very big legs. I've definitely
had my body fetishised quite intensely during sex.' She adds
that she believes her experiences aren't as bad as those of
others: 'Some of my friends who are larger have a really difficult time dating.'

Ashley says people can be better allies to plus-size people in the bedroom by simply treating them the way they'd
treat anybody else. This starts with being upfront about
your intentions without being insensitive or cruel. 'Don't
assume a fat person is up for being fetishised. I know loads
of fat women that love being, like, the BBW, they love
being fetishised and having fat sex with people who identify as feeders and chubby chasers. They love that kind of
fantasy and being part of it. But the assumption is really
dangerous. You could traumatize a plus-size woman if you
take her home and then just inflict this fantasy onto her.
She might just want a shag without her body being part of
the discussion.'

Speaking of discussion, mentioning thin and slim women
to a fat woman while you're having sex with them is a form
of microaggression. Ashley describes a scenario where
someone she slept with kept bringing up 'skinny girls' as
a point of comparison to her while they were having sex.
'I had a guy once have sex with me and the entire time he
talked about how like he always wanted to fuck a voluptu-
ous woman, and kept stressing that he preferred curvy girls
to skinny girls while he was inside me. Like, maybe don't
mention skinny women in comparison to me at all. But definitely not mid-sex.'

Mentioning the skinny girl is something Gina Tonic
addresses in her guide to having sex with fat women: 'I
can see it on your lips. It's dying to jump off. You're deciding between "I've always wanted to fuck a fat girl" or "I
prefer your curves to thin girls". If you've ever wondered

the quickest way to kill a vibe, this is it. You're not special for wanting to fuck a fat girl. There's pages upon pages of Pornhub videos of men fantasising about it, and it doesn't make a girl feel special to be told the reason you're getting shagged is your body size.'[4]

Ashley thinks the mentioning of the skinny girl comes from internalised fatphobia. 'They think we need our bodies to be constantly overpraised or we won't be confident. It's awful to assume that a fat woman doesn't have sexual confidence – that's a load of shit.'

Dating as a fat woman sometimes means painfully coming face to face with fellow daters' internalised anti-fat stereotypes, which result in cruel, dehumanising behaviour. As Stephanie Yeboah, author of *Fattily Ever After*, writes in an article for *Stylist*, 'to date while fat means one of three things: being humiliated, being ignored or being fetishised.' In the article, Yeboah discusses a humiliating encounter with someone who, unbeknown to her, was participating in a 'pull a pig' dating prank. 'I went on a couple of dates with a seemingly nice man and never heard from him again, only to later find out from a friend of his that they had bet him £300 to date a fat girl – a bet he evidently won.' At first, Yeboah says, she felt dehumanised, humiliated and ashamed. 'I like to think that now I am confident enough and maybe numb enough to not let it define me as a woman, but for those of us who are still on our journey to finding self-love, going through an experience where you are basically seen as an experiment can be battering.'[5]

Yeboah is not alone in her experience. In a moving essay for BuzzFeed, author Laura Bogart writes that her sex life as a fat woman was a 'trickle of accumulated humiliations' before she decided to take a year away from dating and sex. That year eventually turned into a decade.

She relays a memory of lying with her head on the chest of a man she's just had sex with. She asks him if he'd like to go out on a date to a museum. His response: 'Cool, cool.' Then his face takes on an apologetic expression. He tells her he wants her to know that he doesn't hold hands. 'But it's not because of, I mean, you know.'

'I do know,' writes Bogart. 'I know exactly why he won't hold my hand in public, why this night went from an electric hum of potential to a dull, familiar drone of humiliation.'

The loneliness she felt at the start of that decade reminded her of how she felt lying in bed with men who were up for having sex with her in private, but not with being with her in public: 'There is nothing lonelier than knowing I'm someone's consolation prize even as they're coming inside me.'[6]

When discussing how people can be better allies to fat women in the bedroom, Beth Ashley brings up people who have sex with fat women as dares. 'This one's horrible but it needs to be said: don't have sex with fat women for a laugh.' The idea of having sex with anyone for a joke is deeply unconscionable. But in addition to the 'pull a pig' prank that Stephanie Yeboah experienced, there's a long-standing violation that's been termed 'hogging'. The term describes hypermasculine men who consciously target fat women to have sex with them for the amusement of themselves and their friends. It is also abuse. Academics see hogging as symptomatic of a broader culture of culturally sanctioned misogyny and fatphobia.[7]

As Ashley says, 'If your interest in a fat woman is for a laugh, or a dare, or because the thin ones have all gone home to somebody else, just fuck off. Don't do it.' She recalls a night out with her partner which ended with him receiving a message from a friend of his. 'We'd basically gone home and left him in a bar, and he texted him saying "because you went home, I got stuck with this fat girl and now I'm on my way back to her house. Now I've got to fuck a fat pig because of you". I know so many men who talk about bigger women like that. If you're fucking someone out of desperation, or a fun experiment, or because your way-too-straight friend started a "pull a pig" challenge or something evil like that, you shouldn't be having sex with anyone at all until you've done some growing up and some internal work on the way you view other human beings.'

Online dating also presents a challenge. Ashley mentions that many fat women feel they need to put a 'disclaimer' that they're fat in their dating app profiles because they're worried they run the risk of turning up and being shunned. 'They're also wondering, why do they want to be with a fat person? Is it a fetish? Or are they actually interested in me? And that's why fat people choose to only have sex with other fat people, because they just don't want to deal with the politics.'

Many of the behaviours detailed in this chapter stem from fatphobia and misogyny. But to blame individuals' behaviour entirely on a wider culture would absolve people of responsibility for their own actions. If you have sex with fat people, talk about sexual boundaries. Ask them how they want to be touched, what they enjoy, what kind of dirty talk they do and don't like. Educate yourself on how fatphobia manifests itself and how your own sexual behaviour can perpetuate anti-fat violence. If dating or sleeping with a fat person is something you've never even considered, ask yourself why. As Ashley advises, 'Work on your internalised fatphobia, because if someone being fat is just an instant no for you, then I feel you need to work on some stuff.'

For plus-size women wanting to feel more empowered during sex, Marie Southard Ospina recommends not having sex with people who don't like your body, or who make you feel there's something wrong with your body. 'This type of sex will never help you feel more confident or empowered in yourself. You need to believe that there are countless individuals who will genuinely find you sexy as hell; they're just waiting to be found.'

She goes on: 'Secondly, have sex with yourself, and often. Don't avoid the fattest parts of your body, either. Learn about the curvature of your stomach, the softness of your arms, or the jiggliness of your FUPA. Find ways of enjoying your softness so that when other people try to do the same, you don't recoil or try to hide it away.'

Gina Tonic says the first step to feeling empowered sexually comes from finding empowerment in yourself. 'If you're insecure about being naked or sexual with yourself, doing that with another person might amplify those worries. Spend more time naked – both in non-sexual and sexual moments with yourself. Fill your screens and Instagram feed with people who look like you. Watch porn with plus-size actors, follow plus-size influencers, find things you love in those people that reflect how you look.'

CHAPTER 9

'If I can't get a hard-on, I'll know I'm definitely racist'

Ella's father is from the West Indies, and was an immigrant to the UK at age six. 'He endured the most vile racism and laboured under the misconception that if his children integrated with white society in private schools, if we were in the same spaces, we would be able to hold the same company, have the same privileges,' she says.

As a mixed-race schoolgirl surrounded by mostly white, upper-middle-class children, Ella was trained to become desensitised to the casual racism that mixed-race and Black people are expected to endure. 'My first jarring memory of being confronted with my otherness was when a girl in my class smugly told me "there are more Black people in prison than white people",' she recalls. 'It's played on my mind ever since that I didn't have a smart answer for her, that I just stood there dumbfounded. I was eleven.'

She struggled with low self-esteem. 'In high school I was never going to be a candidate for being considered pretty or hanging out with the boys from the neighbouring school,' she says. 'I wasn't like them.' This sparked a need in Ella for male approval, a desire to be validated, and a willingness to lower her boundaries to get that approval.

Ella was fetishised throughout school, then at university and beyond. 'Comments ranged from "I've never slept with a Black girl before" to "If I can't get a hard-on, I'll know I'm definitely racist". I don't think it ever occurred to me to be offended. I was used to it.'

She is now divorced and reckoning with the past. 'I've raked over why I didn't feel brave enough not to laugh it off, ignore it, but I'm also very angry that Black women are put in that position in the first place. To ask all of us to be confrontational, to call out the people we're expected to work with, be around, live around, is an exhausting tax for simply being alive.'

While she was dating a white man (who later became her husband), she hung out with him and his all-white friendship group. A group that very few Black people ever associated with, despite the fact her then-boyfriend ran events in one of the most diverse areas in London. 'One of his friends was telling a story and describing walking up a street and being followed. It wasn't the story but the description, "there were three Black men behind me", that caused me

to interject,' says Ella. She asked what that meant, knowing full well what sentiment lay behind those words. 'He
meant scary, he meant dangerous, he meant criminal. I
could feel the disapproval build in my boyfriend as I pressed
for an explanation. I was bringing the "vibe" down.' She
eventually shut up, she recalls. 'I always shut up in the end.'

Later on in the relationship, Ella's father-in-law sneered
while watching a news report about Islamophobia in Britain. Ella didn't stay quiet this time. She told her father-in-
law that when she had children with his son, those children
would not be white, and that she would have conversations
with them that he hadn't had to have with his children. 'I
told him that my father and I had experienced racism; that
Muslims were suffering under the same othering that Black
people still suffer under in a white patriarchal society.'

Eventually, she left the room, and when she and her husband were alone in the bedroom, he was furious with her.
'Furious for arguing, furious for "upsetting his mother",
furious that I would broach such a subject – even though it
was his father's comments that prompted it. He told me I
should laugh it off, ignore it,' she says.

Ella couldn't ignore it, though. She became more and
more outspoken about race. Her husband started to take
exception to some of the things she was saying. 'A major
issue he had was with the phrase "white people", which is
ironic because the phrase "Black people" had been used
around me in a far more loaded sense,' she says. He even
refused to listen to The Read podcast because of his aver-
sion to hearing the phrase 'white people'.

'He began telling me I was "obsessed with race", that I "talked too much about race", but I wouldn't stop this time,' says Ella. She knew something was very wrong. He started to criticise her much more, and would get angry any time race was brought up in conversation. Ella realises that she wanted to educate him. In many ways, she was carrying the burden of race for him in the hope that he'd care about something that was so fundamental to her lived experience – and also to the way society functions. 'I suppose I shouldn't have been surprised when I found out he had been cheating on me with a white girl – a girl I knew, who knew me,' says Ella.

After the murder of George Floyd, the friends in his group posted black squares on Instagram. They had lived in a white cocoon in Black areas for as long as Ella had known them.

'It's a type of violence, having to negotiate your relationship around suppressing a fundamental part of your being,' she says. 'It's a funny sort of violence. The kind where you're lauded when you bear it, and shamed when you defend yourself against it.'

A rite of passage

The comment 'I've never slept with a Black girl before' in its myriad iterations is a racist microaggression experienced by Black women and Black mixed-race women. For Kimberly McIntosh, dating columnist at *gal-dem* – a publication dedicated to telling the stories of women of colour and non-binary people of colour, this microaggression happened to her just before what would have been her very first time having sex. She describes the 'Black girl comment' as a 'rite of passage' for young Black women.

As the 'would have been' qualifier suggests, McIntosh didn't stick around after that remark was uttered. She left the room and didn't go through with the encounter. 'I didn't have sex with that guy, because I was like, is this really going to be how I lose my virginity? This isn't the story I want.' McIntosh often thinks about the next generation of young people and how they'll contend with such microaggressions. 'Especially as a young person, when you're at your most vulnerable in so many ways, to then be hit with a racist microaggression, as well as the vulnerability of being naked, or not being very sexually experienced, or maybe being away from home for the first time, it's a lot to process.'

It's important to note the role of colourism in the experiences of microaggressions. Darker-skinned Black people report a higher number of microaggressions than lighter-skinned Black people do.[1] Not only that, skin-tone discrimination also affects how desirable a person is perceived to be by prospective partners. As Kaitlyn Greenidge writes in an article for the *Guardian*: 'It is a sad and sobering fact to realise that colour – how dark or light you are perceived as being by a prospective partner, who most likely is someone of your own race – sometimes determines who in our communities is deemed deserving of romance.'[2]

Author and blogger Stephanie Yeboah detailed just some of the messages she received on dating apps over a period of six months, in her book *Fattily Ever After*. 'My fat Black queen. Sit on my face pls,' read one message. 'Mm I have such a thing for chocolate. U like white guys hun?' 'I've heard black girls are wild in bed. Wanna prove me right?' 'I'm looking for a fat dominant black.'

As a fat Black woman, in Yeboah's experience dating apps are an extremely unwelcoming and unsafe space. 'Why? Well, for one, people hardly "like" or "match" with me, and when they do, they always seem to be (and I mean ALWAYS) white men who have a fetish for dominating, fat, Black womxn,' Yeboah explains. 'Do you know how tiresome, dehumanising and disgusting this is?'

This type of behaviour doesn't just appear out of thin air. Nor is it a modern phenomenon born out of dating apps. You can actually trace it back to the fifteenth century. During the Age of Exploration – when European ships travelled the world and first came into contact with the African continent – Europeans began to form ideas and indeed fantasies about Black people's bodies. Elizabethan travel books disseminated these ideas, which blended fact with fiction and fantasy, resulting in the spread of inaccurate and fictitious accounts of Africa and its people. Afua Hirsch relays some of these in a *Guardian* article on fetishisation: '"Like animals", one account reported, Africans would "fall upon their women, just as they come to hand, without any choice". African men had enormous penises, these accounts suggested. One writer went so far as to claim that African men were "furnisht with such members as are after a sort burthensome unto them".'[3]

Blackness was seen as the polar opposite to whiteness, with all the deeply negative connotations that Christianity attaches to the colour black. As Dr Akeia Benard writes in her paper 'Colonizing Black Female Bodies Within Patriarchal Capitalism': 'From the 15th century onward, the "vile" bodies of Africans and women were treated as subsets of humanity. During colonialism, Blacks were not a race in and of themselves but a consequence or opposite of Whiteness.'[4]

This notion of Blackness as a deviation from whiteness stems from the ways in which Christianity framed black as a colour. 'The idea of blackness as a colour was already outlined within Christianity and symbolized inherent evilness, libidinousness and disgrace,' writes Dr Kaila Story, associate professor of women's, gender and sexuality studies at the University of Louisville, in an essay in *Imagining the Black Female Body.* 'It was in this context that Africans were compared to apes – with the same animalistic childishness, savageness, bestiality, sexuality and lack of intellectual capacity.'[5]

Enslaved Black women grew to be associated with the sexualised 'Jezebel' stereotype, in direct contrast to the chaste white Victorian-lady ideal.[6] In the 19th century, according to Patricia Hill Collins, white men 'did not have to look at pornographic pictures of [white] women because they could become voyeurs of black women on the auction block'.[7]

Hypersexuality was projected onto Black people, whereas whiteness became synonymous with marriageability. 'The

popular image of the hypersexual Black woman arose
with and was essential to the creation of the White, marriageable "lady" under colonialism – prostitutes and con-
cubines within the colony who were women of color made
White female virginity possible,' writes Benard. 'The jux-
taposition of the marriageable woman and the sexualized
woman demonstrates the oppression of both White women
and women of color but also highlights that White women
have a vested interest in the colonisation of Black bodies.'[8]
White women were also undoubtedly subjugated under
patriarchal rule during this time (though not to the same
extent as Black women) – but in order for them to continue
being perceived as pure, innocent and marriageable, the
hypersexualisation of Black women continued.

As Vanessa Ntinu writes in *gal-dem*: 'Historically, black
women are perceived as objects of sexual exploitation, dating back to days of slavery where the concept of rape was
never applied to the black woman simply because she was
assumed to have been a willing and promiscuous participant.'[9] During the time of slavery and the Antebellum South
in America, Black women were sexually exploited through
rape. As Ruby Hamad explains in *White Tears/Brown Scars*,
'the rape and exploitation of enslaved Black women was
not just rampant, it was endemic'. Hamad adds that the
writing of enslaved women such as Harriet Jacobs has shed
light on the abuses and violations that were the 'defining
features' of their enslavement. Viewed as property and thus
incapable of being violated, Black girls in their early teens
would be bribed with the promises of better treatment by

white plantation workers, and whipped as punishment if they resisted. The abuse of Black women during this time served as 'a sexual outlet that white men took advantage of in order to maintain the illusion of moral superiority in an era of supposed sexual chastity', writes Hamad.[10]

Five centuries on from the start of the Age of Exploration, the hypersexualisation of Black women, men and non-binary people prevails. Stereotypes around Black women's bodies continue to this day and are perpetuated in the media – in the music videos we watch, in the TV and movies we consume, the magazines we thumb through and the pornography we view. 'Sex is,' Afua Hirsch notes, 'in some ways, a very tangible expression of the deeper currents of prejudice in this country.'[11] The insidious racism that pervades every aspect of society and life is right there, plain as day in people's bedrooms.

Kimberly McIntosh went to a suburban school in Berkshire, and there were very few Black people there. Before she started writing at *gal-dem* and sharing her experiences of dating through her work, the things she was experiencing in the dating realm were completely alien to her friends – they had no idea. 'One of my friends read *Queenie*, and was shocked. I was like, that's my diary. Like, nothing in that book shocked me.' To McIntosh, her friend's reaction to the book made her realise that there are some people walking through life experiencing a very different existence and set of experiences to other people.

Queenie, the bestselling novel by Candice Carty-Williams, tells the story of the eponymous heroine Queenie

Jenkins, a Jamaican Londoner, as she navigates the world of dating and casual sex. Queenie's ventures into the dating game are peppered with an abundance of racist micro-aggressions, including non-consensual hair-touching: '"I like your, uh, hair. All this," he said, awkwardly patting the bun on my head. "Don't touch it!" I ducked out of his grasp, losing my footing and falling again, this time against the bar.' Carty-Williams also roves into the territory of non-consensual acts of rough sex – so rough that Queenie presents at a sexual health clinic with internal injuries, shrugging off the cause as 'just some rough sex, I guess?'[12]

White people touching Black women's hair without consent is an act that is charged with white entitlement, racism and misogynoir. A white person choosing to invade a Black person's personal space to touch their hair without consent is an act of objectification and a violation of a person's agency in society.[13] A white person believing that they don't require Black women's consent to touch a part of her body is rooted in white supremacy. For Black women, hair is an expression of their identity, but it can also be a medium for making political statements, for showing confidence and personality, and it is a sacred space for self-expression.

To this day, Black people are still discriminated against because of the texture of their hair, and made to feel they must change their hair to conform to European beauty standards. This pressure can manifest in romantic and sexual relationships. Emma Dabiri writes in *Don't Touch My Hair* that 'while I have had white guys try to "run" their fingers through my hair, Black men tend to know better.

Nonetheless, I've still heard a number extol this "fingers through the hair" malarkey as an ideal.'[14]

Colonialism has had a huge impact on our sexual culture in the UK and the West – one that extends beyond hyper-sexualisation. Almaz Ohene – a journalist specialising in sexual health and a member of the Decolonising Contraception collective – writes extensively on colonialism's lasting legacy in our sexual culture and in the field of sexual and reproductive healthcare.

'The British colonial project kind of took hold massively in the Victorian era and, apart from exporting British values of democracy, they also exported British views on sexuality, which were missionary views,' she explains. Those views included viewing sex solely as a means to reproduce and not for pleasure. 'It meant that to toe the line, indigenous peoples had to conform to colonial ideas of sexuality. So existing family structures like polygamous households, and non-binary people, had to all be suppressed. In order to not endanger your community, you had to suppress that older style of living and become the way the colonisers wanted you to be.' Ohene adds that the legacy of this can be seen in the fact that many former British colonies are still 'staunchly Christian, Protestant and Anglican, even more so than we are now in the West'.

Homophobia is also a British colonial export. Section 377 of the British penal code criminalised all sexual acts 'against the order of nature'. In more than thirty former British colonies, these laws against homosexuality are still in place.[15]

Just as colonisers in the past looked on Black women's bodies and equated them with sexual wantonness, mainstream pornography upholds the very same racist tropes and perpetuates them to this day. 'Non-white bodies have also been eroticised and othered in colonialism, and we can still see this today in mainstream pornography in the way that things are categorised,' says Ohene. If you visit an aggregator porn site, you'll spot that porn is racialised and divided into race categories – Ebony, Biracial, Asian, to name a few. Some sites also let users browse the category 'interracial' to allow them to search out various combinations of characters and scenarios.

'A lot of the time, the situations that those people are being filmed doing are really racist and misogynistic scenarios, rather than just showing a couple engaging in some kind of sex acts as two people making some porn,' says Ohene. 'Often on these aggregator sites, it comes with loads of really problematic issues and tropes behind it as well. And no one really seems to be commenting on this.'

That silence is owed in part to the way that pornography is policed in this country, explains Ohene. This is a reference to the stringent age verification checks the UK government attempted to bring in, which would have made porn harder to access for children – while also adding a blanket complication for all adult consumers of porn. 'In this country, pornography is seen as inherently bad and transgressive. We don't have any kind of critical framework in which to critique the material,' says Ohene. 'It's really sad, because there is a lot of really exciting and really artful pornography being made. It's absolutely pushed to the complete margins in this country.'

Plus-size Black women's bodies are censored on Instagram, further contributing to the othering that pornography already perpetuates. (Othering is the process of setting certain communities apart from what you consider to be a complete and valid member of society.[16]) In July 2020, Nyome Nicholas-Williams posted photos of herself holding her breasts in a common pose that's seen on Instagram.[17] The images, which aimed to show self-love and body acceptance, were removed by Instagram – deemed in violation of the platform's pornography and nudity guidelines. The move prompted Nicholas-Williams to launch the #IWantToSeeNyome campaign, during which it became clear that Instagram was allowing almost identically posed photos of thin white women to remain on people's feeds, while censoring images of Black women in the same or similar poses. Nicholas-Williams, along with fellow activist Gina Martin and photographer Alexandra Cameron, lobbied Instagram and successfully got the app to change its policy on breast-holding. The issue itself is part of a broader culture, however – one that sees Black bodies as obscene and sexually explicit, and champions white bodies as the ideal.

So, how does one go about dismantling centuries of damaging hypersexualisation, fetishism, and micro- and macro-aggressions – all of which are deeply rooted in racism? Is one possible solution to incorporate anti-racism education in sex education curricula? Portia Brown, a sex educator

and founder of Froetic Sexology, a sex education platform
which centres Black women and femmes, tells me she is in
favour of including anti-racism in sex-ed. 'Let me just say
that if your sex education is not anti-racist, and it does not
include information about the history of how sex education
came to be where it is, you're not really doing what you
think you are doing,' she says.

She continues: 'I don't think we have to go as far and be as
explicit as saying, you know, "Don't touch a Black woman's
hair without her consent." I think that there are ways that
we can craft the conversation so that those sort of things
are implied and understood, because it goes further than
anecdotal moments of hair-touching, of non-consensual
spanking, of using certain words in the bedroom, or emu-
lating things that you've seen on television or in media that
are racist or misogynoir.'

Talking about racism in sex education is necessary
for several reasons. First, it's important to understand
how people in the past came to learn about female anatomy. John Marion Sims was hailed the 'father of modern
gynaecology' for developing the surgical repair of vesico-
vaginal fistulae – a complication of childbirth prevalent
in nineteenth-century women. But the Alabama surgeon's
experiments and operations in the 1840s were carried out
on non-consenting Black enslaved women.[18]

'Sex education and our understanding of women's bodies came at the cost of Black enslaved women and people's
bodies, and the exploitation and harm and violation of them
for study by J. Marion Sims and many other doctors – and

I use the term "doctor" very loosely because that man was not a doctor,' says Brown. People need to be made aware of the human cost of the anatomical knowledge scientists and doctors obtained through unethical means.

A lot of the tools and techniques that Sims developed are still in use today. It was Sims who developed the vaginal speculum, the metal or plastic hinged tool that's used in pelvic exams and cervical screenings today. As Brown puts it, 'It cost somebody something for us to have that information – someone had to lose their life or some of their dignity in order for us to get it.'

Just as our sexual culture is firmly rooted in colonialism, so too is the field of sexual and reproductive healthcare. Black women in the UK and Ireland are five times more likely to die in childbirth than their white counterparts.[19] Black Ballad surveyed 2,500 Black women, who reported experiencing substandard care, discrimination and microaggressions during pregnancy care and birth.[20]

'Black physical pain isn't believed,' says Almaz Ohene. 'And that stems from a eugenics belief that Black people just don't feel pain and are somehow lesser. That view still permeates the way that medicine is practised today, which is really disappointing. The high childbirth mortality rate is also compounded by lots of structural and socioeconomic factors as well.'

Birth control and contraception have an equally troubling, racist, paternalistic history. During the twentieth century, medical abuses in the field of reproductive healthcare targeted women of colour, in particular poor and immigrant communities. The contraceptive pill was first trialled on low-income Puerto Rican women in the 1950s, during a period of largely unregulated scientific history. Informed consent was not obtained from participants – and nor was it legally required during that time.[21]

Eugenics programmes in the Southern states of the US enforced coerced sterilisations which were so commonplace that they were named 'Mississippi appendectomies'.[22] Between 1930 and 1970, more than 7,600 sterilisations were ordered by the state of North Carolina – 65 per cent of those were carried out on Black women.[23] In 1965, a survey uncovered that 35 per cent of Puerto Rican women between the ages of 20 and 49 had been sterilised during US population control regimes imposed on the territory.[24]

In July 2020, Planned Parenthood of Greater New York announced it would remove the name of founder Margaret Sanger from the building of its Manhattan health clinic because of her 'harmful connections to the eugenics movement'.[25] In 2016, the Planned Parenthood Federation of America released a fact sheet clarifying Sanger's views on race and her 'outreach' work with the African American community. The fact sheet confirmed that Sanger made a speech on birth control to a women's auxiliary branch of the Ku Klux Klan in 1926.[26]

The national Planned Parenthood organisation also claimed that Sanger 'repudiated the racist exploitation of eugenics principles', but she did agree with incentivising the sterilisation of Disabled people and people with untreatable, hereditary conditions. She also believed in placing 'so-called illiterates, paupers, unemployables, criminals, prostitutes, and dope fiends' on farms in the name of strengthening 'moral conduct'.

In this day and age, we rightly celebrate access to reproductive and sexual healthcare as hard-fought freedoms that are nonetheless still under threat. Access to contraception and safe, legal abortion is fundamental healthcare. But it's also true that those services came at a human cost and hold a legacy that is problematic. In championing the organisations and services we consider central to gender equality, we should also acknowledge the ways in which these services have harmed and violated marginalised communities in the past.

Ohene believes our sex-ed curriculum should include modules on colonialism's role in shaping our sexual culture. 'We don't really get taught in sex education about historical attitudes to sex,' she says. 'It's almost like the way we talk about sex, pleasure and reproductive stuff, it's as if it has always been the way it is right now in contemporary society.'

Is it possible to decolonise our sexual culture? Ohene believes it is. 'What we have to understand is that the way the curriculum is put together, it's by the people who are currently in power, and they have their own agenda to push. I think we have to make people aware that what is most important to the particular government when they put it in the curriculum, it's not the full story. Talking about queerness, polyamory, polygamy and non-mono-heteronormative cultures is the first step towards decolonising sex-ed, because living in units of the nuclear family with a cis male dad and a cis female mum, two to three children, is definitely not how the whole of humanity has lived the entire time.'

She adds, 'I'm not saying that other ways, other family structures, don't have their own problems. But I find it endlessly frustrating that we're sold this narrative that you can only raise children within this heteronormative nuclear family.'

But as well as calling out what's happened in the past, Brown argues that we need to acknowledge the power structures at play that allowed that conduct to occur and call it what it is: racism and white supremacy. 'That was systemic racism at play and that's why we have this information today,' says Brown. 'But we need to honour those people that suffered and were violated so that we can be better humans to ourselves and to each other in the present day.'

Kimberly McIntosh says that anti-racism in sex-ed would need to be carefully drawn up and would also need to delve into pornography's role in perpetuating racist tropes. 'Obviously, I want things to be better for the generation coming up behind us,' she says. 'People are watching porn from a young age, but from a young age you're not analysing it as a social scientist, saying, "Oh, look at this hypermasculine portrayal of Black men."'

Being equipped with the knowledge that porn disseminates damaging tropes about race and sexuality is important – particularly when we know young people often turn to porn to learn about sex. McIntosh believes it would be helpful for people to have that explained to them, so they're aware of how pornography might be shaping their perceptions of Black people. 'You'll have people consuming it and they might not even know any Black people, they might live in a really white area, and one of their first encounters is through that medium.'

In the aftermath of George Floyd's murder in May 2020, as statues were torn down, plaques were removed and building names were changed, one sentence began to be uttered over and over again: 'We cannot erase our history.' This statement was often made by people who didn't believe that statues of racist people should be torn down, and it was uttered by people who in the very same breath argued that 'all lives matter'. Meanwhile, the objectification of Black men and women's bodies at Black Lives Matter protests showed that hypersexualisation was very much alive and well. At rallies, white women wielded placards which read 'I Love Black Dick' and carried black dildos in their hands.

No one is trying to erase history. If anything, we should be *more* aware of our history – but that includes uncomfortable truths about how countries like the UK came to be powerful, and the people at whose expense that power came.

CHAPTER 10

'How could you call me a racist?'

Neha was hooking up with a guy and had a feeling of uneasiness about the situation. 'When you're a Brown girl and you date a white guy,' she says, 'often it's a question of "Am I your in-between person before you end up with someone from your own exact background?"'

It was only when she talked to a friend of hers that she realised the feeling of uneasiness was entirely justified. 'I was talking to my friend, she's another Brown girl, and I told her about the situation with the guy and she immediately goes, "Oh, you didn't want to be the Brown Girl Rebound," and she instantly got it.'

When Neha brought her feelings up with the guy she'd been hooking up with and asked him if she was his 'Brown

Girl Rebound', he reacted badly. 'He was just like, "How could you say that? How could you call me a racist?" and I was like, "I'm not calling you racist, I'm just saying you might have unconscious or implicit bias that you're not aware of."' Neha explained to him that she has definitely had those biases herself. 'It's a process of unlearning those things from a system we were born into. It's not to cast blame, right? But he was just like "no".'

That's when she realised the guy she had slept with cared more about being labelled a racist than addressing his own conduct. 'I feel like sometimes in these conversations, people are more worried about being perceived that way than correcting their behaviour,' she says. The guy ended up calling Neha later and they had a three-hour-long conversation because he was so worried that she would perceive him in a negative light.

This wasn't Neha's first conversation about racism with a white partner. Following the break-up of her last serious relationship, the man she had almost married said something to her that crystallised the fact that breaking up was the right decision. 'When we broke up he was like, "One thing I'm happy about is that I'll get to be with someone where we don't have to constantly talk about race."'

Neha describes him as a little older than her, good-hearted and a good person. 'But he had a photo of himself in a slum surrounded by poor Kenyan children, and I was like, "You need to take that down," and he wouldn't and he didn't understand why that was bad. Even though I explained it a million times, that it's not about you, it's about what it represents – colonialism, history. He was just like, "No, you're wrong."'

In her sex life, the microaggressions have always been almost-imperceptible slights – but present, nonetheless. 'With sex, it's always been more subtle, it's always been almost like, "Have you told your parents I'm a person of colour?"'

With one white guy Neha slept with, she could sense from his behaviour that he hadn't slept with a Brown woman before. 'When we had sex, he almost seemed surprised by certain things, just how I look, you know?' she explains. 'And so, afterwards I was like, "Have you . . . ever had sex with a Brown girl before?"

'He was like, "No no, you're the first one," but he was like, "but one of my best friends is Indian." I was like, "it's not the same."'

As a biracial woman, Neha feels caught between two communities, neither of which treats her well in romantic and sexual situations. 'I have dated a lot of white guys, partly because I'm culturally more comfortable. I am not as culturally Indian, but I get highly fetishised by guys in the Indian community for being biracial. Guys in the Indian community will assume I'm slutty or loose because I'm half white,' she says.

'I get it from both ends,' she adds. 'You get so much sexism from your own community and so much racism from outside your community, you're getting pummelled from all sides.'

After Neha came out as bisexual, she had a lot of guys she knew approach her and say, 'Oh, you're bi, so I can talk to you about girls now.' What they meant by that was that they could talk about women in a way that was less than flattering. 'And I was just like, "It's not erotic to me to demean women."'

Deep down, Neha fears that she'll never be taken seriously in a romantic context. 'If you're mixed I identify with you more because you understand that we don't belong in either world. We confuse everyone,' she says. 'You don't ever know if people will take you seriously because you're always some weird hybrid creature. And they don't quite know what to make of you.'

The fetishisation and sexualisation of Brown women has a troubling legacy, and Disney has played a significant role. A simple Google search of 'Princess Jasmine' will pull up scores of links to porn. In a Medium piece, Nerdy PoC writes that the very way in which Jasmine and Esmeralda are portrayed others them and sets them apart from the white Disney princesses: 'The relationships of both of these girls with the male antagonists are overtly sexual in nature, both of them being seen to "seduce" the men in question with their bodies, their movements sensual and purposeful, a far cry from the delicate waltzes and pirouettes of other (white) princesses.'[1]

Rubina Pabani and Poppy Jay host BBC Asian Network's Brown Girls Do It Too, which is available on BBC Sounds.[2] The podcast centres on British Asian women's sex lives, and is a judgement-free and no-holds-barred space. Pabani and Jay say there is a lot of mystery surrounding British Asian women's sex lives, and they want to break the silence.

Pabani explains that the cultural reason for this mystery is twofold. 'It's about Asian community cultures and us keeping sex secret because of the patriarchy, but then it's about British cultural values that don't make British Asian women feel sexy, that don't put them at the front of magazines, that don't celebrate them as sexual beings,' she says. 'Those are two big things that are pressing down on British Asian female sexuality. We never had space to talk about it. And we never had the kind of inclination to talk about it.'

In episode one of the podcast, Pabani shares an anecdote about a guy she once slept with. 'He was like, "You know how some guys have 'yellow fever'?" As in, they're into East Asian women, which I think is a little bit racist. He was like, "I've got 'brown fever'."'

Pabani elaborates on her thoughts about the fetishisation of Brown women. 'I think that kind of stuff can make you feel uncomfortable, and then you realise that you are being exoticised,' she says. 'But you've also got to remember that the communities of ethnic minorities that have been brought to this country have always felt like they were never attractive and felt like they were never the centre of anything. We're not the protagonists in British films, we're not sex symbols, we're not celebrities, we don't present *Strictly Come Dancing*, we're not Ant and Dec.'

Pabani is honest about the effects of British Asian people being othered and excluded from mainstream beauty ideals. 'A bit of exoticism and a bit of fetishisation, it doesn't go amiss because we're like, "Sick, white people think I'm fit." And I know that sounds terrible, but we do thrive on that. We're like, "Brilliant, we've made it into the mainstream, white people think we're attractive." It's terrible.'

Comments like 'I have brown fever' are deeply problematic, as Pabani points out. Racial fetishism is complicated, because of the fact it is deeply rooted in colonisation. But when a community is desexualised and disbarred from what the mainstream considers sexually desirable, does the term 'fetish' further reinforce the idea that sexual attraction to white people is mainstream, and anything beyond that is a niche fetish?

The mention of the racist term 'yellow fever' is a reference to the sexual fetishisation of East Asian women. Caucasian men fetishise and exotify East Asian and Southeast Asian women, making sweeping assumptions about their bodies and personalities based on reductive stereotypes and homogenising media portrayals.[3] Some of these damaging stereotypes include the notion that Asian women have smaller vaginas, and that they are obedient, submissive, subservient and hypersexual.

As Brittany Wong writes in HuffPost, this isn't a new phenomenon. 'It's been a thing since at least the late 1800s, when the first Victorian men visited port cities in Japan and became transfixed by geishas. French writer Pierre Loti's incredibly popular 1887 novel *Madame Chrysanthème* (later

adapted into Puccini's famous opera, *Madame Butterfly*)
cemented the image of Asian women as doll-like, subservient objects of lust.'[4]

So, these stereotypes are firmly rooted in the past, dating back to a time of imperialism and the colonisation of
Asia. But white men are continuing this centuries-long
legacy of fetishisation on dating apps, and their messages
are being documented on Instagram account @theflesh-
lightchronicles. The messages range from 'I'll eat your
pussy like shrimp fried rice' to 'I need my yellow fever
cured', 'do Asians really have tighter buttholes' and 'I want
to try Asian pussy'. And this hypersexualisation has consequences. When Asian women are viewed as sex objects, it
creates a culture where sexual violence is seen as permis-
sible and normalised.[5]

Though we might not care to admit it, colonialism has left
an indelible mark in Western sexual culture. White people
need to acknowledge and reckon with the uncomfortable
legacy of colonialism, and start to dismantle the damaging
stereotypes that fuel fetishisation and hypersexualisation.
That starts with committing to anti-racism – and recognis-
ing that the bedroom isn't exempt from allyship. In interracial relationships, white people committing to simply not
being racist is not enough.

Gaslighting

Journalist and domestic violence specialist Evie Muir
believes childhood racism can make women of colour

vulnerable to abuse in adulthood. 'The normalisation of racism experienced throughout childhood desensitises us to the point that when we are subjected to it in our romantic relationships, it doesn't present as a red flag,' Muir writes. 'We are gaslit into minimising these experiences and dismissing them as normal. Because we've become accustomed to accommodating whiteness ever since primary school, and because the imagery of victims we see in the media rarely represent us or the nuanced ways racism equates to verbal and emotional abuse, it's harder to recognise that we're being abused.'[6]

In interracial romantic and sexual relationships, people of colour can experience racial gaslighting. Mashable reporter Siobhan Neela-Stock writes that racial gaslighting has happened to her her whole life. 'Whenever I've pushed back when asked the racist question "Where are you from?", argued against someone who says discussing race perpetuates racism (the opposite is actually true), or contradicted members of my white extended family who insist Eric Garner's death was his fault, I'm usually told I'm wrong, it's not that big of a deal, or I'm imagining things.'[7]

Racial gaslighting happens when someone brings up racism as a general topic, or discusses a specific racist act, and is told that they're wrong, that 'not everything is about race', or even criticised for the way in which they've talked about the topic. 'As a brown woman of Indian descent who grew up in Vermont, one of the whitest states in the nation at over 94 percent white, I'm used to these manipulations,'

Neela-Stock continues. 'However it took me a long time to recognize racial gaslighting for what it is: a way to control how a person reacts.'

Sometimes, this gaslighting relies on racist stereotypes – for instance, the 'angry Black woman' trope – as a way of attempting to undermine the veracity of what's being said. This serves to invalidate the speaker's experience, and makes them feel silenced.

In a post on the r/interracialdating subreddit, a woman in an interracial relationship describes how her white husband is gaslighting her about race.[8] 'We've been married for almost 12 years. Together for 14. We have a 12 year old son,' she begins.

'I identify as a Black woman. In a recent argument about race, my husband attempted to minimize my experience as a mixed kid living in VA in the south in the 80s. Like I had to whip out statistics to like prove to him how bad it was when I was growing up. Like I was the only mixed kid and there were maybe 50 black kids at my high school of 1200 people. I was teased and harassed mercilessly throughout school. Prank calls to my house. Being called the N-word, being teased about my hair, called OREO. They followed me everywhere. EVERYWHERE. It was traumatizing.'

The woman describes how her husband attempted to turn the conversation around to argue that Black people are racist against white people. 'So my lovely husband who grew up in a mostly black area and was bused in from the suburbs to go to a black school subsequently pipes up that he was jumped by some black kids and they were racist obvs. And I'm just not okay with him tacitly condoning this backhanded but black people are racist too argument and I can't stop yelling at him and I'm finding it to be a giant turn off.'

The reverse racism argument rests on the premise that Black people are racist toward white people. To be clear: reverse racism does not exist. The belief that it does ignores the power structures that uphold racism, and the vast systemic power white people wield over Black people and other marginalised communities when perpetuating racism.

Reni Eddo-Lodge crystallises this point in her book *Why I'm No Longer Talking to White People About Race*, making a clear distinction between racism and plain-old bad behaviour. 'There is an unattributed definition of racism that defines it as prejudice plus power,' she writes. 'Those disadvantaged by racism can certainly be cruel, vindictive and prejudiced. Everyone has the capacity to be nasty to other people, to judge them before they get to know them. But there simply aren't enough black people in positions of power to enact racism against white people on the kind of grand scale it currently operates at against black people.'[9]

White people in interracial relationships should commit to anti-racism work as a moral obligation, argues Evie Muir. 'Doing so ensures your partner is not intentionally or unintentionally harmed further.' Eboni Harris, a licensed relationship therapist and the founder of Melanin and Mental Health, echoes this in Muir's piece. 'It's no longer acceptable to just *not participate* in racism,' she says. 'When you choose to be in a relationship with a person of colour, you must advocate for their lives and rights like you would your own. Your actions must align with the love you have for that person.'[10]

While anti-racism in sex education will benefit younger generations, we also need to look to those of us who left school a while ago and who are no longer under the tutelage of school curricula. For non-Black people who have sex with Black women, the question to ask yourself is this: 'How can I be a better ally to Black women in the bedroom?'

That starts with listening to Black women in all contexts – not just in the bedroom. 'Listening to Black women and femmes and making it part of your life is going to make you a better ally to Black women and a better partner to Black femme-identified people if you have the chance to be intimate with some of them,' says Portia Brown. 'So don't make it just about being in bed with someone. Make it about: How am I a better ally to Black women in my life? Am I really listening to them? Am I seeking information from Black femmes?'

But that doesn't mean expecting Black women to provide emotional labour and educate people about racism. When seeking information from Black people, rather than contacting them and asking questions about topics that may be deeply triggering and re-traumatising to talk about, non-Black people should instead consider doing their own additional reading and turning to media outlets which centre the voices of Black people and people of colour, like *gal-dem*, Black Ballad and *Aurelia Magazine*.

In this additional reading, books by Black authors should not, however, be treated as 'medicine' to treat racism. As author Yaa Gyasi writes in the *Guardian*: 'So many of the writers of colour that I know have had white people treat their work as though it were a kind of medicine. Something they have to swallow in order to improve their condition, but they don't really want it, they don't really enjoy it, and if they're being totally honest, they don't actually even take the medicine half the time. They just buy it and leave it on the shelf.'[11] Anti-racism literature can be useful, but in order to bring about genuine long-lasting change, we must go further than these works and target the roots of oppression that we might uphold in our personal lives, consumer decisions, and places of work.

Portia Brown says it's important to ask yourself if you're making a point of seeking out Black women's work because you want to hear their experience and the information their work contains, or if it's purely tokenism. 'Or am I just waiting to get into bed with them and then being like, "Oh shit, what do I do?"' She adds that people can't be good allies if we aren't practising that allyship across the board in our lives. Allyship isn't just limited to the workplace or friendships – it applies to all areas of life. The bedroom is not exempt from that.

Allyship extends beyond simply declaring yourself an ally. It is an active state that requires work and showing up. As Aja Barber, writer and fashion consultant, says in Gina Martin's book *Be the Change*: 'Remember that "ally" should be a verb and not a noun. We should all be constantly learning and growing and that means that your work as an ally is never really completed.'[12] Don't view that as a daunting, insurmountable challenge that you'll never be able to achieve, but rather a lifelong commitment.

CHAPTER 11

For your viewing pleasure

Kelly was in her second year of university and was living with a friend she'd made the year prior. They weren't the best of friends, but they grew relatively close and Kelly enjoyed spending time with her.

One night, Kelly and her roommate ended up going out by themselves after an event they'd been at with friends. 'We hung out all night, laughing and dancing, it was so nice,' she says. 'After that night I felt things change between us; we flirted more and teased each other. It was all friendly and playful. Then for my birthday she gave me this amazing gift and flowers and asked me out. Even though all my friends said dating your roommate was a mistake, I said yes. (Spoiler alert: it was.)'

The two of them went out a few times and had a good time. Kelly says their living situation wasn't really affected, and things seemed to be going great. 'Then one morning before I left for winter break we were in her bed kissing and she started to touch me,' she recalls. 'At first it was innocent, over the clothes, and I didn't panic or freak out. I was into it. Then she went under my shirt and I felt kinda weird but I pushed through it thinking I was just nervous about her seeing my body for the first time. Then she pulled my shirt off and I definitely felt weird.'

Kelly describes feeling like there was a rock in her stomach. But she pushed through that feeling. 'Then she went into my pants and I really didn't want to do anything more, but I was a participant and it was already going far so I kept going. But it felt weird and I wasn't having fun or anything. Then she asked me to touch her and even though I was like, maybe this is as far as it should go, she said she was already touching me so touching her shouldn't be a big deal. So I did.'

Afterwards, Kelly left and stayed with friends until she could catch a train home for the winter break. Her roommate called and texted, but Kelly didn't want to talk to her. 'I couldn't get that day out of my head,' she says. 'Every message just reminded me of how uncomfortable I'd felt and that sinking rock feeling in my stomach. Eventually we stopped talking and I met my wife and we started dating. Honestly, it was only two years later that I realised how terrible that situation was and how I should've stood up for myself and said no.'

Research shows that queer women are most at risk of sexual violence. According to the CDC's National Intimate Partner and Sexual Violence Survey in the US, 44 per cent of lesbians and 61 per cent of bisexual women experience sexual violence, physical violence or stalking by a partner, while 35 per cent of straight women experience this type of abuse.[1]

Neha, who shared her experience of being fetishised as a Brown woman in chapter 10, has experienced fetishism as a bisexual woman too.

'I had a particularly awful experience with a white boy who fetishised my bisexuality and tried to use me as a rebound after breaking up with his girlfriend. I called him out for it – and was bullied, berated, gaslit,' she says. 'He was just like, "You're making assumptions." Then flat-out lied. Changed the order of things that had happened, told me I was biased at him for being a white male and that I was projecting.'

Neha had engaged in phone sex with the man and chatted to him for hours. 'We were supposed to meet up at some point, but then he flaked and revealed later he had COVID,' she says. 'During our talk, he also mentioned he was happy more minorities were being hired but was concerned it was more challenging for him – a white male – to get a job because of it.'

At one point, the guy showed Neha a photo of another woman he'd hooked up with. 'She was a woman of colour too,' she says. 'When I think back, he sent me a lot of porn. And we did talk about sex, but I mentioned I was celibate until February. He seemed not to care. Then he sent me an erotic photo of a bunch of women and I replied, "That's not how bisexuality works."'

When Neha confronted him about it, he reacted very badly. 'The first time he called me to yell at me about it, I apologised. I honestly tried to see his point of view, but he's awful.' What she was trying to tell him, though, was that identifying as bisexual, plus the objectification that comes with being openly bisexual, as well as being a woman of colour, affect her sex and dating experiences.

The fetishisation of bisexual women is a problem on dating apps. In an anonymous blog post published by Tinder, a bisexual woman relayed some of the messages she receives from men. 'So, do you have any friends that would like to join us later?' 'Tell me about the first time you were with a girl.' 'You like girls? That's so hot! Are you bringing one of your friends along next time?'[2] She then writes about how the framing of relationships between two women as an erotic fantasy runs rampant in media and society, and about the damaging way women who love women are portrayed in advertising, movies and pornography. 'The loving part of lesbian relationships – the romantic dates, the feeling you get just hanging out with your S.O., the genuine care you have for each other – is seldom shown. As a result, women who like women bear the brunt of an unfair stereotype.'

This hypersexualisation has been linked to the high rate of sexual violence experienced by bisexual women. In the LGBTQ community, bisexual women and trans people experience the highest rates of sexual and intimate partner violence.[3] In the US, the CDC estimates that 61 per cent of bisexual women experience abuse, while other studies suggest 75 per cent of bi women experience sexual violence.[4] That violence also starts young: 48 per cent of bi women who are rape survivors were first raped between the ages of 11 and 17.[5]

Why do bisexual women face some of the highest rates of sexual violence? According to Dr Nicole Johnson, assistant professor of counselling psychology at Lehigh University, who co-authored a paper on the issue in the *Journal of Bisexuality*, there are three main factors: hypersexualisation, substance use and biphobic harassment. She notes that 'sexual violence enacted against bisexual women within intimate relationships may result from social constructions of bisexual women as especially worthy of distrust, jealousy, and other emotions and/or perceptions related to uneven power dynamics and hostility within the relationship'.[6]

Johnson tells me she strongly believes the main reason bisexual women are highly at risk of sexual violence is because of cultural views of bisexuality. 'Bisexual women frequently report experiences of hypersexualisation, being viewed as objects for sexual pleasure and lacking sexual choice or autonomy,' she explains. 'Therefore, if an individual (most frequently a man) finds out a woman is bisexual, they may assume this means that the woman is "sexually available" or "promiscuous" and therefore her "no" or resistance is viewed as "token resistance" and not "real" denial. You'll notice I'm using a lot of quotations because I want it to be clear that they are internalised cultural messages that are not true and do not remove responsibility from perpetrators or place any blame on the victims.'

Bisexual women are both invisible and hypervisible, says Johnson. Bi women are largely invisible in the media, she argues, and on the rare occasion that they are represented, their sexuality is portrayed as a 'phase' before coming out as a lesbian, or a period of experimentation before concluding they're straight.

'Alternatively, the media, and pornography in particular, have a long history of depicting women as "bisexual" while engaging in same-sex behaviours for the pleasure of male onlookers,' says Johnson in an article. This behaviour – known as 'performative bisexuality' – has filtered into our culture. Performative bisexuality occurs when two women perform same-sex behaviour in front of male onlookers for the purpose of attracting the male gaze. 'Many of these women/girls later denounce bisexuality, furthering the "invisible-hypervisible" experience of bisexuality.'[7]

As a society, we have a duty to address these widespread and damaging cultural views that are still perpetuated through pop culture today. We need to address the very tangible harm brought about by the hypersexualisation of bisexual women, and to acknowledge its role in contributing to such high rates of sexual violence against bi women. Johnson argues that combating the myths that surround bisexuality – including that bisexual people 'are attracted to everyone, we are always open for sex, and bisexuality is just a phase' – would be extremely valuable, as would an increase in the representation of bisexual women in the media.

This starts with how we engage with bisexual people in everyday interactions – not just sexual ones. Paisley Gilmour, sex and relationships editor at *Cosmopolitan* UK, wrote about biphobia and how straight people can be better allies to their bi friends. She explains how, years before she came out as bi, she confided in a friend that she wanted to start dating women. 'She laughed and said I should "stop trying to be so edgy" – a remark that in hindsight contributed to me repressing those feelings for another three years.'[8]

Bisexual women aren't alone in having their sexuality fetishised. Lesbians are also fetishised by straight men and more broadly in pop culture. In an article for *Diva* magazine about her experiences of being hypersexualised as a queer woman, Charlotte Summers writes: 'Speaking from experience, online I have faced many DMs and comments asking for threesomes and I often get unsolicited dick pics. My relationship has also faced sexualisation and men have approached us in the streets whilst asking intrusive questions. We avoid all straight clubs, because the harassment is overwhelming and when we tell them "no" because we're in a relationship, it only fuels the fire.'[9]

Mainstream pop culture treats queer women as sex objects that exist solely to cater to the male gaze – whether it's Joey from *Friends* constantly making comments about lesbians being a sexual fantasy of his, or pop stars like Liam Payne singing lyrics that hypersexualise queer women. If you want to see what biphobia in mainstream pop music sounds like, take a look at the lyrics to 'Both Ways' from Payne's album *LP1*. The song drew a great deal of criticism for its biphobic lyrics and fetishism of bisexuality. Payne later issued a rather half-hearted apology for his lyrics. 'I am sorry to anyone who got offended by certain songs or different things on the album for sure,' he told the *Daily Star*. 'It was never my intention with any of the writing or things I was doing.'[10]

But these sexualised songs and TV shows are not without consequences. The normalisation of this fetishism leads to biphobic remarks and microaggressions, in addition to overt violence and aggression.

In 2019, two queer women who'd been on a date were beaten for refusing to kiss at the request of several men onboard a bus. One of the women, Dr Melania Geymonat, told the BBC the group of young men were harassing her and her date Christine Hannigan when they discovered the women were a couple. 'They surrounded us and started saying really aggressive stuff, things about sexual positions, lesbians and claiming we could kiss so they could watch us.' When the women refused, the men started throwing coins at them. 'The next thing I know Chris is in the middle of the bus and they are punching her. So I immediately went there by impulse and tried to pull her out of there and they started punching me. I was really bleeding.'[11]

Misogyny, homophobia and male sexual entitlement combined during that attack. The two queer women on the bus were, in the eyes of those young men, there for the viewing pleasure of their male spectators. The message was clear: kiss on command for our viewing pleasure, or we'll beat you until you bleed.

When I interviewed Ruth Hunt, former chief executive of Stonewall, for my podcast History Becomes Her, I asked her if people in society are aware of the persistent threat posed by homophobia and biphobia. 'I think that there is a degree of complacency about how far attitudes have shifted,' she told me. 'There's an ease with which people say, "Well, it's an older generational objection, and this will pass and change." That's certainly not what Stonewall sees, and it's not what I experience as a lesbian wandering around town. London is no more immune to this than Dorset is.'

Hunt views the attack on Geymonat and Hannigan as a real insight into the persistent anxiety that exists if you're an LGBTQ person in public places. 'What you are constantly doing is risk assessing, and assessing whether a situation is safe or not and whether that situation has changed. There's a reason why I cycle everywhere, in sometimes my three-piece suits and my tweeds tucked into my boots. You know, it is infinitely safer to be on a bike as a dyke, frankly, and get around quickly. My partner and I don't even have to communicate when we're out when we know that suddenly something doesn't feel safe. We'll let go of each other's hands and we'll move away.'

So, how can we as a society work to address the hypersexualisation of queer women and the violence that stems from it? Hunt believes that compulsory sex and relationships education in schools is the answer: 'I think that starts in primary schools with good conversations about how boys treat girls and what good behaviour looks like and how we respect women.'

We also need to think about the impact lesbian porn has on young men who've turned to porn to learn about sex, she says. 'Lesbian porn is designed to demean, diminish and to deride, and if men are only learning about lesbian identities through pornography, then that fuels the misogyny that relates to homophobia.' Hunt believes the answer lies in talking to men much more, talking to boys about respect, what sex looks like, and in talking to women about sexual pleasure. 'I find it extraordinary in this day and age that we don't talk to girls about their own pleasure, and what they need, and what they want, and what they can say yes to, and what they can say no to, and how that's as much part of education as what sex isn't. How we can have a healthy relationship with sex is, I think, incredibly important. And then the way in which lesbians become either a figure of derision or fantasy will hopefully decrease.'

Generations of people were not allowed to learn about LGBTQ people and the issues affecting their lives because of a policy introduced in the 1980s. If you were at school in the UK between 1988 and 2003, then Section 28 will have been in place. Section 28 was a law passed in 1988 by Margaret Thatcher that stopped councils and schools 'promoting the teaching of the acceptability of homosexuality as a pretended family relationship'. It was repealed in 2003. Schoolchildren during this era grew up with a policy that legitimated the erasure of LGBTQ people, and were essentially taught that heterosexuality was the only valid sexual identity. Bullying was rife during this era, and young LGBTQ people grew up without learning about the issues that affect them, sometimes never even hearing the words 'gay', 'lesbian' or 'bisexual' while at school.[12] Ruth Hunt told me about her experience of going to school when Section 28 was still in force: 'I was at primary school. And the words lesbian, gay, bi, or trans or anything like that were not mentioned at all. And any books that positively depicted those things were removed from the shelves.'[13]

LGBTQ-inclusive sex education doesn't just mean educating heterosexual men that lesbian and bisexual women don't exist for their viewing pleasure. It should also work towards eradicating the assumption that penis-in-vagina sex is the most valid form of sex, and that there's a hierarchy of sex acts. Karen Rayne – executive director at Unhushed, a nonprofit dedicated to sex-positive sex education – tells me people often believe that 'sex' means 'partnered sex and by that they mean penis-in-vagina intercourse'.[14]

Hypersexualisation is not without consequences. This chapter has shown that our society's unchecked sexualisation of queer women feeds into heterosexual male entitlement over women's bodies. When queer women are not viewed as human beings, but rather as a straight male's fantasy and as objects for men's viewing pleasure, this objectification leads to violence. And it's about time we started addressing the root cause of this hugely prevalent sexual violence.

CHAPTER 12

'Sex wasn't for people like me'

'My sexuality was robbed from me before I even entered womanhood,' writes Cathy Reay, who's known online as @thatsinglemum, in an Instagram post. Reay has dwarfism and often writes posts about disability and parenting. 'I was desexualised from day dot, told to cover up because "nobody wants to see those" on a Disabled body, ordered to suppress my desires because they were deemed so unrealistic.'

Reay goes on to say that she has long been excluded from conversations about sex. 'People like me didn't appear in any media about sex, dating, or romance except fetish porn; when men showed an interest it was only ever because they wanted to try something new, like they were trialling a different washing powder.'[1]

When I chat to Reay about how ableism manifests itself in our sexual culture, she tells me, 'I feel like conversation around sex and sexual experience, at least when we're first getting to know a sexual partner, is often centred on what we are willing to do in the bedroom. Heterosexual men often enjoy interactions with women that push boundaries of what we might consider a "standard" sexual experience.' She adds that there is an implicit – and indeed sometimes explicit – pressure for heterosexual women to be happy with whatever men throw at them, for fear of guys tiring of them and being driven into the arms of other women.

'It's a little tricky when you're Disabled because there's usually one or more things that we have to do differently in the bedroom,' says Reay. 'Whether that's because we can't reach something, don't have the required strength to do something in a particular way, are fatigued or overwhelmed by certain things. To a new non-Disabled sex partner our boundaries are completely unknown, and I have found that our mysteriousness is often quite a turn-on for men who are actively seeking a different kind of thrill.'

This element of the unknown can lead to assumptions being made by non-Disabled people, particularly if communication is limited. 'Sexual partners, and again this typically applies to men because there's also the element of flexing your misogynistic control muscles, will just decide what we can and can't do, without checking. They might avoid talking to us because they're scared, or they might think we can't really advocate for ourselves so they need to do it for us!'

Reay says it can be very overwhelming entering new sexual situations with a non-Disabled partner for many reasons. 'When we are naked, people often feel very vulnerable, and with a partner we don't know, we're exposing ourselves at this time of peak vulnerability to the chance of ridicule, judgement, disempowerment and/or fetishisation.'

Disabled people experience microaggressions during sex that feel infantilising and demeaning. Some Disabled women report being 'guided' or lifted by men they don't know without their consent, and put in invasive positions. Then there's the comments, like 'you're too pretty to be Disabled', where misogyny and ableism combine. Disabled people also report receiving intrusive questions – 'How do you have sex?' – as well as shocked reactions when they reveal they're dating someone, married or expecting a baby.[2]

Reay says she's not sure how many non-Disabled people actively seek out porn featuring Disabled people and it's not something she enjoys thinking about. 'There's a huge range of porn available and that includes ethical porn, which I totally support, but because Disabled people are not normalised in society, I believe that seeking out any kind of porn that features us will always come from a morbid curiosity that dehumanises our existence before anything else.'

Disabled people aren't just fetishised and hypersexualised by non-Disabled people, they are also desexualised. 'I feel like there's two ends of the spectrum for us: desexualisation and fetishisation, and depending on the non-Disabled person's likes, preferences, past experience and view of the world, they'll do one of those to us, no matter how unintentional,' says Reay. 'It's rare, though definitely not impossible, to meet a non-Disabled sex partner that sees "beyond" the disability from first sight.'

The desexualisation of Disabled people means divesting them of their sexuality, making assumptions about their sexuality, and perpetuating misinformation that Disabled people do not have sex. Being desexualised refers to being regarded by others as someone who is not capable of having sex, someone who is sexually undesirable. This is not to be confused with asexuality, which is a sexual orientation. The Asexual Visibility and Education Network defines an asexual person as someone who 'does not experience sexual attraction – they are not drawn to people sexually and do not desire to act upon attraction to others in a sexual way'.[3] Some Disabled people identify as asexual or aromantic – but societal assumptions about disability and sexuality make it difficult to find space to talk about asexuality and disability.

'It's challenging when you're on the asexual spectrum and have a disability, because disability rights activists have been working to change the dialogue about disability and sexuality for years,' says journalist Alaina Leary in a piece published by Rooted in Rights.[4] Leary often holds back on bringing up that they identify as grey asexual, which means they're on the asexual spectrum and rarely experience sexual attraction. So, here you can see that harmful assumptions that all Disabled people are non-sexual rebound on people who identify as asexual and who feel they are not able to talk about and express their sexuality openly.

If we want to understand where these assumptions about Disabled people's sexuality come from, we need look no further than the way society views and treats Disabled people. Journalist and disability rights campaigner Hollie-Anne Brooks says the reason Disabled people are desexualised is because they are stripped of their humanity by society. 'As Disabled people in British culture, we are first and foremost not seen as people, we're viewed as inspiration porn,' she says. She adds that Disabled people are viewed as 'brave' for going outside, or for doing the grocery shopping alone, and people assume that Disabled people need help. There's also an element of seeing Disabled people as an inconvenience. 'It's a problem for businesses because they've got to install a certain amount of Disabled bathrooms or ramps that then cost them money.'

Brooks says it's deeply ingrained in society that Disabled people are brave and inspirational. 'If we hit back on that and go, "Why? You don't know me, why am I brave?" If people were honest they'd say, "Well, because you're in a wheelchair." They see your physical disability as the definition of you.' Brooks sees this as the root of the desexualisation of Disabled people. 'That's how we're desexualised, because we're not even seen as human in the first place. We are something to be pitied and we are something to be seen as very fragile, and if I touch them, they might break.'

When Brooks's disability became less visible to other people, she realised that non-Disabled people had been viewing her as fragile. 'I learned to walk again, so I am now an ambulatory wheelchair user,' Brooks says. She's noticed a marked difference in the way people behave towards her from when she was a full-time wheelchair user. 'People can't see my disability if I'm just out having a walk around the village. Whereas when I'm in my wheelchair, I'm seen as an easy target.'

Society perceives Disabled people as needy and helpless, says Brooks, and Disabled people are never seen as sexual beings with every possible shade of sex life, from vanilla to kinky. On the rare occasion that a Disabled person is shown to have a sex life, it's 'seen as quite disgusting'. That narrative that Disabled people having sex is 'disgusting' is never challenged, and no one ever asks 'But why is it "disgusting"?' Growing up, Brooks loved the film Notting Hill, but now, looking back, she questions why a non-Disabled actor (Gina McKee) was cast in the role of Bella, a wheelchair user. She also feels that the portrayal of the relationship between Bella and her husband Max plays into the stereotype of fragility. 'She's very dainty and fragile and she gets carried to bed by her husband,' Brooks points out. But there isn't so much as a whisper of sexuality in the portrayal of the relationship between the two – it's gentle and tender, but beyond that, there's no suggestion of sex. 'The only time that we've been anywhere near sexualised,

I suppose, is around the TV show *The Undateables*, which, again, I hate because it is the definition of inspiration porn.'

Here in 2021, there's not been much progress at all when it comes to society's view of Disabled people and their sex lives. The erasure of Disabled people's sexuality asserts itself in dating app culture too. 'A really hard decision if you're dating is: do you put in your profile that you're Disabled, because you're a proud Disabled man, woman, whatever gender you are, and that's a huge part of your identity?' says Brooks. 'On the flip side, you're also putting it in your bio to potentially warn people because society isn't ready for that.' She's heard from friends who won't put in their Tinder bio that they're Disabled. They'll message back and forth with someone and when everything seems to be going well, they'll say, 'So, by the way, I'm a wheelchair user, I have cerebral palsy,' and the conversation ends there.

Society is too scared, says Brooks, to ask itself the following questions: 'Why do you think you can't date a Disabled person? Or have sex with a Disabled person? Or marry a Disabled person?' Fear plays a big role in fuelling the idea that Disabled people aren't human, that they aren't sexual beings. 'You can become Disabled overnight, you can have a fall, you can get ill. I got meningitis. Overnight you can become a wheelchair user, overnight you can become Disabled, overnight you can become somebody in that minority. And that's actually quite terrifying to think of. And I think the reason why we don't see Disabled people as sexual beings is because we're kind of too scared to acknowledge that that Disabled person could be us.'

These deep-seated, inward fears that non-Disabled people harbour come from the fact that they do not get to see the positive side of life for Disabled people on television screens. 'It's so hard because I want to see more Disabled people having sex, or more Disabled people in relationships with non-Disabled people on TV and represented, but then it will always be used as a PR stunt,' says Brooks. That doesn't mean creating storylines where somebody is building up to have sex with a Disabled person, but rather that a character just happens to be Disabled, and their disability isn't an issue when it comes to their romantic or sex life. And that storytelling needs to be done in a natural, almost nonchalant way.

More on-screen representation might elicit another type of reaction that doesn't disrupt stereotypes. 'If we put it on TV, then we become a hot topic to talk about because of the shock factor,' Brooks explains. 'We're either hidden away and we're like fragile eggshells or we are the big-bang shock factor right in your face. We live among you, we are you.'

The assumptions that Disabled people are fragile and desexualised have a tangible impact on Disabled people's sex lives. When Brooks became Disabled, she and her boyfriend – who doesn't have a disability – were unsure how to adapt. The couple met six months before Brooks became a wheelchair user. 'I don't remember googling it and going, "How do I have sex when my legs don't work? Like, will it feel the same?"' she recalls. 'Masturbation was the answer. But we didn't know what to do.' Sex education for

Disabled people doesn't happen at school – it's not part of the syllabus.

The fact that consent is ongoing and can be withdrawn at any time is a core tenet of ethical sexual relations – but it's one that many of us did not learn about when we were growing up. 'We're not taught in general that it's OK to change our minds,' says Brooks. 'And I think when it comes to disability and sex, that's a really important thing. I'll be having sex with my boyfriend and my body will just start to ache a bit and we're in a great place where I can say, "Yeah, we need to stop now because ouch," and we can laugh about it or whatever.'

Brooks says we're never taught as a society that consent is ongoing and can be withdrawn at any point. 'It might start out OK, but we also need to be very much aware that if it's not OK during because it's uncomfortable, because for whatever reason, then that needs to be an open conversation that we also have during sex.' That becomes more complicated if it's within the context of a one-night stand or if you're having sex with someone for the first time, 'We're too scared to not give consent during sex, to say "can we stop for x, y, z disability reason" or "this is painful, this is uncomfortable".' There's a reluctance to withdraw consent, to stop the sex for fear of judgement.

'As Disabled people, no matter what point you become Disabled, because of internalised ableism, which is a societal problem, you are told directly or indirectly that you should be grateful for this,' Brooks says. She adds that she's wondered 'who else would have me?' if she and her boyfriend broke up. 'Each time, I feel like, "Gosh, never think like that." I'm a catch. But again, we have that idea of, "I should feel lucky to be experiencing this." It's a very female thing.'

As a wheelchair user, this idea that you should feel grateful is particularly reinforced. 'We're told to be grateful for what we've got,' Brooks explains. 'We're supposed to be grovelling and so thankful that you've installed a ramp or that you've dared to go down on us, to the point that we can't actually point out that, no, that ramp isn't safe, or no, you're not doing that right.'

Neurodivergent people are often subjected to the societal misconception that they are desexualised. 'Sex wasn't for people like me,' says Amy Gravino in her TEDx Talk 'Why Autism is Sexier Than You Think It Is', in which she reflects on the ideas that became entrenched during her teenage years. 'Even if I wanted to, no one would ever want to have sex with me, an autistic woman, would they?'[5]

In her talk, Gravino, who is a writer and autism consultant, unpacks how this stigma affects autistic people. In 1986 sexologists Thore Langfeldt and Mary Porter defined sexuality as "an integral part of the personality of everyone, man, woman, and child. It is a basic need and an aspect of being human that cannot be separated from other aspects of human life". Gravino notes that the definition, published by the World Health Organization, states that sexuality is not synonymous with sexual intercourse, but that it influences actions, thoughts, interactions and feelings, in addition to mental and physical health.

'But somewhere along the way, a stigma built up around the sexuality and sexual expression of autistic people. The world decided this definition didn't apply to us,' Gravino continues. She adds that society as a whole doesn't like the thought of autistic people having sex. 'Somehow it became easier to think of autistic people as sexless, uninterested, and repulsed by the idea of sex.' But if we reflect on Langfeldt and Porter's definition of sexuality as central to the human experience, you can see the issue with overlooking autistic people's sexuality. 'To act as though having sexual desires and thoughts is something that doesn't happen is to deny autistic people a huge part of the human experience,' says Gravino.

When it comes to conversations about sexual violence, the experiences of Disabled people, neurodivergent people, and people with mental health conditions are erased and rarely discussed. Hollie-Anne Brooks is a rape survivor. When she attempted to report the incident to the police, the process did not bring the closure she needed. 'The police don't know how to handle it, in my experience,' she says. 'It was four years ago, it was before I became Disabled, but I had a very bad mental health problem at the time. And that was used against me, that was one of the main reasons it didn't go to court. I remember the police going, "Well, you've had to spend time on a mental health ward, that will go against you."'

Research has found that men and women with disabilities are at an increased risk of sexual violence compared to non-Disabled people.[6] In a 2019 overview of data and crime statistics for the UK, Disabled women were almost twice as likely to have experienced a recent sexual assault compared to non-Disabled women.[7] It's estimated that 40 per cent of women with disabilities experience sexual or physical violence in their lifetimes.[8] People with intellectual disabilities experience sexual violence at a rate seven times higher than non-Disabled people, according to an NPR investigation.[9]

More broadly, ableism in society results in the erasure of Disabled people's experiences of sexual violence and prevents those experiences being heard, acknowledged and believed. 'Nobody likes to think of it happening,' says Brooks. 'I don't like the term "vulnerable" but we are more vulnerable to sexual violence, whether it's because we're blind, whether it's because we're wheelchair users and can't run away, whether it's conducted by carers, whether it's emotional sexual violence, because people can pick up on insecurities and manipulate you that way.'

When people do hear stories of sexual violence perpetrated against Disabled people, the reaction is often disgust. 'We're not seen as sexual beings full stop, and there's a disgust at the idea of somebody, say, raping a wheelchair user. I think there's more disgust that they would do that. I think that's because they're raping somebody who's a wheelchair user and there's a bit of like, "Why would they fancy that person?"' The focus, Brooks says, is not 'How could someone do such a thing?' but rather 'Why would they rape a Disabled person?' Some people would frame it as 'something they're into' rather than a horrific violation for any human being to endure.

Brooks says she now expects sexual violence to happen to her at any point when she's in public. 'I expect somebody to grope me, I expect somebody to put their hand between my legs, I expect every time I go out – maybe not in my village, if I was in London and in my wheelchair – because it's easy. And what am I going to do about it?'

We've reached a point where sexual violence is so deeply normalised in society that people don't even recognise when it's happening. This is in part because of a lack of education as to what constitutes sexual violence, but also in certain types of violence being seen as less valid, or 'not that bad'. 'The lines are so blurred about what is sexual violence?' Brooks remarks. 'When do you report it? Is there any point?'

Brooks wants some key things to change, starting with advocacy and education around disability and sexual violence. She says she's never seen a campaign or even a leaflet for adults about what to do if you're a Disabled person who's subjected to sexual violence. And when it comes to reporting sexual violence, there needs to be the assurance that accessibility is being considered by police forces. 'If you were raped, and you had to go for your examination, are there hoists in there for wheelchair users or people who are Disabled? If not, why not?' she says.

Sex education also needs to change. Cathy Reay says she'd scrap sex education and start again, because sex education does nothing to normalise sex for or with marginalised people. 'We don't appear in these classes; our anatomy internally or externally may look different to the dolls provided, but there's no forum for discussion on this. There needs to be, massively.'

'Sex educators need to address the disability elephant in the room,' she adds. But that doesn't mean calling on Disabled students in the classroom to educate non-Disabled peers – it means thinking how the subject can serve all students in the class effectively.

For Reay that means 'promoting healthy attitudes towards Disabled people in the bedroom. Hammering home consensual sex and the benefits of setting boundaries, particularly for women. Addressing why and how disempowerment and fetishisation are harmful. And also teaching about all different kinds of contraception – not just male condoms! – to recognise that there isn't one single product that works for all (Disabled) people.'

'I think we just need to know Disabled people have sex. Hey, there's a lot of us,' says Brooks. Disabled people account for 15 per cent of the world's population, according to the World Health Organization.[10] In Britain, there are more than 11 million people with a disability, chronic illness, or impairment.[11] Brooks believes the government should look to using Disabled sex-education advocates in educational programmes. 'I'd love to go into a school and speak to a load of sixteen-year-olds and go, "Right, tell me what you want to know about disability and sex," and just have them ask,' she says. 'I'd rather a sixteen-year-old said to me, "Can you still have a penis inside your vagina?" or "Can you feel anything?" than have a thirty-six-year-old man I'm about to have sex with say something like "I'm surprised you actually want this. I didn't think you lot could feel this.'"

Learning about sex isn't something that starts and ends in a classroom. We each spend our lifetime learning new things about sex. That's why it's important for adults to have access to articles, books and online resources that can fill in any gaps in their knowledge. 'There is no leaflet on how to have sex once you become a wheelchair user, so then I went and wrote about the best sex toys for Disabled people for *Cosmopolitan* because it just wasn't out there,' says Brooks. People often turn to Google's search bar for questions about sex. But misinformation about sexual health thrives on the internet. This is where the need for accurate, intersectional, reliable, sex-positive (and high-SEO-ranking!) journalism on sex and relationships becomes really clear.

If we want to radically change our sexual culture for the better, Disabled people need to be included in the conversation. 'This means that yes, we should appear in your ethical porn, but we shouldn't be treated as fetishes in the footage. Disabled people should guest speak in sex-ed classes. We should write about our sexual experiences and desires and this should be published,' says Reay. 'Disabled people should appear in magazines – in fact, in all media – because this is how you normalise our existence. The more you see us, the less you're surprised. And the more modelling we do of healthy communication and boundaries around what goes on beneath the sheets, the more Disabled people will feel safer when engaging in sex or sexual conversations with non-Disabled sex partners.'

Fundamentally, attitudes towards disability and sex need to change drastically in society. 'We're having all of the variants of sex lives, some people having no sex lives by choice, not by choice, we're living literally the same thing that non-Disabled people are,' adds Brooks.

Just as desexualising Disabled people strips them of their humanity, so too does hypersexualising and fetishising Disabled people. 'Please don't fetishise us. Please don't slide into our DMs on Twitter and ask if you can fuck me while I'm in my wheelchair,' Brooks says. 'Don't hypersexualise disability, don't use disability as your fetish to get off.'

CHAPTER 13

Seeking closure at closed doors

J amie Windust was sitting on a bench alone in the rain just a few metres down the road from where it happened. When the police showed up, Jamie got into the car before being driven to a quiet side street. 'Do you understand what you're saying?' the officer asked Jamie.

'I was just completely bewildered,' Jamie says. 'But I was like, "I think so." He wouldn't say what he was trying to say, which was: "Do you understand what you're accusing this man of?"'

Jamie is a trans rape survivor. Their experience of reporting the crime to the police shows a glaring issue in the way the criminal justice system treats trans people who've experienced violence. 'What I found was when I rang the police and when they arrived, the level of compassion or care was almost non-existent,' they explain. 'It was an incredibly robotic situation. They weren't horrible, but they also weren't lovely.'

That question Jamie was asked in the back of the police car has stuck with them. 'As someone who's vulnerable, that question could be taken in many ways. If I was really on the fence about reporting, if I'd been in that car with the police officer and he'd said that, who knows where that could have gone. I could have been like, "Oh fuck, no, I didn't actually, bye."'

From the moment they got into the police car, Jamie was misgendered by police officers dealing with their case. Jamie understood it initially, because they hadn't yet told police that they use they/them pronouns. But after talking with an LGBTQ officer and sharing their pronouns with that officer, the misgendering continued. 'There were many times with the detective on the case where he would get quite defensive when I would challenge him. That was quite an issue,' says Jamie.

That night, Jamie was handed a leaflet for male survivors of sexual assault after stating that they're trans. The forensics and the rape kits were all binary-gendered. 'So there was lots of me adding extra boxes, or being told off for adding extra boxes,' they recall. 'They were like, "Um, I don't understand what you've put here."'

When they think about the incident itself and the process that followed with the police, Jamie feels they were equally traumatising. Jamie came away from this experience feeling that the criminal justice system isn't fit for purpose when dealing with trans and non-binary survivors of sexual violence.

According to the 2015 US Transgender Survey, 47 per cent of transgender people will be the victim of sexual violence in their lifetime. That figure increases to 53 per cent among Black trans people.[1] 'Statistically, trans people are more likely to be in the criminal justice system as survivors and it's not equipped for them in any way, despite the overwhelming statistics that say that they are more likely to be there,' says Jamie. 'So I think definitely the criminal justice system is not tailored for transness. The criminal justice system in the UK does not understand the complexity and the nuance of transness, the intersectionality of transness. So it fails a lot of people, but it fails trans people without giving them a chance for it to be successful, if that makes sense.'

The police had taken a digital download of Jamie's phone and the accused's phone. 'In it were messages from before we met, detailing what I was and wasn't happy to do,' they say. 'And a message after from him basically acknowledging that I wasn't happy.' Jamie later found out that no further action would be taken on their case. That meant that they were told they weren't allowed to go through court. The police told Jamie this decision had been reached on the grounds that there was insufficient proof beyond reasonable doubt. In that final meeting with the police, Jamie asked them, 'Was this not enough?' – referring to the evidence gathered in the digital download.

'They said "no", because I could have changed my mind after I sent the messages. So I sent the message to him saying "I'm on my way." And before that, I'd been like, "I don't want to do this, I'm happy to do this." The police were basically saying the reason for the no further action was that there's no evidential proof that when I got to his house, I didn't say, "Oh, fuck those text messages. Let's do whatever."'

Jamie can understand that, from an evidence perspective. They also feel that if there isn't enough evidence, then it's best not to go to court, because it could end up being a worse experience. But Jamie also came away from the ordeal feeling they hadn't been heard. 'That was the kind of nail in the coffin for me to be like, you never understood me. I never felt like you believed what I was saying,' they say.

After finding out that no further action would be taken, Jamie wrote down what they would have said in their victim statement, and what they would have said to the jury. It was later published by *Gay Times*. In it, Jamie says: 'The system rendered me powerless, unable to make people understand who I was. That I was trans. That I wasn't lying. That I'm not just fulfilling a stereotype of promiscuity. I was powerless to myself.'[2]

After reading the piece, people have asked Jamie, 'If you can't get justice through the criminal justice system, how are you going to get it?' They have ruminated on the idea of justice and closure, and come to realise there is a lot more to what people consider justice than is commonly thought.

In the aftermath of their negative experience in the criminal justice system, Jamie has given a lot of thought to what the word 'justice' really means for survivors. 'From the second that they no-further-actioned my case, I almost felt relieved, because I was like, I don't have to go through the criminal justice system anymore.' Being free from that process opens up the possibility of finding justice or closure on one's own terms. 'I don't have to abide by what they define as justice, I can decide whether or not I even want justice, or if I just want to move on, or if I just want to recover,' says Jamie.

What Jamie has come to learn is that closure, for them, has nothing to do with the accused. 'For me, that closure and processing has come through therapy, it's come through understanding the reasons why I went to see him – not to victim-blame – and essentially having to just break everything down in my life to then rebuild it. I think that'll be my closure, being a happier, better, recovered person. Because I'm not necessarily recovering from what happened.'

Shut out of support services

'Trans' is an abbreviation of 'transgender', which is an umbrella term referring to people whose gender identity differs from the sex they were assigned at birth, according to GLAAD. The terms 'trans' and 'transgender' refer to a range of identities – including trans women and trans men as well as non-binary people, whose gender identity cannot be defined within the gender binary.[3]

All too often, trans people are erased from conversations about sexual violence. And in conversations about whether trans people should have the same rights as cisgender people – which means people who are not transgender – to use certain bathrooms, trans people are framed as threats to the safety of cis women. The argument that trans people using bathrooms that align with their gender identity poses a risk to cis people's safety has been debunked by researchers. A 2018 study from the Williams Institute at UCLA School of Law found there is no evidence that trans people using public facilities increases safety risks.[4]

When I ask Jamie if they feel we need to centre trans people in mainstream conversations about sexual violence, they tell me, 'The short answer would be yes. But a more thought-through answer would be no, because right now in this country, if you were to highlight trans survivors or if charities were to come out and say, we've actually got a whole new, trans-specific wing to what we're doing, there would be absolute uproar.'

Jamie thinks that charities and organisations need to make their services trans-inclusive without shouting about it to everyone. At the same time, those organisations need to make trans people aware. 'In terms of trans people being profiled in the media or speaking out, it's a frustrating one, because the conversation does need to happen, but the UK is inherently transphobic. You can't let that stop you. But you can therefore predict what's gonna come,' Jamie says.

'Trans people are strong. And I think the time will come when we do that. There are many trans people who have spoken up in the #MeToo movement. But I think this country has a real problem. But that shouldn't be a hindrance to people telling their story.'

Jamie has been reporting on the state of support services for trans and non-binary sexual assault survivors and speaking to others about their experiences. 'A lot of trans survivors, I think, fear that the process is going to be inherently transphobic so they just don't report,' says Jamie. It was a challenge for them to find trans and non-binary people who had reported their assault to the police and not been deterred by concerns about how they would be treated by the police because of their identity. 'The few people that I did speak to were treated equally as heinously, they were disbelieved, and race intersected with that.'

Jeff Ingold, head of media at Stonewall, says more needs to be done by the justice system to ensure trans survivors are able to safely report what's happened to them in ways that align with who they are. 'This could include updating systems to offer gender-neutral options, along with training for all police officers and front-line staff on how to better support trans survivors.'

He emphasises that more needs to be done to include and centre trans people in conversations about sexual violence. Stonewall research found that one in five trans people has faced domestic abuse from a partner, including 21 per cent of trans men, 16 per cent of trans women and 19 per cent of non-binary people.[5] 'These are not just statistics, they represent the lives of trans people who have experienced horrific abuse from those closest to them, and it's vital they are able to access non-judgemental, safe support when they need it,' says Ingold. 'This means there needs to be enough sustainable funding available for support services to meet demand, including specialist providers that have experience with LGBT issues.'

In addition to facing dehumanising behaviour when seeking justice, trans people are also being refused care by support services. An investigation by *gal-dem* journalist Moya Lothian-McLean found that support services for violence against women and girls (VAWG) are rife with transphobia and transmisogyny, and are refusing care to trans survivors of sexual violence.[6]

One former employee of a high-profile organisation for domestic violence survivors told Lothian-McLean she witnessed hostile transmisogyny while working there. The employee, referred to in the report as 'Lily' (not her real name), explained that she and her colleagues had been concerned that the helpline wasn't inclusive enough and that the organisation didn't have a gender inclusion policy. When they asked the director of operations who the helpline was for, the response was extremely telling. 'The reply from [the director of operations at the organisation] and another senior staff member was that "if they sound like a woman on the phone, talk to them . . . If they don't sound like a woman, it doesn't matter if they say they are, hang up. We're not supporting them".' Lily says she also overheard transphobic references to people as 'men-women', along with statements claiming that only 'biological women' should be able to access refuges.

Another worker, identified in the report as 'Cora' (not her real name), told Lothian-McLean that she realised transmisogyny was essentially normalised in her workplace – a South London organisation serving sexual violence survivors – towards the end of 2017. 'I just remember there being far more comments like "Yeah we only support real women".'

The *gal-dem* investigation found that trans survivors were met with a hostile culture when attempting to get access to urgent front-line services, shutting them out of the gender-based violence sector due to an ideology that excludes trans people and doesn't consider trans women to be 'real women'.

One in six trans women experienced domestic violence between 2017 and 2018, according to Stonewall's report on trans women and domestic and sexual violence.[7] Trans women of colour are nearly 20 per cent more likely to experience multiple counts of sexual harassment than other women, per a study by Australia's National Research Organisation for Women's Safety. The same study found that trans women of colour reported having to rely on themselves for support, while other women reported finding support from partners, friends and the police.[8] Professor Jane Ussher, the project lead on the research, said 'what was really disturbing in the research was that the trans women of colour were almost invisible and marginalised in the support services and the legal recognition around sexual violence'. The trans women of colour were not believed, not taken seriously, and were sometimes ridiculed.[9]

Time and time again, academic studies and landmark reports find the same thing: that trans people are at the highest risk in society of experiencing violence, and trans women experience sexual violence at a higher rate than cis women. So why are support services turning trans survivors away? Why are the most vulnerable people in society being discriminated against when they find themselves at their lowest ebb?

This hostility, this unwillingness to help trans survivors, goes hand in hand with the toxic rise of so-called gender critical feminism and trans-exclusionary feminism in the UK.

In the mid-2010s, trans people started to gain more visibility in the mainstream media. In 2018, that visibility turned into 'outright toxicity', according to Hannah Ewens, features editor at *Vice*, who wrote a piece charting the rise of transphobia in this country. 'The consultation on the now-outdated Gender Recognition Act, which allows trans people to have their identity legally recognised, changed everything.'[10]

The Gender Recognition Act sets out a lengthy and dehumanising medicalised, bureaucratic process that trans people are expected to go through in order to be legally recognised as trans. The process of applying for a Gender Recognition Certificate comprises medical assessments and psychiatric interviews, in addition to providing two years of proof that they've been living according to their gender identity.

'The reforms suggested by LGBT charities like Stonewall were fairly minimal,' Ewens writes. 'The recognition

of non-binary identities, no medical diagnosis or presentation of evidence needed and self-determination through a
more streamlined process. The media commentary around
the subject suggested otherwise.' Suddenly, articles about
trans people were all over the news. Tea Uglow, author of
Loud and Proud and creative director at Google's Creative
Lab, searched a year's worth of media coverage from a
handful of outlets between August 2018 and August 2019
and found 878 articles about transgender people published
in those 365 days. One of the key things that stood out to
her when sifting through the results was the volume of stories dedicated to covering trans people, despite the fact that
trans people make up a small percentage of the population.
'Nearly three stories a day, every day, all year (from only
nine sources) is just not normal. It's not a news cycle. It's a
campaign,' she says.[11]

That campaign stoked hate, fear and distrust towards
trans people. The conversation became, as journalist Shon
Faye wrote in British *Vogue*, 'a vicious and distressing media
debate on the validity of trans people. You may be hearing
more about us, but when there are no openly trans editors,
staff writers, directors or producers at major media organisations, and no openly trans people in Parliament, very
often we are not in control of the terms of the discussion.'[12]

In the end, the UK government published its response to
the consultation on the Act, announcing small administra-
tive changes.[13] The process, at the time of writing, will not
be de-medicalised, and nor will a self-determination process be introduced. Legal recognition will not be given to

non-binary people or under-18s.[14] Trans-exclusionary feminists were vehemently opposed to the idea of making the process of legally identifying as trans or non-binary quicker.

As the *gal-dem* investigation notes, the focus then turned to women-only services for survivors of sexual and domestic abuse, and so-called gender critical feminists began to stir up fears around trans women accessing those spaces. 'For trans-exclusionary feminists, the argument goes that allowing self-determination through GRA reforms would open up "single-sex" sites to "predatory men", who would supposedly pretend to be women in order to perpetuate abuse,' writes Lothian-McLean.[15]

The thing is, trans people have legally had the right to access single-sex spaces since the 2010 Equality Act was passed.[16] Not only that, 'single-sex spaces' like refuges already undertake risk assessments to determine who is safe to enter. 'They have to do this, otherwise they could unwittingly unleash an abusive or violent lesbian on their female partner who is seeking refuge. That won't change,' Helen Belcher of Trans Media Watch told *Gay Star News*.[17]

Taylor is a non-binary sexual violence survivor, and says that for trans people and non-binary people, the act of reporting to the police can add additional layers of distress to an already deeply traumatic incident. 'Even before I came out as non-binary, if I was thinking about myself going, I would ignore my non-binaryness, and just rely on the fact that I'm femme-presenting. That is a privilege I have to be able to rely on that,' says Taylor.

They feel they would need to conceal the fact they're non-binary in order to be believed as a survivor of sexual violence. 'If I really pushed the non-binary part of myself, then I don't think it would be taken as seriously. It would kind of get in the way of actually what happened and what I'm trying to report and what I'm trying to talk to the police about or, say if I was airing it publicly, say on Twitter, if I was brave enough, because it is quite a bold move.' They add that they feel terrible for saying that they'd hide the fact that they're non-binary, but that it would come from a place of wanting to protect themself.

'Because imagine going to the police, you're already traumatised, you're already like, having to deal with it. I just think it's insanely brave that trans people and non-binary people do go to the police. But I hate myself for saying that as well. Because it shouldn't be brave. That should not be brave at all.'

A lot of Taylor's friends who are trans and non-binary would likely not seek help from the authorities, they say, and wouldn't regard the act of going to the police as something that would make them feel better. 'I guess that's the thing, would it give you closure, for example, give you a sense of justice? And I think certainly for myself, and I think for most of my friends who are trans or non-binary, they'd just think no that wouldn't. That wouldn't help at all.'

Taylor has experienced sexual violence and 'grey area' experiences. But when it comes to seeing those experiences reflected in mainstream conversations about sexual violence, they don't hear about non-binary or trans people in those narratives. Taylor says we're only really now getting to the point where we're getting our head around sexual violence that occurs to cisgender straight women – and, even then, there is still so much victim-blaming that occurs, and it's still so hard to get justice, and to be believed.

'So then when I think about trans and non-binary experiences of sexual violence, we're just not there yet. Then I think the fact that people are trans or non-binary takes away from actually what happened. And it kind of becomes the focus when, actually, it doesn't really matter what someone's gender identity is – like, they've experienced that violence. Obviously we need to think about the people who are more vulnerable to it. But in that case, trans people and non-binary people are more vulnerable. I don't really understand why we're seen as so separate from cishet women, and yet we're seen as like, in opposition to, which is just not true at all.'

Taylor tells me about a personal experience that felt like a grey area. 'It was harder to think about or voice and talk about because it was me as a non-binary person, but very femme-presenting.'

Taylor's partner at the time, who was a cis woman, had been sexually assaulted while they were together. 'A couple of days afterwards, she really wanted to have sex, almost like she needed to and she needed to be the dominant one in that role. It was almost like reclaiming the power that she'd had taken away from her; she needed to reclaim it in a sexual setting,' they recall.

'At the same time, there was me being like, "I don't want any of this."' Taylor says they found it shocking what had happened to their partner. At the same time, it brought up their own experiences of sexual violence.

'I think that kind of clash was a real issue for her because then she was kind of coming up against a wall of her trying to reclaim this power. And I was saying no, and she did end up pushing and pushing to the point where she had me up against a wall. And she was forcing herself onto me and I was like, "What the fuck is actually going on?"'

'It wasn't scary in the way that sometimes it can be with men, if that makes sense. Because it was a different dynamic but it was kind of a bit of a mindfuck of like, what is going on here? Why are you doing something that you've just experienced?'

Taylor couldn't understand why their partner, as a victim of sexual assault, would push that onto someone else, particularly someone more vulnerable than themselves. 'It does feel like, in that instance, if you are wanting to reclaim power and you're feeling vulnerable yourself, I do think trans or non-binary people are at the bottom of the stack in that sense.'

Taylor thinks a lot more can be done to make sex education more inclusive for trans and non-binary people, particularly in the way consent is taught. They feel that we still talk about consent in a very binary and hetero- and cisnormative way. 'One person initiates, typically the man. And then you've got the woman who is the limit-setter or the person saying yes or no. Then you've also got that they just say yes or no, and that's another binary and that it's either good sex or bad sex. I think that's a problem.' Taylor believes there needs to be more nuance when it comes to the way we discuss sex and consent.

'You could also be more trans-inclusive, and non-binary-inclusive, by bringing it out of normative ideas of sex as well – just this whole idea of, you start kissing, and then you move on and get a bit handsy, there's a normative script of what goes on between a boy and girl,' says Taylor. That heteronormative script, where kissing leads to heavy petting, then to oral, before moving to penis-in-vagina sex, might resonate to some straight people – but it's not representative of, or indeed relevant to, the sexual experiences of trans people, non-binary people and others who are LGBTQ.

When we only teach young people about what boundary violations look like or feel like within the context of a cishet sexual encounter, trans people and non-binary people aren't being equipped with the relevant examples and knowledge to be able to identify when their boundaries are being crossed, and when sexual violence is happening to them. 'If we're talking about sexual consent in that way, it's no wonder that trans young people, non-binary young people, grow up and think, "Well, where do I fall into that? Was that a violation against my boundaries? Or was it not?"' says Taylor.

But it goes beyond consent. In a world where trans-inclusive sex education happens, trans young people would learn about navigating gender dysphoria during sex. As

Angie Gunn, sex therapy expert for Talkspace, explains in a *Teen Vogue* article on this topic: 'Gender dysphoria, the experience of distress when your assigned gender does not match your experience of yourself, can make the complexities of navigating sex, pleasure and connection exponentially more challenging'. Not every trans person experiences gender dysphoria, and it can vary in intensity for those who do experience it, says Gunn.[18] Knowing how to keep yourself safe while experiencing dysphoria during sex means communicating your boundaries about where you're comfortable being touched, determining what feels good to you, and knowing that not everyone's experience of dysphoria will be the same.

From every angle, we can see trans people and non-binary people being shut out of important conversations. Trans and non-binary people are not centred in discussions of sexual violence, despite being at risk. They are denied support services and treated inhumanely when seeking justice.

Look to the way in which society views trans and non-binary people, and the picture doesn't improve. Some trans women who have sex with cis men experience a mixture of transphobia and misogyny which can take the form of abusive or dehumanising behaviour, mistreatment and disrespect. In 2019, I interviewed Paris Lees for an article I was writing about the power of being single when misogyny pervades dating culture. Lees – a *British Vogue* columnist and the author of *What It Feels Like for a Girl* – told me about her experience dating as a trans woman, and the way some cis men behave towards trans women. She said that there are some men who are happy to have sex with trans women but feel shamed about dating trans women in a serious capacity. 'It's really interesting when you tell guys that you're trans because immediately it's like, "Oh we don't have to treat you with as much respect now." Not all of them, but a lot of guys, they think "Oh, this is the one I'm gonna fuck, but I'm not gonna take home to meet mum and dad."'[19]

Lees said that hearing people debate whether trans women are 'real women' has exacerbated misogyny for trans people. 'At the height of the "are trans women real women"[20] debate in the British media about a year ago, I was actually dealing with bullshit from a man and I just remember thinking, "This is bullshit." Seriously, these people are telling me I'm not a real woman, and I'm out here getting all the misogyny.' This intersection of misogyny and transphobia is called transmisogyny – a term that was coined by Julia Serano in her 2007 book *Whipping Girl*.

These so-called debates which attempt to discuss whether trans people are 'real' people only serve to give people licence to treat trans people in dehumanising and disrespectful ways. Trans people's lives are not a debate. Helping trans and non-binary survivors of sexual violence shouldn't be a debate either.

CHAPTER 14

Unprotected

Sophie Gallagher, a journalist and editor at the *Independent*, was heading home from work on the Victoria Line in 2017 when a stranger Airdropped a photo of his penis to her phone. 'I felt angry and violated,' Gallagher tells me over email. 'It felt like such a clear act of sexual aggression and threatening behaviour – which stemmed largely from the perpetrator's anonymity and not knowing if he'd follow me home – that surely it would be punishable by law.'

She assumed that flashing via digital means would be regarded in a similar way to traditional 'trench coat' flashing by the law. But Gallagher soon discovered that cyberflashing – the act of sending someone a sexually explicit photo without their consent – was not legally classed as a sexual offence.

'It goes without saying that with the advent of the internet, sexual violations no longer needed to be analogue, they could move online,' says Gallagher. 'While this seems entirely obvious to anyone who is semi-digitally literate, it does not mean legislation has kept pace to protect people against such developments. In fact, the law as it stands has gaping holes. A Women and Equalities Committee published a report over two years ago, in October 2018, calling for a law against cyberflashing to fill the vacuum.[1] Yet, we wait.'

Gallagher has worked tirelessly over the past three years to give a voice to people who've experienced cyberflashing. 'In this time I have interviewed nearly 100 women on the record (and plenty more off) about their experiences of cyberflashing, more commonly known as unsolicited dick pics.'

Gallagher says the evidence shows that online sexual violence doesn't sit in a separate arena to offline violence. 'It exists on a spectrum of harm. And let's be clear, the harms – which include everything from humiliation and distress to fear, changing behaviours such as routes home or how they engage with their smartphones – are no less extensive than those experienced with old-school flashing. It is certainly not as black and white as being less damaging online.'

As for our cultural understanding of cyberflashing, Gallagher says there's a lot of work still to be done. 'Generally, cyberflashing is still seen as either a non-existent problem, or a joke. Much like other harmful behaviours in this space (upskirting, for example), cyberflashing sits in a Venn diagram of public perception that encompasses female hysteria and female imagination.'

Tara Jane O'Reilly told me about her experience of cyberflashing in 2019 for a Mashable article. When she got on the tube at Baker Street station, a photo of a penis was Airdropped to her phone. It was 10 p.m. and she was the only woman sitting in a packed carriage. She felt targeted, shocked and grossed out. 'Like as though as soon as they saw a new iPhone connect they knew it would be my phone,' she explained. After declining the Airdrop request, the sender didn't give up. 'Then it popped up again, and again. So I started to go into my settings but the fucking photo kept popping up until I finally switched Airdrop off. I couldn't work out who did it – the tube was relatively packed and it was just really grim.' The ordeal left O'Reilly feeling unsettled.[2]

So, how can we go about addressing the cultural minimisation of this act of sexual violence? We can start by looking at the language we use. We live in a world where terminology like 'unsolicited dick pics' exhorts a giggle from people who haven't grasped the seriousness of this violation. Cyberflashing is alarmingly common, research shows: 41 per cent of women aged between 18 and 36 have been sent an unsolicited photo of a man's genitals, per You-Gov data.[3] Cyberflashing is also a highly gendered violation, with researchers at City, University of London, saying women are overwhelmingly the target.[4]

Currently, 'cyberflashing' is a term that doesn't exist in legal language in the UK. As Siân Brooke, researcher at the Oxford Internet Institute, tells me, 'there is no official definition of cyberflashing within UK legislation'. Professor Clare McGlynn, who is an expert in the legal regulation of image-based sexual abuse, told me in 2019 that referring to cyberflashing as unwanted dick pics can 'sensationalise and minimise' this crime. But she also recognises that 'flashing' is a term that's not taken very seriously either, despite it being a highly traumatic violation.

Campaigners are calling for the creation of a law on cyberflashing to bring about cultural awareness of the violation and greater protections for victims. In September 2020, the Law Commission – the body tasked with reviewing the law in certain areas and coming up with proposals – published its recommendations for how to better protect victims from online violations. The proposals suggested that cyberflashing be included as a sexual offence under Section 66 of the Sexual Offences Act 2003. In the document, Professor Penney Lewis, Criminal Law Commissioner, said that a rise in abuse had gone hand in hand with the internet and social media becoming an everyday part of our lives. 'Unfortunately, the law has not kept up and isn't giving victims the protection they need.'[5]

So, what is the law's role in changing public perceptions about the seriousness of this violation? 'Laws not only give recourse to justice for victims, they also provide avenues for educational moments,' explains Sophie Gallagher. 'Without clarity on how those in charge see something like cyberflashing, why shouldn't the public continue to doubt its importance or that it counts as legitimate sexual violence? To look at historic examples of sexual violence – like spousal rape within marriage, which was only made illegal in the UK in 1992 – until the law asserts its position, society is slow to catch up.'

Gallagher wasn't alone in realising that something that happened to her wasn't illegal in England and Wales – and she's also not alone in doing something about that fact. Activist and writer Gina Martin was watching The Killers at Hyde Park in London with her sister when she was upskirted by a man in the crowd. Upskirting is the violating act of taking photos or videos under a person's clothing without consent, to capture an image of their crotch, underwear or genitals.

Martin was 25 at the time and had just moved back to London after living in Greece, and she hadn't seen her sister Stevie in a long while and wanted to spend some quality time together. 'This group of guys were hitting on me and Stevie and making loads of comments and I was just like, "Listen, I've not seen my sister in forever, I just wanna have a good night with her,"' Martin told me when she came on my podcast History Becomes Her.[6]

It didn't end there, though. One of the guys made a really loud joke, saying something along the lines of 'I bet she's good at giving blowjobs'. Martin clapped back at him and told him he sounded like a 12-year-old. 'And then he just got really angry and then, I didn't see him do it, but he stuck his hands between my legs and took photos of my crotch up my skirt,' she recalls.

'I remember him brushing up against me and me thinking it was just someone in the crowd. And then a couple of minutes later, one of the guys was standing in front of me, and they were all laughing and I could tell they were laughing at me but I didn't know what's going on.'

When Martin looked at the guy's phone, she could see he was on WhatsApp and was looking at a photo of her crotch. 'I grabbed the phone out of his hand and held it up and was like, "What are you doing taking pictures of my vagina?" and I started crying and we got into a scuffle,' she says. A woman and two men helped her escape and Martin ran to security with his phone in her hand. The man ran after her. Security then called the police.

'The police were like, you know what, you should be able to go to a festival in thirty degrees and wear a skirt and this not happen to you. But we've had a look at the photo – it shows more than you want it to show. But you won't hear much from us because there's nothing we can do,' Martin explains. 'He said because you've chosen to wear knickers it's not a graphic image.'

What Martin later learned was that upskirting was not legally classed as a sexual offence under the law in England and Wales. 'So, the police officer was quite understandably confused because there wasn't a law in place. Upskirting didn't exist in legal language in England and Wales, so he didn't know what to do about it.'

The police told her there wasn't much they could do. 'I went home and was like, geez, what if I was a kid though?' The Metropolitan Police later informed her they'd dropped the case. 'I got super angry and I was like, I'm so bored of brushing stuff off,' she says. 'I remember being like, I'm not going to take the underpass near my house on the main road because I'm more scared of what will happen in the underpass than about crossing a main road and traffic, because I'm scared of guys I don't know. It's just been twenty years of brushing stuff off and I'm just not doing that anymore.'

Martin decided to start a campaign. Initially her aim was simply to raise awareness, but she soon changed her goal. She got the law changed in England and Wales, making upskirting a criminal offence. On 12 April 2019, the 'upskirting' law was introduced in England and Wales.

Digital sexual violations are alarmingly prevalent. And the language we use to describe this type of violence is not fit for purpose. A 2019 report found that as many as one in ten British people have experienced image-based sexual abuse, and as many as 30 per cent of people know someone affected by it.[7] This form of abuse is commonly referred to in the media as 'revenge porn' – a term which survivors find harmful because it implies they have done something to deserve it.[8] Research by the Cyber Civil Rights Initiative in 2017 found that the use of the word 'revenge' is a misnomer, given that revenge or hurting the victim is not the motivation for 79 per cent of those sharing non-consensual images or videos.[9] Legal academics also argue that the term 'revenge porn' does not fully convey the distress, trauma and humiliation that this type of abuse causes, and they suggest 'image-based sexual abuse' as a more fitting term.[10] 'Non-consensual pornography' is another term favoured by victims.[11] For the survivors, the consequences are devastating. Some are forced to resign from their jobs when the images or videos are published in public. Some die by suicide,[12] and research carried out in the United States found that 51 per cent of survivors contemplated suicide.[13]

Currently, the main UK legislation relating to image-based sexual abuse is in Section 33 of the Criminal Justice and Courts Act 2015, says Emily McFadden, an abuse lawyer at Bolt Burdon Kemp. 'This sets out that it is an offence to share private, sexual materials, either photos or videos, of another person, without their consent and with the purpose of causing embarrassment or distress.' Those found guilty face up to two years in prison and a fine.

This applies online and offline – so that includes showing someone a physical or digital image. It also applies to sharing by text or email, as well as uploading content to the internet. But McFadden says there are many practical difficulties faced by victims who report this type of crime. A major one relates to anonymity. 'A problem with the current legislation is that the offence is not categorised as a "sexual offence", so victims have no right to anonymity through the criminal court process under the Sexual Offences Act, as they would if they had been physically touched by someone; meaning their names can be published.'

Reporting the existence of the photos to the police presents another challenge. For some victims, the knowledge that reporting it to the police will result in more people seeing the images adds to the existing trauma that the victim has suffered in the first instance.

The need for the images to have been shared 'with the purpose of causing embarrassment or distress' is another issue. 'This part of the offence means that the police and CPS need to assess the intention of the perpetrator,' explains McFadden. 'I have spoken with a number of victims who have been told by either the police or CPS that they cannot be confident that they would get over this hurdle in a criminal trial, and therefore close the case.'

Threatening to share intimate content is another area where the law is only just beginning to play catch-up. One in fourteen adults in England and Wales have experienced threats of sharing intimate images or videos – and those threats are most common among young women, affecting one in seven women aged between 18 and 34, according to research conducted by Refuge, the domestic violence charity.[14] Following Refuge's campaign, on March 2021 the UK government announced that 'revenge porn' laws will be expanded to include threats to disclose intimate images.[15]

It is unconscionable that the survivors of digital sexual violence have very few legal protections when seeking recourse – if any. But turning to a criminal justice system that has effectively decriminalised rape doesn't inspire much confidence.[16] Rape convictions in England and Wales fell to a record low in 2020, with only 1.4 per cent of sexual violence cases being prosecuted, according to Crown Prosecution Service figures. The CPS is reportedly 'refusing to take cases to trial out of concern that jurors will be swayed by myths and misconceptions about what a rape victim should look and sound like, especially when alcohol or mental health problems are involved,' according to a *Guardian* report.[17] Meanwhile 90 per cent of rape and sexual assault survivors know their attacker,[18] but despite the prevalence of sexual violence carried out by people known to us, these cases are 'difficult to prosecute'.[19] Since 2019, CPS prosecutors were reportedly told to drop weak cases.[20]

Alarmingly, sexts are being used as evidence in rape trials and, according to a *Vice* investigation, 'innocuous data obtained from mobile phones has been consistently cited by the CPS as reason to stop pursuing rape or sexual assault cases'.[21] That data could be flirty texts or explicit photos exchanged between the complainant and perpetrator, but might also include the victim's wider digital data too, per the investigation. Looking at these findings, it's clear the current system isn't keeping survivors safe.

We should be wary of automatically accepting an approach that considers increased policing, prosecution and imprisonment – aka carceral solutions – as the solution to violence against women and marginalised genders. As prison abolitionist Victoria Law writes in *Jacobin*, a carceral-led approach – also known as 'carceral feminism' – 'ignores the ways in which race, class, gender identity, and immigration status leave certain women more vulnerable to violence and that greater criminalization often places these same women at risk of state violence'.[22]

Nonetheless, it's clear that the absence of legal protections plays directly into the hands of the recalcitrant tech companies hosting the abusive content on their platforms. Survivors of this type of digital sexual abuse seeking help from tech companies in removing the abusive content have found that the only way to get a response is by threatening legal action.

In 2020, British journalist Ash Sarkar was informed that there were 'hatewank' videos of her on a porn website. Crucially, these videos featured photos of her wearing bikinis that had been taken from her Instagram account. One of the videos, titled 'racist hatewank for Ash Sarkar', had been uploaded onto xHamster. 'The racist hatewank was literally a guy masturbating to images of me,' Sarkar said when I interviewed her for a Mashable article.[23] 'After I'd read this tweet that it was out there, my partner was the one who looked it up to confirm that it was all there.' Sarkar's partner began to research how to get the video taken down and discovered that flagging copyright infringement could be a possible avenue to pursue, given that the images were taken from her personal Instagram. 'I sent them an email and, to their credit, very quickly, they took it down,' Sarkar said.

During my investigation into hatewank videos for Mashable, I discovered this type of abusive content is increasingly used to target and harass women in the public eye, and particularly high-profile Black and Brown women – including

Meghan Markle and BBC presenter Naga Munchetty. But while copyright infringement proved successful in getting Sarkar's content removed, the legal avenues for removing such content are limited.

'Women in public life who are the target of hatewank pornography – either of their own images or deepfakes – will find that their legal options are limited, and often ineffective,' says Emily McFadden. 'This is due to its nature, its accessibility, the perpetrators' anonymity online, and that perpetrators often post images/videos on multiple sites. Practically, it's almost impossible to completely remove media once it's been posted online.'

Some porn aggregator sites have been known to essentially ghost victims of image-based sexual abuse by not responding to requests to remove videos unless legal threats are made. As we saw in chapter 5, Rose Kalemba urged Pornhub to remove the video of her rape, and sent them 'begging emails' countless times, pleading with them and informing them that she was a minor. She got no response. Only when she posed as a lawyer and threatened legal action did Pornhub respond to her requests and remove the content.

If tech companies only respond when there's a clear breach of law, where do you stand when the law in this area is still playing catch-up? While some tech companies have made changes to address revenge porn on their platforms,[24] other platforms, like Telegram, have key features that make them perfect places for spreading revenge porn – as identified by Mashable reporter Rachel Kraus. Telegram's features allow for anonymity, the ability to replicate groups and create back-up groups in the event of a suspension, and bots that automatise abuse.

Non-consensual porn is a borderless crime, as Kraus points out in her investigation. This is because laws on image-based sexual abuse differ from country to country, and within the US from state to state. 'One of the most challenging aspects of nonconsensual pornography is that it's a borderless crime, that it can travel across countries, can travel across the world and you can have a perpetrator in one state, you can have a victim in a different country,' Mary Anne Franks, a lawyer and the president of the Cyber Civil Rights Initiative, told Kraus. 'There are all these kinds of moving parts that make it really difficult to be able to effectively prosecute these kinds of cases.'[25]

The law in England and Wales has not kept pace with technology and image-based sexual violations. Clare McGlynn says that, currently, the English law in this area of sexual violence doesn't go far enough and is extremely piecemeal. 'It's not comprehensive,' says McGlynn. 'You've not got cyberflashing clearly covered. You've not got threats to share images clearly covered, you've not got the [deep] fake porn covered. Even non-consensual sharing – you can only bring a criminal case if you can prove the perpetrator did it to cause distress. So there's this huge range of gaps in the law there.' (Following my interview with McGlynn, the government announced that threatening to share images will be covered by revenge porn laws.)

McGlynn says that she doesn't think closing those gaps will necessarily bring about immediate change, because you still need police and prosecutors to bring cases to trial. Currently, the law in its piecemeal state requires certain criteria be used to determine whether an offence falls under voyeurism, or upskirting, or non-consensual sharing offences. Some of those laws offer anonymity to victims, but not others. McGlynn feels a more comprehensive approach would bring cohesion to this messy set of laws. In addition to legal clarity and closing gaps, having an exhaustive digital violations law would have a societal awareness impact. McGlynn believes that there would be 'powerful expressive value in seeing all of this is clearly criminalised and unlawful'.

A comprehensive law covering digital violations is something that's currently being considered by the Law Commission. One of the areas currently being examined by the commission is image-based sexual abuse. In 2015, it became a criminal offence for someone to disclose 'private sexual photographs and films with intent to cause distress' under the Criminal Justice and Courts Act.[26] At the time of writing, the Law Commission is conducting a consultation to review the law that applies to taking, making and sharing intimate images without consent. The review will look at 'image-based sexual abuse' and 'deepfake pornography' – which uses deepfake technology to superimpose a person's face onto pornographic photos or videos – in addition to cyberflashing, upskirting and downblousing.

The problem, as identified by the commission, is that there is not currently a single criminal offence in England and Wales that covers the taking, making and sharing of intimate content without consent. 'Instead, we have a patchwork of offences that have developed over time, most of which existed before the rise of the internet and use of smartphones,' reads the Law Commission report. 'Each offence has different definitions and fault requirements, and there are some behaviours that are left unaddressed.'[27] There might be a bit of a wait before we see any legislation, though, warns McGlynn. It could take until 2022 for any new legislation to be discussed.

The Law Commission has two ongoing projects relating to image-based sexual abuse, pertaining to the reform of communication offences as well as the taking, making and sharing of intimate images without consent. McFadden says these projects do give some hope. 'However, the government is not obliged to enact reform suggested by the Law Commission,' she adds. The Online Harms Bill, currently going through Parliament, names revenge porn as a harm.[28]

When it comes to digital acts of sexual violence, the law quite simply does not protect survivors. McGlynn believes a comprehensive law that brings expressive value with it would make it easier for victims to know what the situation is and for educators to be clear about what is unlawful, as well as ethical behaviour practices.

The law in this country is lagging behind the ways in which sexual violence is being perpetrated. This is why defining sexual violence outside of a legal framework is vitally important. As it stands, we have far too many legal grey areas when it comes to digital sexual offences, and those grey areas are impacting survivors as they try to get abusive content taken down and gain some kind of closure. These legal gaps also highlight the need for greater action from society as a whole – as well as tech companies – on the matter of digital sexual violence.

CHAPTER 15

The ones who didn't get away

The women I spoke to in chapter 3 all lived to tell the tale after being choked without their consent. But that's not always the case. Women and people of marginalised genders are dying because of the rise of sexual violence.

Grace Millane's name might be familiar to you – for weeks it was emblazoned on newspaper front pages, and the details of her sex life were used against her in the reporting of her murder.[1]

Grace was a 22-year-old British tourist who was murdered in New Zealand. It was supposed to be the trip of a lifetime, a round-the-world adventure. But it ended with her death. Her bruised body was stuffed into a suitcase and buried in a shallow grave in bushland outside Auckland. Grace died from manual strangulation so violent that blood vessels burst in her face and left eye, and her nose bled heavily, two forensic pathologists confirmed.

Grace's death would have required unrelenting physical pressure and sustained strength for five to ten minutes, three medical experts confirmed. There was deep bruising on Grace's upper arms, left shoulder, and neck – 'typical of restraint', per the forensic pathologist who examined her body.[2]

In the press, the reporting focused instead on Grace's sex life. 'Grace Millane was member of BDSM dating sites and asked ex-partner to choke her during sex,' read one headline.[3] 'Grace Millane gave man on BDSM site list of sex fetishes like electric shocks and being "a submissive slave",' declared the *Sun*.[4] 'Grace Millane "encouraged date to choke her during sex and apply more force",' read another headline, in the *Mirror*.[5] Grace was being slut-shamed in the news and blamed for her own death.

The defence claimed this was 'an accident', arguing that 'acts designed to enhance sexual pleasure went wrong'.[6] 'If the couple engaged in consensual sexual activity and that went wrong, and no one intended for it to go wrong, then that is not murder,' Ron Mansfield, the lawyer defending the man, told the jury.[7] It was portrayed as a 'sex game gone wrong'. But the man, whose name wasn't revealed for legal reasons, had taken intimate photos of Grace's corpse, watched eight clips of hardcore pornography, and proceeded to go on a date with another woman while Grace's body was still in the room.

The court heard evidence from other women who'd had sex with the defendant. One woman said she was in bed with him when he pinned her down and she couldn't breathe. 'He had grabbed my forearms and put all the pressure on my arms so I couldn't breathe and I couldn't move my arms. I started kicking, trying to indicate I couldn't breathe. I was kicking violently. He would have felt me fighting. I was terrified.'[8]

Grace was murdered. Her killer was found guilty and jailed for life, with a non-parole period of a minimum of seventeen years.[9]

Increasingly, the phrases 'rough sex' and 'sex game gone wrong' are used as a defence in murder trials as though they're get-out-of-jail-free cards. It should go without saying, but it bears repeating: the stories being described in these murder cases are categorically not consensual rough sex. As journalist Franki Cookney has identified, the stories told in courtrooms where the 'rough sex defence' is used overlook the fact that people who engage in consensual rough sex do so responsibly and with a duty of care to their sex partners.

'In a murder case where the rough sex defence is argued, we are asked to concede that if someone is willing to engage in such risky practices, they must take on themselves the possibility that it will go wrong,' writes Cookney in the *Independent*.[10] 'But in truly consensual sex no one person is ever solely responsible for what happens. Taking responsibility not just for yourself and your own wellbeing, but for the wellbeing of your partners, is the cornerstone of safe BDSM (as it ought to be for all kinds of sex, frankly).'

Abusers and killers have co-opted the term 'rough sex' and exploited the stigmatisation of BDSM and kink as a way to excuse their abuse and avoid facing consequences. I believe that some people have seen the efforts to destigmatise BDSM as an opportunity to wilfully misunderstand the central tenets of this practice (consent and boundaries being chief among them) and instead appropriate its terminology as a disguise for their own misogyny. These people are not practising BDSM or consensual rough sex.

We Can't Consent To This led the campaign to ban the use of the 'rough sex' defence – also known as the '50 Shades of Grey' defence – in murder trials. 'This is a response to the increasing use of "rough sex" defences to the killing or violent injury of women and girls,' they write in their mission statement. 'There are 60 UK women killed and many more injured.' Of those sixty women, nearly a third were killed in the last five years.[11]

So, what exactly is a rough sex defence? As anonymous author the Secret Barrister explains in a lengthy Twitter thread: 'In order to prove murder, the prosecution have to prove that the Defendant *either* intended to kill the deceased, or intended to cause her really serious harm. If the prosecution can't prove that intent, they can't prove murder . . . A common "defence" in murder cases generally, therefore, is a defendant saying "I may have intended to cause *some* harm, but I didn't intend to kill or cause really serious harm." And it's in that context that consensual rough sex can become relevant.'[12]

Over the past five years, the rough sex defence has been successful in seven of seventeen of the killings which went to trial, according to WCCTC. This resulted in the defendants being found not guilty, or convicted of manslaughter. The use of this defence is tantamount to saying 'she asked for it' and suggests that the women consented to their own deaths – something that, in technical terms, is legally impossible under UK law.[13]

Following Grace Millane's death, the campaign to ban the rough sex defence gathered momentum, and magazine *Grazia* joined forces with campaigners to create a petition, which has since been signed by 68,000 people.[14] In July 2019, MPs Harriet Harman and Mark Garnier pledged to take action over the use of the rough sex defence, and they eventually gained the cross-party support of more than eighty MPs. The Home Office subsequently said it would look into including 'rough sex' laws in the new Domestic Abuse Bill for England and Wales.

In July 2020, the UK government published a clause banning the rough sex defence in that bill.[15] Harman said in *Grazia* that sexual liberation shouldn't come at the cost of women's safety: 'It's ironic that women's sexual liberation should be used against them to justify men killing them.'[16] In an appearance on *Woman's Hour*, she said, 'The new version of men being able to blame the woman they killed for her own death is by saying "she wanted the violence".'[17]

Legally, the rough sex defence shouldn't actually be admissible when used by defendants in England and Wales.[18] Almost thirty years ago, the aforementioned R v Brown case ruled that you cannot consent to being seriously injured or killed. Under English and Welsh law, anything beyond 'transient or trifling' injuries cannot be consented to. As the Secret Barrister wrote on Twitter, 'It is a long established principle of the common law that a person cannot legally consent to being injured or killed . . . If you read the Bill, you'll see that all it does is put down in statute the common law principle that you can't consent to being injured or killed. But that was already the law.'[19]

There is an understandable hesitation in criticising this development when so much is riding on it. For families of victims, the law change represents hope that other families won't have to go through what they have. Grace Millane's family hailed it as 'fantastic news'.[20] Campaigners have worked tirelessly to bring people's attention to this issue and to get the government and media to care about it. Professor Clare McGlynn shares that hesitation in condemning the law change, but expresses concerns about its impact on a broader level: 'When you talk about how do we change things, one of my concerns is that the assumption is that it's now been done, and we have sorted that, but these cases are going to keep continuing,' she says.

'The proposal that's actually in the legislation, all it's doing is putting into legislation the existing law, which says you can't consent to certain levels of violence. On the one hand, that is a good thing, because it certainly seems that the Crown Prosecution Service were being reluctant to take some cases because they thought the existing case law might be changed or might not stand up in court. 'But that only applies in cases of assault. It's not going to make any difference to these murder cases. So it is a good thing, but it's not the end of the rough sex defence.'

In the context of domestic violence, non-fatal strangulation is a highly gendered crime. Every two weeks a woman is strangled to death by her partner in the UK.[21] Domestic abuse survivors who've been throttled by their partner are seven times more likely to be killed than those who haven't been.[22]

New research published in January 2021 looked at the harm that non-fatal strangulation causes. Strangulation often leaves no visible signs of harm or injury. But a review of thirty empirical, peer-reviewed studies found that non-fatal strangulation can bring about serious neurological and psychological consequences – including stroke, cardiac arrest, miscarriage, incontinence and memory loss – some of which take days or weeks to take hold. Neurological consequences include brain injury, paralysis, seizures, and motor and speech disorders. The psychological outcomes include PTSD, depression, suicidality and dissociation.[23]

Rachel Williams is a domestic abuse survivor who campaigned to change the law and make non-fatal strangulation a standalone criminal offence. When Williams was pregnant with her first child, her husband grabbed her by the throat and lifted her off the ground. It was only when her lips turned blue that he loosened his grip. Her husband was charged with common assault, the lowest charge to levy against someone. To clarify, acts like pushing someone are also classed as common assault. Yes, you read that right: starving someone of oxygen until their lips turn blue is classed as the least severe form of assault.

'If someone is putting their hands around your neck to obstruct your airways, to me that needs to be a stand-alone charge close to attempted murder. If perpetrators are doing that to you then your risk of homicide increases seven-fold,' Williams told *The Times*. 'They [throttle you] on a regular basis to show the control they have got. You are one step away [from death] and the intent is there. By someone putting their hands around your throat they only have one reason to do that and that is to cut off the air supply.'[24] Her husband went on to throttle her several more times; the final time, her two sons intervened by calling the police. Six weeks later he showed up at her place of work and shot her with a sawn-off shotgun. Her husband died by suicide.

In the context of domestic violence, throttling, choking and non-fatal strangulation aren't being met with a robust response from the criminal justice system in the UK. Choking perpetrators are usually charged with common assault or actual bodily harm, but the prosecution rate is extremely low. And those offence types carry lower sentences – anything from a fine to five years in prison. According to Dr Catherine White, director of St Mary's Sexual Assault Referral Centre in Manchester, prosecution is 'very rare' because the law needs proof that strangulation occurred as a means to carry out a further violent act like rape or assault.[25]

Williams called on lawmakers to create a separate piece of legislation or for an amendment to the Domestic Abuse Bill, and in March 2021 it was announced the new Domestic Abuse Bill would make non-fatal strangulation a specific criminal offence in England and Wales, punishable by five years' imprisonment.[26] Prior to this development, the government had stated it had no plans to change the law.[27]

When women die after being choked or strangled during sex, details of their sex lives are plastered on the front pages of newspapers, as if to blame the victim for her own death. Op-eds have subsequently claimed that 'rough sex has gone too far'. But, in reality, it has nothing to do with consensual rough sex, and everything to do with misogyny.

Reinforcing in legislation the principle that you cannot consent to your death is a positive step, but it does nothing to remedy the rampant, deep-rooted hatred of women that exists at the heart of these killings. How many more women will die before our society decides to do something about the root cause of this epidemic of violence?

CHAPTER 16

Prata om det

In December 2010, Swedish-Finnish writer Johanna Koljonen tweeted something she'd never said out loud to another human being, describing events that had taken place years earlier, when she was 24 or 25 years old. What she couldn't have foreseen was that these tweets would herald the start of a national movement in Sweden, prompting people to look inwardly and think about their past sexual experiences and how their behaviour might have impacted others.

Koljonen had been asked out on a date by an older man she knew professionally – a man she greatly respected and was somewhat in awe of. She gave little thought to the age difference between herself and the man in question, who was about 40 years old. But now that Koljonen is that very age, the disparity sits less comfortably with her.

Early on in the date, the man said very clearly that his goal was that they would have sex later. Koljonen tells me, 'I was like "yes!" and we had dinner, then went home to my place and we had sex – very consensually and very enthusiastically. But in the morning I woke up to being anally penetrated in a completely non-consensual fashion and in a very direct conflict with agreements around condoms that we'd had.'

In that moment, she froze and, after a while, realised what was happening to her. 'I was like, "I'm just gonna wait for this to be over." And then I gave him breakfast and then I sent him home. I can't remember if I realised then – or even years after that – that was me being raped.' Her experience, she says, did not fit the rape narratives she'd grown up hearing about.

When Koljonen told this story on Twitter, a movement called #PrataOmDet (#TalkAboutIt in English) was born. It was then that the term 'grey area sex' was coined.

Koljonen's impetus to speak out came in the wake of the Swedish media's reaction to sexual assault allegations against Julian Assange, and the stark contrast to media responses in the international press. Sweden has since dropped the rape investigation against Assange after a review of the evidence.[1] 'In Sweden the baseline assumption was: here are these allegations and we don't know what happened, but it's feasible to assume they may be real,' she says. 'Whereas the international press in the English-speaking world primarily was saying: there have been these allegations in Sweden and obviously they're false. People were saying things like, "as we know, when people have sex this is what happens", "when people sleep with people at parties", "when you take someone out this is how it always goes" or "men are like this, women are like this" or "drunk people having sex is always like this".'

Around this time, Koljonen was concerned by the sweeping generalisations about 'how sex usually is' being spouted in the social media discourse prompted by the Assange allegations. She reflected on whether she'd ever experienced something that might be considered complicated if it were discussed as part of a public debate. Then she remembered what had happened to her in her bedroom the morning after her date with the older man.

Koljonen believed that if she'd reported what happened, it would have been unlikely to get a conviction. She says that, to be honest, it hadn't even crossed her mind at the time, because 'frankly we have pretty low expectations' when it comes to conviction rates. Despite this, Koljonen felt in some way responsible for what had happened that morning. 'I somehow felt that I didn't deserve being treated well. Which is ridiculous because I'm pretty sex-positive, I shouldn't be ashamed of having sex consensually, but weirdly I did. And especially in that situation I felt it was somehow my fault.'

After her rape, Koljonen said she set it aside and didn't think about what happened. But when she tweeted her story, people began reacting strongly to it. It seemed to be resonating with people.

A spark of curiosity had been ignited for Koljonen. It occurred to her how rarely we discuss the reality of our sexual experiences – particularly ones which don't fit certain narratives. This kind of information usually remains largely 'hidden away in everybody's private souls'. She hadn't really reflected at all on that incident. 'Possibly never in my life have I gone back and thought about a sexual experience afterwards in an analytical way,' she says.

When it comes to talking about sex, we often talk about the good, but we seldom discuss the experiences that are bad, traumatic, or ones that we're not quite sure how to label. Those grey areas deserve conversation, but what is the appropriate medium for dissecting those experiences? We're not talking about spilling about fun sexcapades over cocktails with mates here. This is about having nuanced conversations about experiences that didn't fit those narratives – the experiences we might have pushed into the furthest reaches of our memories.

Talking to Koljonen made me wonder about what might have happened if I'd shared the real version of events with my friendship circle back in university? Perhaps those friends, upon hearing my honest, unfiltered account of what transpired, would have felt more able to share the reality of their own experiences. I'd hazard a guess that we all might have felt a little less alone.

So, how do you start to talk about the broad spectrum of harms? How do you normalise conversations about such a nuanced and sensitive subject matter? How do you talk about aspects of sexual violence that don't fit the narratives you've been brought up hearing about? How do you talk about an experience you're still trying to make sense of?

The experiences that are riddled with misogyny. The experiences that were pleasurable for one person, but painful for the other. Experiences that were violent and traumatic. Experiences that you told yourself didn't really 'count' or weren't 'that bad'.

Koljonen wanted to find a way to temporarily suspend the embarrassment and shame that stands in the way of talking about these things. She knew that if she was able to get everybody to divulge an intimate story in a detailed and analytical way at the same time, it would be 'an appropriate thing to do', as part of a collective moment.

In order to make this collective moment happen, Koljonen – who was working as a freelance journalist at the time – enlisted the help of fellow journalists and newspaper editors. Together, they orchestrated a plan. They coordinated the publication of stories in every major Swedish national newspaper on the exact same day. Koljonen describes the brief given to the other journalists as follows: 'Tell a story, any story of sex that didn't work, sex that was bad, that made you unhappy. How and why did it happen? What led you to the situation? What did you do? What did the other person do? How did you react? How did you wish you'd reacted? What did you do after?'

The journalists wrote stories about 'really painful things that they had probably never told anyone'. These were, as Swedish academic Lena Gunnarsson puts it, 'personal experiences of sexual/violent interactions that, in one way or another, involved difficulties with boundary-drawing in terms of whether to label an experience as sex or sexual assault, in terms of knowing and communicating one's own boundaries'.

While the journalists were writing their pieces in preparation for the coordinated event, Swedish journalist Sofia Mirjamsdotter tweeted that she was working on her piece but she had so many experiences that fit the brief that she didn't know which one would be most meaningful. She tweeted some of the experiences and asked her followers to tell her which one she should write about. 'She started tweeting big and small stories, sexual harassment, but also "grey zone" sex,' says Koljonen.

Mirjamsdotter tells me over email that she was one of a few people who began tweeting about sexual assaults they'd been through. 'At the time I had many followers and my tweets had a great impact. A day after I had told a lot of stories about assault and harassment in the media business, people all over Sweden did the same.' From that moment on, Mirjamsdotter became one of the key voices of the movement. Hours after she'd shared her experiences, thousands of people in Sweden began sharing their own experiences, sometimes anonymously via separate accounts specifically registered for this.

People responded to her stories in a very positive way. But Mirjamsdotter provides a caveat to that by saying, 'This was also before Twitter was invaded by trolls, so it was in a way easier to talk about private stuff and controversial subjects . . . Many were shocked, mostly men of course, but then my inbox started to overflow with people telling me their stories, some of which they had never told anyone before.'

In a way it was liberating to read all the stories, and to know that you weren't alone. 'It became so much easier for a lot of people to talk about these things, and I guess that is why also #MeToo went so huge in Sweden. We were somewhat prepared for it,' she says. 'It was also very clear that it's so much easier to not be alone, the power of hundreds of stories cannot be underestimated, and it made more people believe us.' Despite that, it was also very sad to hear that so many women had experiences like this and that it was so common. 'I have also met a few men during the years who have told me how they changed in both thoughts and behaviour thanks to #PrataOmDet,' Mirjamsdotter adds.

The long-term consequences of the movement were that it was easier for people to talk about sexual violence and it created a space for survivors to share experiences without feeling ashamed, says Mirjamsdotter. 'About the long term, I am sorry to say that there is still a lot of work to do, which was proved when #MeToo came. But for a lot of individuals it did make a difference for life, of that I am sure.'

Mirjamsdotter believes we need to talk about sex a lot more than we do. 'About difficulties, about consent, and so on. And yes, the conversation must be held at all levels, from the private bed to international debate. Still there are far too many women having bad, even unacceptable experiences, and we must keep on talking until that situation is changed.'

The publication of those stories in well-regarded national papers lent credence to the experiences being shared, Koljonen says. '#PrataOmDet was very much about looking at complexity and looking at the massive gap between how sex is talked about in culture and our actual personal experiences of having sex in our lives.'

By this point, thousands of people all over Sweden had joined the conversation, sharing their stories. Most of the accounts were written by women, but men also contributed their experiences 'both of victimhood and of having (possibly) violated someone else's boundaries', according to Gunnarsson, who translated and analysed many of the accounts in her academic research.[2]

When people participate in a large-scale public movement like this, telling stories that have not previously been discussed with anyone else, it's possible to build a bigger picture of a society's sexual culture – and to spot patterns and problems within that culture.

Unwanted sex

One common thread that united many of the stories being shared was that of unwanted sex – sex that people consented to, but didn't want or desire. A crucial takeaway from #PrataOmDet was that people who identified as liberal-minded and sex-positive had unconsciously internalised harmful gender roles, Koljonen tells me. 'What we were learning was that even people who are what we would now call "woke" are pretty bad at seeing internalised gender norms in themselves.'

There were situations where women didn't feel their pleasure was important, or felt they 'didn't want to be a bitch' or to cause any trouble. In instances of unwanted sex, an individual might reflect on that experience afterwards and think, 'I had consensual sex with them, but I couldn't wait for it to be over.' These gender norms had given people ideas about what it meant to 'be a man' in a sexual situation, what it meant to 'be a woman' during sex, and whose role it was to initiate sex. 'A lot of people end up having sex they don't want, a lot of people end up forcing themselves into situations or remaining in situations that they could have prevented,' Koljonen adds.

Among the #PrataOmDet stories were scores of people who relayed experiences of having sex when they didn't feel like it for a broad spectrum of reasons. Lena Gunnarsson believes unwanted sex is one of the biggest contributing factors to the existence of the grey area. In her research, she interviewed people of different sexual orientations to find out why they consent to unwanted sex. 'I make the case that the main factor behind the grey area can be found in the fact that what people want is not always clear,' she tells me over email. As explored in chapter 6, reasons for consenting to unwanted sex may be love, care, fear of abandonment, or something else. 'It's indeed possible to have sex with someone for the sake of the other as a generous, loving act, and it can be altogether constructive and positive for both parties. But it's also very common to do it in a way that is destructive for the accommodating person.'

While there are myriad reasons why the 'accommodating person' may engage in unwanted sexual activity, there's one very significant reason in heterosexual sex – gender roles.

'The gendered problem here is that women are socialised to tend to others' needs generally and, more specifically, to downplay their own independent sexual needs in favour of pleasing men's sexual needs,' Gunnarsson says. 'So, when a woman repeatedly "wants" to have sex with her male partner although she's not really into it, this "wanting" can of course be problematised.'

When misogyny shows itself to you, believe it

The #MeToo movement has had a profound effect not only in giving survivors space to share experiences of sexual violence, but in challenging the general public's ideas and stereotypes about rape, assault and harassment. You might have also noticed that the #MeToo movement brought to the fore a lot of long-held ideas about sexual violence – some of which were deeply problematic.

In late 2017, in the wake of the *New York Times* investigation into Harvey Weinstein's sexual abuse, I noticed a polarising effect in the ways in which #MeToo was perceived among older and younger generations. I was sitting at a kitchen table with a family friend in their fifties when they told me they were concerned we were in danger of entering an era of extreme sexual correctness. In this person's blueprint of our sexual future, men would feel under constant scrutiny if they so much as made eye contact with a woman.[3] And that conversation was not an isolated incident. Research at the time looked into generational differences in opinion when it came to what constitutes sexual harassment. A survey by YouGov found older British women viewed certain behaviours as acceptable, while younger women deemed them inappropriate. Wolf-whistling was deemed to be the most divisive behaviour, with 74 per cent of 18- to 24-year-olds and 59 per cent of 25- to 39-year-olds considering it inappropriate. But four in ten women over 55 said wolf-whistling was acceptable, and 27 per cent even thought it was flattering.[4]

Generational differences aside, recent research has highlighted the prevalence of public sexual harassment experienced by young people. UN Women data from 2021 shows that 97 per cent of young women in the UK have experienced sexual harassment in public spaces. That same research also found a lack of faith in authorities. Just 4 per cent of women said they'd reported incidents of harassment to an organisation, and 45 per cent of women said they didn't think reporting it would change anything.[5]

The #MeToo movement made me realise how much of an echo chamber I live in. If you carefully curate your Instagram and Twitter feeds to show you only sex-positive accounts, and only befriend people with similar value systems to yourself, it's easy to think that everyone thinks the same way you do.

Never before in my lifetime had I heard so many differing views – and so many problematic views from people that I knew. Some of those views pertained to what does and does not 'count' as sexual violence, and how people – usually women – should behave or react in those scenarios.

At parties, old friends' new boyfriends told me – unsolicited of course – what they thought about 'this whole #MeToo thing'. From people my parents knew I'd hear their thoughts on how they felt sorry for young people who would no longer be able to flirt with their colleagues. 'How are you supposed to meet people now?' they'd ask me.

At a charity supper club event at the height of #MeToo, I ended up sitting with a group of people I'd never met before. The woman beside me struck up a conversation. 'I'm sorry, but I just don't buy it,' she told me. She'd asked me what I did for a living, one thing led to another, and somehow I'd ended up telling her about a story I was working on. I wished I hadn't.

'I think that if a woman says yes at the outset then she can't claim any harm has occurred,' she said. I shuffled the salt and pepper shakers around on the table while I waited for this stranger to finish explaining to me what did and did not 'count'. We were discussing the Babe.net story, and the allegations of sexual misconduct by Aziz Ansari. This woman wasn't convinced. 'Why didn't she just leave?' she asked.

The #MeToo sceptic shook her head at me in disbelief. As she spoke, my mind flipped through the sexual experiences I'd lived through that had left me feeling uncomfortable, as if I were going through a Rolodex of personal violations. Experiences that, in this stranger's eyes at least, did not technically 'count'. These experiences were to be filed under 'N/A' and never spoken of again. Too difficult, too confusing, best left alone.

In the cab home, I kept thinking about the woman's words: 'If a woman says yes at the outset then she can't claim any harm has occurred.' I couldn't remember the last time I'd heard a statement I disagreed with so vehemently. Consent is a constant negotiation, and it can be withdrawn at any time.

But this woman wasn't alone in her take on the situation. All over the internet, people were posting their takes on what Grace 'should' have done in that situation with Aziz Ansari. I wrote a response to this problematic rhetoric, explaining why saying no isn't always possible: 'The responses to the woman's story are peppered with the word "should". She *should* have said no; she *should* have walked out; she *should* never have taken off her clothes; she *shouldn't* have been there in the first place. These responses, which are disturbingly widespread, not only shift the blame and responsibility onto the woman, they also fail to recognise an important truth. For many women, uttering an explicit "no" is not as easy or straightforward as you might think.'[6]

American conservative political commentator Ben Shapiro took issue with my assessment of the responses in his book *Whining Doesn't Win*. (Remember the guy who criticised Harry Styles for donning 'floofy dresses' because it was an attack on masculinity? Yeah, him.)[7]

In a chapter called 'Stop Feministsplaining Sex to Men', Shapiro outlines his grievances. 'Well, as it turns out, reading minds is not quite as easy or straightforward as feminists might think. It was feminists who boiled down sexual relations to the issue of consent. Traditionalists always argued that physical intimacy and emotional intimacy ought to be linked. But they were accused of removing female agency with such linkage and condemned for "mansplaining".' Shapiro goes on to argue that we put an end to both mansplaining and 'feministsplaining' when it comes to sex, and instead focus on the 'communication between men and women'. Aside from the heteronormativity of his statement, Shapiro's assertion that it's 'feministsplaining' to bring up that saying 'no' isn't always an option feeds into the tired argument that talking about sexual violence makes you a feminist killjoy. His suggestion that we should all just communicate better is laudable in theory, but in this context it ignores the power imbalances and systems of oppression that impact people's sexual agency.

If you happened to be on social media at the height of the #MeToo era, you might have stumbled across the odd tweet that pondered 'Why didn't she report it at the time?' Ah, that old chestnut. The question reared its ugly head once more when Dr Christine Blasey Ford alleged that the then-Supreme Court nominee Brett Kavanaugh sexually assaulted her thirty-five years prior. 'I have no doubt that, if the attack on Dr. Ford was as bad as she says, charges would have been immediately filed with local Law Enforcement Authorities by either her or her loving parents,' Trump tweeted at the time. 'I ask that she bring those filings forward so that we can learn date, time, and place.'[8]

Trump's tweet prompted survivors to begin sharing their reasons for not reporting abuse, using the hashtag #WhyIDidntReport. 'I was 16yo the first time I was raped,' reads one tweet. 'I didn't understand consent, rape, and thought it was my fault. For this and many reasons are #WhyIDidntReport.'

'I was humiliated. I knew everyone would find out. I was afraid it would ruin my professional reputation before I had even started. I was afraid they would not believe me and let him hold my grade back. I was afraid they would not let me graduate from law school. #WhyIDidntReport,' reads another.[9]

It goes without saying that no one should really have to explain their reasons for not reporting sexual assault. But this hashtag brought to the fore the ways in which our global culture's deep-rooted propensity for blaming victims makes survivors feel they're at fault for what happened to them, makes them feel they won't be believed, and makes them afraid of the repercussions of taking any action.

Activism can play a really important role in challenging social views on sexual violence, broadening our definitions of what constitutes violence, and revealing how internalised gender roles play out in our sex lives. In the UK, activism has also brought awareness about sexual violence to the corridors of power, taking these issues to the doors of lawmakers. But it's worth noting that white privilege plays a role in ensuring some activists' voices are lifted higher than those from marginalised communities. Gina Martin, in her book *Be The Change*, talks about how white privilege opened doors for her when she was campaigning for upskirting to be made a crime: 'My whiteness, among other things, benefited me because we prioritise whiteness.

White is the main power source. White is the default. Our industries are owned by white people. Our country is run by white people. Our media showcases white people. White people prioritise white people.'

The value of activism and social movements lies in their ability to challenge and change widely held assumptions about sexual violence. But it's also clear that more work is needed to ensure these movements speak for all survivors, not the few. Our work is far from done.

CHAPTER 17

The new sex scene

'In that place where rules, clarity, law, separation, cease to exist we will show you exactly what we mean by violation.'

—Arabella, *I May Destroy You*

'Is that what you want?' Connell asks Marianne in episode two of *Normal People*, which aired in 2020 on BBC Three. The 'that' refers to sex, and the question is a method of seeking affirmative consent.

Two people in a state of undress, shyly making small talk at first before giggling at the awkwardness of being naked together. In hushed tones, they talk to each other about what they want, one of them seeks affirmative consent from the other. As a viewer, you feel two things at once: this intimacy is refreshingly ordinary; this consent negotiation is unlike anything I've seen on TV before.

'Is this your first time?' he asks from the corner of his bedroom as he fetches a condom. 'Yeah,' she replies nervously. 'Is that OK?'

Connell emphasises to Marianne that consent can be withdrawn at any time. 'If you want to stop or anything, we can obviously stop . . . If it hurts or anything, we can stop. It won't be awkward.'[1] That sentence might sound like common sense to many of us in theory, but to see it on television felt like a big deal. Viewers at home found this moment arresting and refreshingly different to typical TV sex scenes. What we were witnessing was a consent exchange – some people called it the 'consent chat'. It was a scene infused with authentic intimacy and, watching it, you felt a tug of recognition. There was an awkwardness and shyness that is so often present in our real life sexual interactions. For anyone who's ever thought consent negotiation is a mood killer or not sexy, watch this scene and disabuse yourself of that false notion immediately.

Journalist Almaz Ohene points out the rarity of seeing conversations like these playing out on our television screens. 'We hardly ever get shown consensual conversations before any kind of sexual contact is happening. In *Normal People* when Marianne and Connell have sex, the whole first scene is nine minutes long. There's loads of consent conversation, but also chit-chats about what was happening. They giggle about taking her bra off. And actually, that is what happens in real life. But people think that it doesn't.'

If we think about the significance of that moment for Marianne, who's never had sex before, then this is a really positive example of someone being treated with the care and attention they need in that moment. For many young women, their experiences of first-time sex could not be further from what takes place in Connell's bedroom. If we can move closer towards normalising conversations about consent and boundaries in on-screen sex scenes, we can begin to challenge people's ingrained belief that consent negotiations 'ruin the mood'. The entire nation was practically transfixed by the *Normal People* sex scenes – proof, perhaps, that there's nothing remotely unsexy about letting someone know they can withdraw their consent.

When it comes to our sex lives, the sex scenes we watch on our screens play a role in shaping our ideas and expectations about what sex is like. When we watch media featuring intimate content – be it a TV programme, a film or online porn – our brain forms ideas and messages from those portrayals as sexual scripts, or stereotyped ideas about sex. Half of young people rated their school's relationships and sex education as poor or terrible, per a 2017 report by the Terrence Higgins Trust.[2] But when we turn to other sources of information to satisfy our curiosity about sex, we aren't equipped with the skills that help us differentiate between positive depictions and problematic ones. TV sex scenes which rely heavily on gender roles and traditional heterosexual ideas were found to have an impact on young women's sexual agency in real life, according to one study.[3] The more realistic the sex scene, the more likely we are to internalise those ideas as scripts.

Problem is, the sitcoms, dramas, reality shows, and movies we watch are typically made with entertainment as their main objective – not education. Though that's not to say that directors and writers don't set out to challenge our ideas, perspectives and stereotypes.

But whether they like it or not, directors and screenwriters have a responsibility to ensure that sex scenes do not perpetuate unhelpful and harmful ideas of sex. And it should not end there. When making sex scenes for the screen, directors and writers should ask themselves the following questions: Does this sex scene serve the narrative or is it entirely gratuitous? Does this sex scene feature any consent negotiation? Is this sex scene believable and realistic? Does the sex scene misrepresent or hypersexualise marginalised communities and feed into damaging stereotypes that already exist? Does this sex scene portray kink or BDSM without showing the robust consent protocols at the heart of this community? Do the sex scenes in this production only show thin, white, cis, straight, non-Disabled people having positive sexual experiences? If so, why?

Things are changing, though. Over the past couple of years, we've started to see some small but positive differences in the way sex scenes are shown on our screens and also in the way they're filmed.

Let's talk more about consent. Annie Lord, British *Vogue*'s dating columnist, would like to see more examples of people asking if their behaviour is OK in sexual scenarios. 'In *Love Island* when Luke T and Siannise were in the hideaway and she gave him a lapdance, he was asking: "Is this okay?" I'd love to see more of that kind of behaviour on TV,' Lord tells me over email. 'Not only did it show how sexy consent is – if you talk through what you are doing together, it makes you both hyper-aware of what's happening – but it also showed how to ensure both adults are comfortable throughout the sex.'

In December 2020, I took to Twitter to ask people for examples of consent being portrayed in a progressive way in TV or film. I had been thinking about this question for weeks trying to come up with positive examples, but truthfully they are few and far between. One person replied to me saying, 'I just finished watching *Normal People* today and now I'm wracking my brains to think of anything that is even vaguely similar. It's pretty depressing that I can't, to be honest.' As journalist Beth Ashley told me, 'It seems consent is usually explored in film for educational or awareness reasons via a rape or harassment plot, rather than one of pleasure.'

Ashley's words about consent often being shown in storylines about sexual violence stayed with me. Because when you think about it, when do you ever see consent conversations or negotiations in positive, pleasurable sex scenes? The sad reality is, I can't think of any examples. That's not to say there isn't value in portraying sexual violence that challenges stereotypes and serves as educational viewing. All too often, however, sexual violence on our screens feels entirely gratuitous – a device for viewers' entertainment. But what's entertaining about watching a woman or marginalised person being raped, assaulted or abused?

Until 2020, I hadn't seen a programme on television that portrayed sexual violence in a way that felt representative of survivors' experiences, or that moved the needle in the conversation about sexual violence. *I May Destroy You* is without a doubt the best on-screen portrayal of sexual violence and its aftermath I've ever seen in my 32 years on this earth. Created by Michaela Coel – writer of *Chewing Gum* – the show tackles the intersection of sexual violence, race and consent in a way that overturns widely held misconceptions and stereotypes. Shows had previously come close to depicting the everyday acts of violence that women endure in relationships and sexual encounters – but few did so in a way that felt devoid of harmful stereotypes.

In episode one, Arabella (Coel) is trying and struggling to finish a book when she decides to take a break and grab a drink with friends. It's here the night changes course. The morning after, Arabella cannot recall how she made it back to her desk. There's blood coming from a cut on her forehead and her phone screen is smashed to smithereens – neither of which she can explain. Amid the haze and confusion, an image keeps replaying in Arabella's mind. It's a vivid flashback of a man violently thrusting in a toilet cubicle. It is the memory of a rape.

For a while, she cannot explain where this image has come from. Nor can she identify the person who is being raped. What she later comes to realise and eventually accept is that she is the person who's been raped.

In the first two episodes, we witness this unacknowledged rape – an aspect of sexual violence that is rarely explored on screen. As previously discussed, psychologists employ this term to refer to a violation that meets a legal description of rape or assault, but is labelled differently by the survivor. In episodes one and two, Arabella does not realise she's been raped. When the police officer repeats back to Arabella her interpretation of the night in question, Arabella urges caution and tells her to be careful with how she's describing the events which unfolded.

Arabella's difficulty in naming what has happened could be explained by cultural rape scripts – the difference between the reality of rape, and how it's shown on television, and how it's described by the media. Not only does *I May Destroy You* challenge the stereotypes that we've all absorbed from inaccurate media descriptions of sexual violence; it also shows the damaging aftermath of growing up in a culture that fails to equip people with the information to identify when they have been raped. If what happens to us doesn't fit the mainstream media narrative of the violent stranger rape, how do we know what to call our experience?

Later in the series, while Arabella is reeling from the trauma of what happened to her, she's introduced to another writer called Zain. The pair end up having sex, but Zain removes the condom midway through and throws it across the bedroom. Arabella is unaware at the time, but afterwards asks Zain what he did with the condom.

Arabella and Zain then go out together to get the morning-after pill. While she's listening to a podcast in a later episode, she later learns there's a word for it: 'stealthing'. Arabella publicly confronts Zain, taking to the stage at a literary event and delivering a blistering speech about what he did to her. It is a moment that brings goosebumps to your flesh, a moment of reckoning, and it is glorious to behold. 'He gaslighted me with such intention, I didn't have a second to understand the heinous crime that had occurred,' Arabella announces to the audience. 'He is a rapist under UK law.'[4]

I May Destroy You didn't just bring the relatively little-known act of stealthing into public consciousness, it also helped give language to real-life survivors of this violation and made them feel 'vindicated'. Journalist Sophie Wilkinson interviewed stealthing survivors about the show's impact on them in an article for British *Vogue*.[5] Kelly, who was just 17 at the time of her incident, said she knew immediately that the condom had been removed. 'To be really graphic, I had come inside me.' Kelly told Wilkinson she'd insisted on condom use: 'I was inexperienced and that was the one thing I was certain of. I was scared because I knew you're not supposed to have unprotected sex.'

Kelly described the experience as 'pretty grim', and once she'd realised he'd taken off the condom she felt 'so grossed out'. When she told her friends, they judged her for sleeping with him. 'Yeah, fair enough, it is a bit my fault,' she replied to her friends. In the months after, Kelly said she grew 'obsessed with the idea I had AIDS'.

Fifteen years later, the trauma of that violation lives on. 'I get weird about things during sex and I wish I could be more free. Sometimes I think it's my personality, but maybe it's been informed by those early years when sex started for me.' But watching *I May Destroy You* was helpful – and it was the first time she discovered that what had happened to her was a criminal act. 'I felt a jolt of vindication,' she said to Wilkinson. 'I needed someone to tell me it was 100 per cent wrong. And it was good to be able to tell my husband and acknowledge it.'

Black women are frequently erased from conversations about sexual violence and rape. That omission is a historic one that dates back to the time of slavery, when rape was considered a violation that happened uniquely to white women. Under the chattel slavery system introduced by French colonists in Louisiana in the United States, the rape of a Black woman – whether she was enslaved or free – was not a crime. Under state law at the time, rape was viewed as a crime that only white women experienced. But, under the very same system, the rape or attempted rape of a white woman by an enslaved Black man carried a sentence of capital punishment.[6]

I May Destroy You centres Black people's experiences of sexual violence, rape and racism. It's not only Arabella's storyline which makes this show so compelling to watch. Arabella's friend Kwame (Paapa Essiedu) is raped when he meets up with a Grindr match. Their mutual friend Terry (Weruche Opia) undergoes a racist microaggression during an audition, when a white casting director asks her to remove her wig so she can see her hair. We also learn Terry engages in a threesome that wasn't quite what it seemed. Terry believes that she has agreed to a random threesome, but she later finds out that it was planned by the two men. The scene raises questions about consent and being fully informed of all the circumstances you're consenting to.

In an interview with *Variety*, Opia says that the threesome storyline delves right into the grey area. 'She felt empowered in the moment, that she made this decision as a woman who was exploring her sexuality. But there is that grey area conversation: was that circumstance actually given, or was it stolen because she wasn't privy to the whole situation? Some people might think she was completely in control, and others may feel like her consent was stolen. I felt it was important to play both sides of it and allow everyone to take what they would from it. It's interesting to watch and to think about these situations, because everyone's is unique.'[7]

In recent years, a number of television programmes have looked at our sexual culture in radical new ways, kickstarting productive conversations.

In stark contrast to the teen movies that many of us grew up watching – with their problematic messaging about sex and consent – Netflix's *Sex Education* has managed to include educational elements in a really fun show. And one of its most powerful moments is Aimee Gibbs's sexual assault storyline in season two.

It starts with Aimee carrying a birthday cake onto a bus on her way to school. The bus is packed full of people, standing room only. As she grapples with the handle over-head, trying not to damage the cake, she becomes aware of a presence behind her. At first, she apologises to the man, thinking she's bumped into him. But then she real-ises what he's doing. 'He's wanking on me,' she exclaims to the crowd of onlookers. No one intervenes. They simply look away.[8]

It's only when Aimee tells her best friend what hap-pened that she's made to confront the seriousness of it. She doesn't realise until then that it is actually sexual assault. 'No, you've been assaulted,' Maeve tells her. Aimee says she thought the perpetrator was 'just lonely'. She plays down the impact it's had on her. 'It's silly. I'm fine. Honestly.' But when she tries to get on the bus the next time, she can't cross the threshold. She's patently traumatised.

I interviewed actress Aimee Lou Wood in 2020, a year after this powerful scene aired, and asked her how TV rep-resentations of consent are changing.[9] 'The fact that she puts on that brave face and goes on with this cake and says "Happy Birthday" to Maeve, I just thought it was such good storytelling because it's what so many of us do in those situ-ations,' she told me. 'And actually, not even just put on a brave face, but don't even allow yourself to go there, don't even allow yourself to believe that what just happened to you even happened, you just sweep it under the carpet.'

I asked Wood if she thinks we're entering a new age of television when it comes to reflecting the reality of women's experiences. 'I really think we are,' she replied. 'It feels very, very powerful right now. I think that it's shifting massively.'

She said that one of the first things that struck her about the *Sex Education* scripts was that she'd never seen anything like this on TV before. 'This is real, rather than the sex scenes that we've been shown in the past.' She then talked about watching scenes that seemed 'steamy' and 'sexy' when she was growing up, and revisiting those assessments through the lens of a grown-up. 'Is it steamy? Or is it just rough? And not consensual.'

So, should sex scenes that reinforce outdated stereotypes and perpetuate misinformation about consent like 'no means yes' be eradicated? Wood told me she is concerned about the impact those scenes have on young viewers and how they might shape their ideas of what consensual sex looks like. 'What we see when we're growing up has such an impact on what we think sex is.'

In the opening episode of *Sex Education*, Aimee's first-ever scene illustrates the very kind of impact Wood is talking about. In those opening moments, she's having sex with her boyfriend and mimicking the acts and sounds you'd typically see in porn. 'She's obviously watched some porn, and she's gone, "Right, I'll pretend like I'm having an absolutely great time right now," even though she's never masturbated, she doesn't actually know what she wants, she doesn't know her own body or own vagina,' said Wood. 'She's just going, "Do you like my tits," she's just repeating what she's seen. And it's not connected to any of her own desires, or what she actually wants.'

Television is edging ever closer towards mirroring women's sexual realities. But it's worth pointing out that these two radical programmes – *I May Destroy You* and *Sex Education* – both take inspiration from their screenwriter's lived experiences.

Laurie Nunn, the writer and creator of *Sex Education*, has spoken about the inspiration behind Aimee's storyline in a YouTube video. 'The inspiration for Aimee's storyline in series two came from a personal experience that I had myself,' she explains. 'This thing happened to me about five years ago where I was on my local bus and I was on the way to King's Cross station.' The bus was largely empty, except for another woman at the back. 'This man got on and he just made a beeline straight for me and came and sat right next to me. Which was just so weird, I was like, you have so many seats you could sit on but you've come and sat right next to me. I had my bags on the floor and he put his feet on my bags so that I couldn't move and he started inching himself toward me and then he was rubbing himself on me and touching himself.'[10]

I May Destroy You also draws inspiration from real life events. While delivering the MacTaggart lecture at the Edinburgh Television Festival in August 2018, Michaela Coel said that she was raped when she was working on season two of *Chewing Gum*. 'I was working overnight in the [production] company's offices; I had an episode due at 7 a.m. I took a break and had a drink with a good friend who was nearby.' When she regained consciousness, she was back typing season two. 'I had a flashback. It turned out I'd been sexually assaulted by strangers. The first people I called after the police, before my own family, were the producers.'[11]

Both powerful scenes are informed by personal experiences, and that realism shines through in the writing and the acting. There is merit in having a writers' room that reflects the characters you're portraying on-screen, as well as a roster of experts and advisers on hand to ensure the script is accurate and that the filming doesn't leave actors feeling violated. Alix Fox, a writer and sex educator with over fifteen years' experience, works on *Sex Education* as a script consultant. Fox's job is to make sure the show doesn't disseminate misinformation, which could harm young viewers.

In season one, Fox informed Gillian Anderson's role as Dr Jean F. Milburn, a sex therapist, providing examples of the issues she might treat in her job and the kind of resources she might make use of. In an interview for Mashable, Fox told me that for season two – which featured a number of complex and important storylines – her job became more involved and specific. She was sent chunks of the script to read, and had to decide whether they were factually correct. 'It was all about making sure that the information contained within the show was as accurate and as realistic as possible,' she told me. 'Often it's about balancing what people do in real life with what is best practice. It has to be believable but we also don't want to give young people the wrong idea of things that are dangerous.'[12]

In the second season, Lily's vaginismus storyline is one that was particularly significant for Fox. For the past five years, Fox has really focused on vaginismus in her writing and broadcasting work. Until a few years ago, the term 'vaginismus' was not in most people's lexicon. 'Actually getting it on a major TV show like *Sex Education* can be utterly transformative for people who are going through this or if their loved ones are affected by it too,' she says.

This transformation has been mirrored in the kinds of messages Fox has received. She's been inundated with emails and even letters from people of all ages, who have told her they were 'overjoyed to see something they've been coping with very privately' brought to a TV screen.

Portraying BDSM

I grew up watching on-screen kisses that weren't preceded by the words 'can I kiss you?' I grew up seeing sex scenes that didn't show any protection being used, that didn't feature any consent negotiation. But TV sex scenes are transforming before our eyes. These scenes are prompting conversations over dinner tables, over pints at the pub, across desks with colleagues, and on our timelines on social media. Change is happening. And that gives me great hope for the future.

But that's not to say things are perfect. Annie Lord has criticised *Normal People*'s presentation of BDSM, stating that the show seems to pathologise consensual rough sex and position it as the result of abuse.[13] 'In *Normal People*, it would have been so hot to watch Connell be like "Is this OK?" while binding her hands together or closing her mouth, rather than just freaking out when she said she wanted to be hit, as though there was something weird about it,' she says.

Sally Rooney clarified her position on BDSM in an interview with *Esquire* in 2019. 'I think some people have read this as me saying it's bad to accommodate violence into sex. For me, it was that Connell doesn't like BDSM, so people shouldn't do things they don't like . . . It's about him coming to terms with the fact that actually he has, in many ways, been dominating her all along, without wanting to admit it in himself.'[14]

Overall, Lord thinks the way BDSM is characterised on-screen is flawed, and it's often presented like consenting to one act is a no-holds-barred permission to mete out whatever you want on a woman's body. 'Normally in film and TV, if a woman character says she is into BDSM, her sexual partners tend to behave towards her in a very entitled way, as though they have been granted free rein over her body,' she says. 'In reality, this woman might be interested in a very small set of behaviours. Maybe she likes her hair pulled but doesn't like being slapped. Maybe she likes her hands tied up but hates being spat on. It sets a very dangerous precedent, as though saying you are into BDSM is the same as asking to be traumatised.'

She adds: 'As a culture, we tend to pathologise consensual rough sex as stemming from trauma and abuse. That because you've been hit before, you will want to be hit again. While this is true in some cases, the overemphasis on it as deriving from trauma makes BDSM sound like a sad by-product of something awful when it could just be that some people like pain and power play more than others.'

The BDSM community has stringent rules when it comes to consent and safeguarding. What's often absent in TV scenes depicting BDSM is any kind of conversation surrounding consent. If television did a better job of demarcating consensual rough sex from sexual violence, we could attempt to unlearn the dangerous messaging that inaccurate on-screen portrayals of BDSM have disseminated. Showing that clear difference on TV could also serve viewers by giving them a firmer grasp on what is and is not OK in real-life sexual scenarios.

Behind the scenes

As sex on our screens moves towards a greater realism and more positive portrayals of consent, that change should not come at the expense of an actor feeling traumatised or violated, however. The existence of on-set intimacy coordinators is proving vital in safeguarding the actors who bring these scenes to life. In an interview for *Attitude* magazine, Sharon Stone said they didn't have intimacy coordinators in the 1980s when she started her movie career. She then spoke about a terrifying experience she had during her first-ever nude scene. 'When I did my first movie, which was *Irreconcilable Differences*, I had a topless scene. And they didn't even clear the set. Everybody's on set, like a million people on the set. And I take off my top and this actor screams, "Would you get out of the fucking way? I can't even see her tits."' Stone says she was 'terrified' in that moment, and all she could hear was her own heartbeat in her ears.

It's not just about what we see on our screens, it also matters what goes on behind the scenes in order to bring that intimate content to our TV and laptop screens.

Ita O'Brien is an intimacy coordinator whose credits include *Normal People*, *I May Destroy You* and *Sex Education*. Her role involves developing best practice when working with scenes that involve sexual content and nudity in film, TV and theatre. O'Brien is a pioneer in the emerging field of intimacy coordinators, which is gaining adoption in major production companies like HBO, Netflix and the BBC.

Sex Education, O'Brien tells me, was a turning point in the television industry, because a professional structure hadn't been in place before when sex scenes were filmed. 'There wasn't the idea of a structure, or that even the need of a structure to allow you to work professionally, with open communication, transparency, agreement and consent.' That consent refers to consent of touch, of sexual content and of nudity.

O'Brien will then begin to choreograph the sex scene and bring clear techniques and physical structure to the intimate content, while also serving the director's vision and the writing. 'Without that structure, it meant that there was a real confusion of who that person was performing the scene personally, and who they were professionally,' she says. 'Before, because that consent wasn't invited, the idea of a no, as in "I'm not comfortable", was absolutely fraught with concerns from the actor that they would be considered unprofessional if ever they brought a no into the conversation; that they would be considered a troublemaker or a diva. And they absolutely would be concerned about losing the job, or certainly not being employed again.'

Actors are still grappling with the worry of 'Can I really say no?' O'Brien often tells the individuals she works with that 'your no is a gift'. 'We want to know your boundary, we want to know what is not suitable for you so that you can work freely, so you can be free as the actor to really serve the director's vision, free to be able to bring all of your glorious, beautiful skills as the actor, an actor can't do that unless they feel empowered, autonomous, comfortable, happy, and then they can do their best work.'

O'Brien does still experience resistance from some entertainment professionals who do not want the intimate content to be choreographed and who, as O'Brien puts it, 'are still working with the old-fashioned attitude of "oh for God's sake, just let her act it".' But those kinds of attitudes used to be endemic. She recalls working with an actress who had a scene featuring oral sex coming up, who said to O'Brien, 'Help, I've never done a scene like this before.' Each time she tried to rehearse the scene, the director would say, 'No, we'll rehearse this later.'

When *Sex Education* came along, O'Brien talked to director Ben Taylor and producer Jon Jennings, who told her they wanted the show to have an educational storytelling quality that would give young people an alternative to watching pornography and for porn being the main learning tool in their lives.

'At that point it was 2018, my kids were eighteen and twenty, so I was very aware of what he was talking about. I have my daughter saying to me that as soon as her girlfriends became sexually active, they felt they instantly had to shave their pubic hair because that's the only thing that they saw on pornography,' says O'Brien.

When it comes to keeping actors safe on set while filming intimate scenes, understanding an actor's personal boundaries is vital. O'Brien draws a parallel with preparing for a stunt scene. 'If someone's going to be jumping off a high building, that is dangerous, someone might die or someone might get injured. So they're going to check in with the actors and stuntpeople and find out their skill level.'

The danger involved in filming sex scenes and scenes involving nudity might not be quite the same as filming a death-defying stunt, but it's a danger of another kind. 'There is danger within this work, but of course when the danger isn't so clearly physical, but it's also absolutely emotional, psychological, and that's what we're taking care of,' O'Brien says. 'That's what we're not so good at doing as a society – really acknowledging the reality of that danger.'

The level of risk, she explains, is dependent on each and every person's life journey. If, for instance, an actor has been asked to stand completely naked in a scene and that actor has a very comfortable and open relationship with their body, that isn't necessarily going to present a risk for them. But if an actor's relationship with any part of their body means that this scene would overstep their boundaries and make them feel vulnerable, then that will be a damaging moment for that actor.

In the past, if a production wanted an actor to be completely naked and they weren't prepared to do that, the attitude was that 'they're not a good actor', according to O'Brien. Now, those two things – being a good actor and having clear boundaries – are regarded as entirely separate. 'We need to honour their boundaries,' she says. 'And then the intimacy coordinator can work creatively in facilitating those conversations, looking at working with modesty garments, working with camera angles, so that as a production you can still get the inference of the nudity that you require for your storytelling while also honouring the actor's boundaries.'

In *Sex Education* series one, episode eight, actors came to understand their own boundaries, and production worked around those boundaries, finding solutions to make the scene work. In the scene where Adam and Eric are in detention together and they start fighting before ending up kissing, 'both of the actors spit onto each other's faces. And when I checked in with them, they both said, "Hmmm not too sure,"' explains O'Brien. 'Part of the consent is your yes is your yes, your no is your no, and if it's a maybe then it's a no, because you can't be free and open as the actor.'

Instead of requiring the actors to spit in one another's faces, the production team set about finding solutions to

replicate that action without violating the actors' boundaries. They found a solution that involved some clever camera angling, a piece of paper that each actor's spit would
land on, and the make-up team concocted a mixture of
glycerine and rose water that was daubed onto their faces
to mimic the effect of being spat on. If an actor communicates a no, then the intimacy coordinator will then work
creatively with choreography, with camera angles, or facili-
tate casting a body double.

O'Brien says that, on *I May Destroy You*, it was outside
Weruche Opia's (who plays Terry) agreement and consent
to perform the intimate scene of the threesome. 'So again,
really clearly stated her boundaries, and production set
about finding a body double.' Opia was able to have input
in the scene involving the body double, and stated that she
wanted to make sure that it was visible that a condom was
used in the scene.

As well as supporting actors to assert their boundaries
and ensuring they're respected, there is another important element to the job of an intimacy coordinator – helping the actor differentiate their private sexual self from the
intimacy their character is portraying. 'The intimacy work
helps the actor to separate out who they are personally and
privately so that they can then really serve the character
professionally,' says O'Brien. 'And really separating out
boundary-wise who we are in the loving of our most loved
ones in our lives is a very precious and personal thing. It
doesn't mean that you're not going to perhaps draw from
your experiences, but you don't have to have that narrative

of laying who you are in your personal, private, intimate body out in the workplace. This is a workplace.'

So, how does the sex on our screens need to change? O'Brien believes it's paramount that sex scenes bring in more anatomically realistic details to make the scenes credible to audiences. 'I really feel that when something is anatomically correct, we just get it as humans, as an audience, and then we can stay believing in it and investing in the narrative of these characters.' It's the job of the intimacy coordinator to ensure that the positions are anatomically correct – for instance, making sure the actors' legs aren't too straight when the scene portrays vaginal sex, or that viewers can tell when the moment of penetration occurs. All too often, TV and movie sex scenes uphold unrealistic ideas about sex, whether that's two male characters having anal sex without the use of any lube, or that penis-in-vagina penetration would happen without any build-up and without the opportunity for the woman to be aroused, or that women orgasm through vaginal penetration alone.

O'Brien cites episode two of *Normal People* as a positive example of realistic storytelling. Consent is sought 'without losing sexiness,' she says, and you witness the moment of penetration and see Marianne's discomfort as she is having sex for the first time. 'It was really important that we included that moment of discomfort, so that reality was shown and it wasn't just "oh, she's asked for a condom and it's all angels singing".'

She adds: 'I would like to continue just as with *Normal People*, *Sex Education* and *I May Destroy You*, to lift the lid and keep on telling a more truthful story that actually will liberate everybody.'

What we've seen on television recently is certainly a step in the right direction. It shows us what is possible, and how audiences notice and respond to positive change. At present, television shows that feature consent negotiation are seen as the gold standard. What we should work towards is making that aspect of a sex scene so normal, so commonplace, so mundane, that we cease to see it as a rarity on our screens.

CHAPTER 18

How do we change our sexual culture?

A s a society, we tend to see the bedroom and our sex lives as a zone that is separate from the systems of oppression that invade every arena of life. That logic is deeply flawed. Sex is not the great equaliser we perceive it to be – sex is a realm where power imbalances exist, where a person's privilege can take centre stage, where larger power structures can manifest themselves. While it's true that the culture we exist in fuels many of the problems outlined in this book, it would be a mistake to place the majority of the blame on collective power structures. Doing so absolves individuals of any responsibility to look inwards, to educate themselves and to change their behaviour. We can acknowledge our proximity to systems of oppression and accept that these power structures have shaped us, while also understanding that we as individuals are capable of benefiting from and upholding those systems through our own actions and interactions.

So, where do we go from here? How do we change our sexual culture for the better? And is it even possible to change aspects of our culture that are so deeply ingrained? Laina Bay-Cheng believes we have to eradicate misogyny. 'It's not easy, but the only way to help women is to change our misogynist culture. Just because that's a tall order, and because it will be hard, doesn't mean that we shouldn't try.' She says that 'ending misogyny is more possible than protecting women within misogyny – that can't happen, but that's what we're currently trying to do. Misogyny, racism, economic injustice, cishet centrism – all of those things are mechanisms of dehumanisation.'

Bay-Cheng argues it is vital that we understand 'women are sexually vulnerable, not only because of misogyny but because we think it's okay to deprive whole, massive segments of our society of basic resources, which is also why women are sexually vulnerable anyway. If we become unwilling to live in such fundamentally and grossly dehumanising conditions, that's actually what will protect women.'

So many of the experiences written about in this book stem from bigger power structures like white supremacy, racism, misogyny, ableism, anti-fatness, transphobia, biphobia and homophobia. If you're someone with privilege who considers yourself an ally to marginalised communities, think about whether you're bringing that allyship with you when you enter the bedroom with someone with less systemic power than you. Consider the ways that your own actions within sex and intimate relationships can perpetuate microaggressions that might retraumatise a marginalised person.

Ethical sex

There's a basic point that we keep coming back to time and time again – whether it's about intervening when you witness blatant racism, not voting for politicians with policies that will almost certainly harm others, or wearing a mask in a pandemic. It's a fundamental truth that we should care about other people. Even if we don't know that person, let alone love or like them, we should still care that no harm comes to them. To draw on author Lauren Morrill's oft-cited 2017 quote about the Affordable Care Act debates: 'I don't know how to explain to you why you should care about other people.'[1]

I believe that same concept should be applied to our sexual interactions with one another too. And I'm not just talking about the sex we have with our partners, the people we love; it's a rule should apply across the board – to the strangers we fuck, the one-night stands, the encounters with exes, the casual sex, the fuck buddies, the friends with benefits. A guiding principle should be this: You don't have to like them or love them, but you should care about them. You should afford them a modicum of basic human respect, and you should behave towards them in a way that's in line with the values and morals you uphold in all other aspects of your life.

During my conversation with Laina Bay-Cheng, she put forward the idea of ethics-grounded sexual relationships. 'What we should be doing is, like, infusing all sexual encounters with a sense of ethics and commitments to one another. Even if it's like, one night, you should still care about that human as a human,' she explains. 'With ethics-driven and ethics-grounded relationships, that's where we can make headway on all of these things. That starts with ethics and how we treat one another individually, like on a one-on-one basis.'

The way we see sexual consent needs to focus on morality rather than legality. Consent is often framed as a 'rule' or a barrier that one has to climb over once at the outset of a sexual interaction. Jaclyn Friedman, co-editor of *Yes Means Yes!*, a book which redefined consent, writes that 'on the way to codification we've replaced some of the old rape myths with this new one: That consent is just a hurdle you have to clear in order to Get The Sex.'[2]

You might have seen headlines about consent apps or consent contracts, both of which position consent as a kind of legal document you have on record in case someone accuses you of something.[3] 'We've forgotten that enthusiastic consent is so much more than a string of legal language – it's a humanising ethic of sex,' says Friedman.

Sex educator Portia Brown agrees that our sexual culture needs to move towards a more ethics-driven model. 'So often we talk about what's been labelled "hookup culture", and everyone is presumed to be into casual sex.' Brown explains that studies have shown that millennials are having less sex than previous generations.[4] But despite the fact that millennials and Gen Z are having less sex, there's no denying that dating apps have made sex more readily available to many. 'Sex is more accessible to people because of dating apps, you can have more casual sex, it's more widely accepted to do so. But it's also expected to not speak to the person afterwards, which is fine if both people consent to that,' says Brown.

'However, when you are in that interaction, whether it's for five minutes or five hours, you do need to begin to engage in a more ethical practice. It starts with ourselves, right? If you are not caring for yourself in your own self pleasure interactions in a way that is ethical, then how can you extend that to the people that you are engaging with?'

Taking responsibility on an individual level for your own actions is an important step in this process. 'If we're to zoom out, we are looking at a societal overhaul of the way that we treat sex and sexuality and how we treat women, non-binary people, and basically non-men when it comes to sex,' says Brown. 'But if we're to zoom in, we really have to look at our own homes, we have to look at our own circles of friends. And we have to look at our own daily activities and start to think, "How can I change?"'

Changing our sexual culture can also come from challenging other people in our lives and being more vocal when we witness behaviour that is abusive, toxic or unethical.

If you're someone who engages with sex-positive conversations in podcasts, articles, Instagram guides and books, Brown advocates reaching out to the people around you to encourage them to model better behaviour and thinking patterns. 'It comes down to being a little bit braver and pushing back against people when they don't ask you for consent in platonic situations, or when they say things that are sex-negative or homophobic.'

She concludes: 'At the end of the day, most of us will never have that much control to change macro, big-picture things, so it really is about looking at your circle, at the people you surround yourself with, and thinking "How can I influence that person and influence them to influence the people around them?" Because it's a domino effect.'

Kimberly McIntosh from *gal-dem* says 'it is really about what you owe to other people. A one-night stand shouldn't be different to how we interact with other people in other areas of our lives. Why should my behaviour be different from when I go to the Sainsbury's Local across the road? I care about the staff, and I wear a mask, and I like chatting to them. Even though I don't know them, they're not my friends, it's not a particularly deep relationship, I still value them as individuals and would want all my interactions to be positive ones and fair ones.'

McIntosh believes we haven't quite figured out as a culture what the rules are around what we owe people we're having sex with. 'Sex is so intimate, and yet I think there's kind of a disposability to thinking that you're not going to see someone again, or that it's not really clear what you owe them. I don't think we've got necessarily a really clear cultural script as to what that looks like, in a fair way, where everyone is treated with respect no matter the length of the interaction or relationship. It's just the way you treat people that you don't really feel particularly close to.'

This sense that our sexual partners are disposable is a symptom of the wider online dating culture that we're immersed in. At breakneck speed you can swipe, match, and set up a date with a stranger. But it's just as easy to remove any trace of a person's existence from your app by unmatching them, blocking them, and thus absolving yourself of any responsibility.

McIntosh likens the dating app dynamic to being a consumer, with the obvious caveat that 'it shouldn't be – it is a person': 'That makes it easier to then obviously not message someone back, and ignore them. I've done it before. But I don't think you would treat someone in real life with that same lack of care. And I think casual sex is an extension of that. I think we need to kind of reevaluate that and maybe try and come up with some new cultural norms as to how it's OK to treat someone, and part of that is obviously making sure it's as equitable an experience as possible, if that's what you want.'

Male allies, we need you

In 2021, the death of 33-year-old marketing executive Sarah Everard prompted an outpouring of collective grief and sparked a national conversation about gendered violence. In the wake of Everard's suspected murder after she disappeared walking home in South London, men asked what they could do to make women feel safer in public. People began replying with suggestions of one-off gestures, including crossing the road to avoid walking or running close behind us. The request for suggestions was well intentioned, I'm sure, but one man's journey across a street so a woman will feel less threatened isn't going to solve this epidemic of violence anytime soon.

Aside from the cry of the #NotAllMen brigade, men's voices were notable by their absence in the conversations that followed. It was disappointing to see. At the time, I asked men I knew for the reasons for this silence. Some said they didn't want to appear performative; others said they believed it was time for men to shut up and listen; and some even said that they didn't believe change was possible. Change *is* possible – but we need help in achieving that. What we need is for men to step up as allies, and join the fight against misogyny and the systems of oppression that allow this violence to operate unchecked in our society.

That allyship can take many forms – from speaking up when your friend makes rape jokes or misogynistic comments, to educating yourself on misogyny and its consequences, to talking to the other men in your life about their views on and behaviour towards women and marginalised genders, and understanding that silence is complicity. If you see red flags in a friend's behaviour towards women or marginalised genders, do you turn your back, or do you acknowledge that red flag and consider saying something about it? As well as looking at other men's behaviour, it's important to look inward too. Reflect on your past behaviour and ask yourself if misogyny might have manifested in your own words and actions. How can you learn from those mistakes and ensure it never happens again? Thinking back might be uncomfortable, but imagine the constant discomfort of living with the threat of violence just because of your gender.

Know that your allyship shouldn't be directed solely to women you're attracted to. Nor should you have to be a brother, partner or father to women to care about this violence. And your allyship shouldn't only serve white, cis, straight, non-Disabled, thin women.

Know that silence makes you complicit in a dehumanising system.

It's time to talk about masculinity

It shouldn't be the job of women or marginalised genders to 'fix men' or solve the problems stemming from traditional masculinity. Rather, I think we have a collective responsibility to look at the ways in which patriarchy affects people of all genders. I believe men should also start having conversations about masculinity with their peers, their brothers, fathers, partners and friends.

'Boys will be boys, right?' These are the words said by Ben Hurst, head of training at the Good Lad Initiative, at the start of a TEDxLondonWomen talk about masculinity.

'That's what they say,' he goes on. 'It's kind of like a get-out-of-jail-free card for any given situation.'[5]

'Boys will be boys' are four words that have become synonymous with the low behavioural standards attached to traditional masculinity. In the TEDx Talk, Hurst describes the work he does in schools with boys aged between 11 and 18 – he talks to them about masculinity and gender equality. One of the techniques he uses for engaging these boys in conversations is something called a 'word race', which involves splitting the boys into two teams and playing a word association game. The boys are given words like 'men' and 'women', and they have to write down all the words they associate with these terms. 'As you can imagine, the boys come up with a whole host of words to describe genitalia and body parts, so they say things like "dick", "pussy", "cock", "cunt" – anything you can imagine, it will be on those sheets of paper or on those whiteboards,' says Hurst. The boys also list characteristics they associate with men and women. Words like 'dominant' and 'strong' come up for men, while 'kind', 'mother' and even 'kitchen' are written about women.

When Hurst ran this activity in a workshop with youth workers, he gave them the topic of 'boys and girls' to elicit a conversation about the stereotypes they have about these genders. 'What they came up with was slightly disturbing,' says Hurst. 'So for boys, they said that they are smelly, dirty, porn addicts, violent, lazy, all kinds of horrible adjectives. Bearing in mind that these are the people that we pay to work with our young people, it leads me to ask the question: What is it that we actually expect of boys? And I think that we're setting the bar very low.'

At this point in his speech, Hurst refers to something called a 'man box'. This term, coined by Tony Porter in a 2010 TED Talk, refers to a list of characteristics we ascribe to manhood, and our definitions of what it means to be a man.[6] Porter talks about his own man box in his TED Talk, relaying some of the things he was told when he was growing up: 'We were taught that men had to be tough, had to be strong, had to be courageous, dominating – no pain, no emotions, with the exception of anger – and definitely no fear; that men are in charge, which means women are not; that men lead, and you should just follow and do what we say; that men are superior; women are inferior; that men are strong; women are weak; that women are of less value, property of men, and objects, particularly sexual objects.'

Porter refers to this as the 'collective socialization of men', also known as the 'man box'. 'Now I also want to say, without a doubt, there are some wonderful, wonderful, absolutely wonderful things about being a man,' he continues. 'But at the same time, there's some stuff that's just straight up twisted, and we really need to begin to challenge it, look at it, and really get in the process of deconstructing, redefining, what we come to know as manhood.'

Hurst talks about the man box in his powerful TEDx speech, and how he gets young men and boys to see the ways they're being conditioned to believe they have to be emotionless, dominant, protective, powerful and not feminine. 'When we do this activity with boys, it's like something clicks for them, and they realize that they've been tricked for their whole lives,' he says. The boys sometimes want to cling on to some of the qualities in their box – like being athletic or courageous, which aren't bad things to strive towards.

Hurst then describes the kinds of ensuing conversations he has with the boys as they begin to examine where they've inherited these ideas from. Some cite films like James Bond and 'how he never says no to sex unless he's trying to kill someone. We talk about consent and how boys never feel like they have agency to actually give consent in any given situation. We talk about how we view women as the gatekeepers of sex.'

These gender constructs are harmful to the men who've subsumed these ideas, and they have devastating consequences on men's mental health. For heterosexual men, these gender norms have a destructive impact on the women in their lives too. As journalist Liz Plank writes in *For the Love of Men: A New Vision for Mindful Masculinity*: 'When half the population gets trained to block emotions, they lose the ability for empathy.'

'Every man can remember the first time that they were called a pussy, right?' Plank told me in an interview for Mashable. 'Or called the F-word, or when they were told that they were not being a "real man", and that they needed to hide their weakness, that they needed to hide this empathy, that they needed to be strong and stoic.'[7]

What we're talking about here is sometimes referred to as 'toxic masculinity', a term that has entered the mainstream lexicon in recent years but which for a long time was only really heard by gender studies students in lecture halls or read in textbooks on the topic. Toxic masculinity – also known as 'traditional masculinity ideology' – is defined as a cultural attitude which results in beliefs and behaviours like hiding your emotions, exhibiting 'tough guy' behaviour, and using violence as a demonstration of power. So, how do we start to address toxic masculinity and its consequences in society? We need to begin to have conversations about what it means to be a man, and where we've inherited those ideas from – and which of them are positive and which are negative.

Ben Hurst believes that we need to have conversations with boys and talk about masculinity and the myriad forms it comes in. 'The men in my life never told me that the patriarchy was shit for everyone,' he says in his TEDx Talk. 'Boys won't just be boys; what boys will be is men, and that is when we will all have an issue.'

He believes the way we talk to men and boys about masculinity sets the bar really low. 'We tend to talk to them and say this is what you have to do to not get in trouble, this is how you don't break the law, this is how you don't rape someone or how you're not labelled as a sexual abuser or a harasser.'

But what if we were to change this conversation around and turn it into a discussion centred on what Hurst calls 'positive masculinity', which focuses on men building healthy relationships – be they friendships, sexual or romantic. 'We need to move towards a new version of masculinity, one where we celebrate being a man and celebrate all of the good parts of being a man, but also one where we give men spaces to unpack all of the problematic messages that they have learned about what it means to be a man and we give them space to relearn what it means to be a man,' Hurst suggests.

How do we even go about talking to the men in our lives about toxic masculinity? I put this very question to Liz Plank and she had some useful advice. For starters, we should avoid even using the term 'toxic masculinity'.

'I think that the term "toxic masculinity" is not the most useful term to bring up especially with someone who is a gender theory virgin,' Plank told me. 'These are words that are being used as weapons by like, Tucker Carlson and Jordan Peterson to signify this idea that people who use these words want to come after your way of life, they want to criticise the way that you were raised by your father that you love and the way that you raised your sons.'

The term 'toxic masculinity' has been co-opted by the far right and used in arguments to suggest that masculinity is under attack. Canadian psychologist Jordan Peterson, a right-wing thinker with a big far-right following, refutes the idea of toxic masculinity and says there's a 'backlash' against masculinity and 'a sense there is something toxic about masculinity'.[8]

Toxic masculinity isn't the only term that Plank advises steering well clear of when discussing masculinity with men, however. 'Someone who has no idea that gender has even impacted their lives is going to feel very uncomfortable about any acknowledgement that this has shaped their decision-making and their behaviours, attitudes, and who they are in the world,' says Plank. 'Even the word "gender", the word "patriarchy", words that if you have read books and have a lot of knowledge about this, these are words that are familiar to you.'

Focus instead on asking simple questions that will foster more productive, positive conversations. Plank says she often doesn't mention the word 'masculinity' at all. 'One of the most impactful questions I asked men for this book was, "What is hard about being a man?" This is a question that I've not had a single man not stare at me for a full ten seconds before even starting to begin to think about answering that question. Because it's a question they're not really asked and they've never really given permission to ask themselves.'

The first step, says Plank, is encouraging self-reflection during these talks. 'Instead of coming in with, "You have all these behaviours that are hurting all the people that you love around you, and you need to take responsibility for it." Yes, they need to do that. But that's like the second step. The first step is self reflecting. That's where empathy is really important.'

Knowledge is power

Misconceptions about consent and sexual violence are deeply ingrained. It took me until my thirties to figure out things that had happened to me could be considered sexual assault. And yet, even then, I didn't believe I had the right to label my experiences as such; I didn't feel I'd suffered enough to be able to characterise the events in that way. Part of that comes from not receiving solid sex education – I think all I got was a tutorial on putting a condom on a banana, and a few photos of genitals exhibiting symptoms of STIs.

Layla, from @lalalaletmeexplain, tells me she's made some disturbing realisations while running 'poll time' on her Instagram account. 'Recently, I did a whole thread about sexual assault,' she explains. '11,000 women took part in this poll and 61 per cent of women said that they had been sexually assaulted. One of the next questions was, "Have you ever been groped, touched by some random stranger in a bar or at carnival or whatever?"' And 91 per cent of women said they had. So there was this disparity of 30 per cent of people who were saying, "Yeah, this has happened to me" but weren't calling it sexual assault.'

Layla went on to post the results of the poll and talked about how non-consensual touching or groping is sexual assault. 'I got so many messages from women who were like, "You've blown my mind because now I'm looking back at the amount of times I've been sexually assaulted."'

Layla believes there's a culture of normalisation that results in people minimising and dismissing the harm that's actually befallen them. 'You could be with some male friends even and you go, "Oh my god, that guy just hit my bum," and then your mates will go, "Oh, come on, don't make a fuss about it, boys will be boys,"' she says.

'That small stuff makes room for the bigger stuff. If we're unsure about whether it's OK for a stranger to slap her bum and if we're unsure about whether it's actually impolite to say something to him, then how do we manage when you have all the added complications of it being with someone you like and know?'

The way we talk about these situations amongst our friends can actually play a pivotal role in helping us acknowledge that an experience was in actual fact a violation. A recent academic study by researchers at the University of Essex found that taking another person's perspective can help women label ambiguous sexual experiences as coercive or violative. The researchers said that the study reflected the 'more nuanced and complex ways in which people tend to experience sexual encounters'.[9]

'Because people often rely heavily on nonverbal communication to signal the presence and absence of consent, and because many people engage in sex under the influence of drugs and alcohol, people do not always know how to make sense of their sexual experiences,' the researchers wrote. 'Our research suggests that while people will use contextual cues to help fill in the gaps, they are also more likely to believe that a sexual encounter was untoward when they imagine it happening to another person.'

The study found that women who thought about their own sexual experiences from 'a distanced perspective' were 'more open to acknowledging that the experience was nonconsensual, that it was likely a sexual assault, and were also more open to learning about sexual assault resources'. The researchers also advocated further research into whether people can be trained to use spontaneous self-distancing strategies so that women can then reflect on their own sexual experiences in a way that's more conducive to acknowledging occurrences of sexual violence.

Misinformation about how consent functions is rife due to a lack of education. Dr Veronica Lamarche, one of the authors of the aforementioned study, believes better education about consent and assault early on in people's lives is the best way to reduce unacknowledged sexual assaults in the future. 'People need to understand the complexity of interpersonal interactions, that sexual assaults can happen in lots of different contexts, and that there is no shame in standing up against one's victimisation,' she says. 'As a relationship researcher, I think it is highly problematic that consent and sexual assault are often framed in a casual encounter type of context.'

She goes on to say: 'Research shows that the majority of sexual assaults are committed by romantic partners – people we're supposed to trust and be able to share intimate moments with. I believe that better education on how to navigate consent in established relationships will help empower people to acknowledge sexual assaults more readily.'

It's never too late to educate yourself – and your friends and family – about consent. Talk to your children about consent, talk to your siblings, talk to your friends, talk to your partners. Don't wait around for sex education to suddenly sort itself out. We can't afford to delay this any longer.

Everything you've ever heard about sex is probably wrong

If you grew up online, chances are you also grew up with unlimited access to less-than-reputable sources of sexual health information. Or rather, misinformation. And the way we talk about sex also gives way to myths about the amount of sex other people are supposedly having.

One thing I grew up believing is that everyone was having loads of sex all the time. This idea, which I believed to be fact, made me feel like I was never having enough sex, and made me feel like I should be having more and making a more proactive effort to put myself out there sexually.

This worry that I wasn't having enough sex, that my 'body count' wasn't high enough, that all my friends were way more sexually active than me, honestly filled me with so much shame and anxiety in my twenties. The truth is, as a long-term single person, I've had long periods when I didn't have sex – there were times I didn't have sex for a calendar year and didn't think anything of it. But the moment that sex hiatus was discussed in a friendship group, it was treated as some great anomaly, something that needed to be rectified, something that was even greeted with laughter. Those reactions from others caused me shame and made me question my own decisions, drove me to worry that I wasn't making the most of my youth, and even led me to believe I'd regret the lack of sex when I was older. Sometimes there's absolutely no reason for a gap in sexual activity, it just happens that way, but other times there are genuine reasons like prioritising your own mental wellbe-ing, dealing with trauma, needing time on your own, not feeling like you're up for dating right now or focusing on your career or studies. But it's also not something that requires any justification or explanation.

Rachel Hills writes about this cultural pressure in *The Sex Myth*: 'In the sitcoms I watched on TV, the single charac-ters dated (and by implication, slept with) new people each week. In the conversations I had with acquaintances, sex was at once a subject of nervous excitement and an unspo-ken assumption – something it was expected *everyone* was doing.'[10]

The assumption that everyone needs sex to be happy is also very damaging to people on the asexual spectrum. As Leni Morris writes for Stonewall, 'ace people are often told they're defective because they don't experience attraction in the way others do.'[11]

In the world of dating apps, certain apps have grown to have connotations attached to using them. These per-ceptions can lead us to believe we 'should' have sex even if we don't want to or don't really feel like it. Hilda Burke – psychotherapist, couples counsellor and author of *The Phone Addiction Workbook* – tells me she once had a client who slept with every man she went on a Tinder date with because 'that's what she thought Tinder was. So, even though she found a lot of the men unattractive and the sex not very enjoyable, it was what she felt was expected in the "Tinder World" so she did it. In time, she learned to check in with herself, what she wanted and, crucially, what she didn't, which led to a much more content love and sex life.'

Burke recommends giving ourselves permission to be honest about our needs and wants. Do I actually want to have sex with my Tinder date, or am I feeling pressured by the expectations other people have about this app? Am I attracted to this person, or do I feel some kind of obligation to sleep with them because I suspect they might be expecting that from me?

Looking inward and examining the myths we might have absorbed while growing up can be a really positive thing. Ideas about what constitutes 'too much' or 'too little' sex are not just sweeping generalisations, they're tools for instilling shame in people's lives. And that shame can be incredibly destructive.

Let's talk about sexual boundaries

Talking about sex is hard. Especially with a new partner. But we need to be equipping every single person with the ability to identify and set sexual boundaries, to communicate those boundaries, and to honour and respect other people's boundaries.

When it comes to navigating any kind of relationship – be it sexual, romantic, familial, platonic, professional, whatever – boundaries are your best friend. They are not just essential for your mental health and self-esteem, they are also vital in making you feel safe and comfortable in sexual situations. 'Boundaries set the basic guidelines for how a person wants to be treated,' says psychotherapist Neil Wilkie.[12] In sex, boundaries are used to communicate hard and soft limits. If we've experienced sexual trauma in our past, asserting a boundary can help protect us against being triggered or retraumatised.

Sexual boundaries are very personal and vary from person to person – hence the importance of communicating those boundaries to new partners. They can mean literally anything in sex, from drawing a line at facial ejaculation to ruling out certain sexual positions or sex acts.

Learning where your boundaries fall takes a bit of time. None of us are born with a list of dos and don'ts that we carry through life, and often we only realise a boundary exists after it's been crossed. Understanding what your sexual boundaries and limits are is the first step in the process of setting them and ensuring that they are respected.

Sex therapist Massimo Stocchi-Fontana describes a useful technique that can help people figure out where their boundaries lie: 'A simple mechanism I use with my clients is getting them to identify where they feel resistant to certain suggestions, or pressures from the people around them or their partners. The moment they can consciously identify the emotional resistance that arises in a relational situation is the moment that they can begin to question what the resistance is about. Once there is clarity on what the resistance is about, then it can be communicated more effectively to one's partner.'

As Erin Taylor writes in *Allure*, 'I have a hard limit on spankings. I never want to be spanked and I communicate that with any person I have sex with. How people react to the expression of boundaries can also be telling and reveal possible red flags. If someone communicates their yeses, nos, and maybes and the person they're having sex with doesn't respect their boundaries, that may be a sign that the relationship should not continue in such an intimate way, at all.'[13]

As Taylor explains: 'There were many times in my early sexual experiences where I'd leave an experience feeling gross and wrong even though I technically didn't say "no" to what was happening. This feeling was the result of not understanding I could say no while also being unaware of what my emotional, physical, or sexual needs were at the time.'

She says in the piece that she's taken the time to get to know what her boundaries are, in addition to practising small boundary-setting, 'such as saying no to a kiss at the end of a date'. That setting of smaller boundaries makes it easier for her to assert bigger boundaries 'such as stopping in the middle of sex because I felt unsafe'.

Neil Wilkie says that sexual boundaries are rarely talked about openly, but that it's actually really important to understand each other's preferences and desires in order to create a healthy and evolving sex life. 'I am amazed at how few couples actually talk about, for example, boundaries of sexual preferences and desires, until after many years the stored-up frustration and resentment explodes,' says Wilkie. 'In the early days of a relationship it is rare for a couple to discuss boundaries, which will mean that the ground rules are unclear and uncertain.' But despite this, introducing boundaries early on in a relationship can be easier than bringing them up later – perhaps after lines have been crossed and boundaries transgressed.

'It is so much easier to talk about boundaries in the early days of a relationship, as that will be coming from a place of growth and clarity rather than resentment and blame,' says Wilkie. That's not to say that you shouldn't bring up boundaries in a long-established relationship, however – you should definitely still do that.

And discussions of sexual boundaries should happen in all sexual contexts – not just in long-term relationships with people you love and trust. Sexual boundaries should be discussed during one-night stands, casual hook-ups, friends-with-benefits situations and fuck-buddy relationships – in short, any sexual encounter.

The idea of setting a boundary with a stranger or someone you hardly know seems daunting. If you are in the early stages of a nebulous relationship with someone you like, you might feel worried about being perceived as 'difficult' by someone you'd like to date. Firstly, setting a boundary does not make you difficult. And if someone responds badly to boundary-setting, this is a red flag. I write this as someone who used to feel guilty when I began setting sexual boundaries with men I was dating. My approval-seeking tendencies made me worry that these men would like me less or perceive me as difficult or 'no fun'. When I expressed these thoughts aloud to both my best friend and my therapist, they both responded with a definitive 'Rachel, no!' I now try to quiet those doubts and remind myself that these boundaries are necessary to keep me safe.

Massimo Stocchi-Fontana says there is always a way to set a boundary in a one-night encounter or casual situation. 'It's something called transparency,' he explains. 'We too often fall into the trap of not being transparent enough with people that we meet, out of fear of being judged or rejected, and this can be deeply rooted in our shame and guilt. The manner in which I see casual encounters is like this: if I am transparent as to what I like and what I don't like, there is less assumption from the person I know very little about.'

There are several techniques for discussing boundaries. You can each write a list of what your boundaries are, deciding which are hard and soft limits. Drawing up a list of 'Yes, no, maybes' is one way of approaching this. Erin Taylor suggests a Yellow/Red traffic light system. 'Yellow means "let's do something else" and Red means "stop entirely",' writes Taylor. 'These can be helpful both in vanilla and kink scenarios because everyone, irrelevant of what kind of sexual experience they are having, should be able to revoke consent at any point.'

Beth Ashley believes that discussing sexual boundaries is paramount – but it's also something that's often missing from mainstream porn. But boundary-setting in sexual relationships is something she's relatively new to. 'I never used to do it. For probably most of my sexually active life, I've not engaged in those important conversations. But now I consider the discussion of sexual boundaries as part of the intimacy,' she says.

'That discussion of what's on and off the table can be a turn-on,' she adds. 'And it's an important stage of communication, it means that you're going to have safer and more enjoyable sex, but it's a turn-on itself to discuss those together.'

It wasn't until Ashley started a new relationship and had a conversation about sexual boundaries for the first time in her life that she realised just how important it actually is. 'When I think about the sex I had before my partner, there was always something I didn't like. Even if overall we had a good sex life, there was always just that one incident that made me feel "Why did that happen? Why did he have to do that?"' she explains. 'But when I first started dating my partner, I was really shocked and impressed when he immediately started a discussion when I mentioned that I liked rougher sex. And he was like, "OK, so let's talk about what we want to do together and what we definitely don't."'

She realises now that conversations like these are actually bare-minimum requirements in sexual relationships, and that this is how all sexual relationships should begin.

Navigating trauma and triggers

We know how prevalent sexual violence is in society. We know how many of us don't even believe what happened to us 'counts'. But what we don't know or rarely talk about is: how to live with trauma. Emily Nagoski writes in *Come As You Are* that it's 'impossible to talk about women's sexual health without spending some time discussing trauma', given just how many women are affected by sexual assault (conservative estimates place that figure at one in five; it could be more like one in three).

Trauma doesn't necessarily come from a one-off major incident. 'It can also emerge in response to persistent distress or ongoing abuse, like a relationship where sex is unwanted, though it may be technically "consensual" because the targeted person says yes in order to avoid being hurt or feels trapped in a relationship or is otherwise coerced,' Nagoski explains. 'In that context, a survivor's body gradually learns that it can't escape and it can't fight; freeze becomes the default stress response because of the learned pattern of shutdown as the best way to guarantee survival.'

In my final few days of writing this book, Alexandria Ocasio-Cortez spoke out about the long-lasting impact being an assault survivor can have on your life. 'I'm a survivor of sexual assault,' Ocasio-Cortez said in an Instagram Live video about the 2021 storming of the US Capitol. 'And I haven't told many people that in my life. But when we go through trauma, trauma compounds on each other. And so, whether you had a negligent or a neglectful parent or whether you had someone who was verbally abusive to you, whether you are a survivor of abuse, whether you experience any sort of trauma in your life, small to large, these episodes can compound on one another.'

She's right. Your body doesn't forget trauma. Bessel van der Kolk wrote in his 2015 book *The Body Keeps the Score* that trauma leaves 'imprints on body, mind and soul'. 'Traumatised people chronically feel unsafe inside their bodies. The past is alive in the form of gnawing interior discomfort. Their bodies are constantly bombarded by visceral warning signs, and, in an attempt to control these processes, they often become expert at ignoring their gut feelings and in numbing awareness of what is played out inside. They learn to hide from their selves.'[14] Just as we're upfront about our sexual boundaries, talking about past sexual traumas to a partner (if you're comfortable) can build a safe sexual environment for you.

We cannot place our faith in the law or in education syllabi – both of which are controlled by lawmakers looking to serve the interests of their own political agenda. Changing our sexual culture has to start on an individual level, through thinking about how you treat other people – even if they're complete strangers – on a human level. But on a macro level, we also have a collective duty to understand and fight the ways systems of oppression operate in our sexual culture.

Conclusion

I started writing this book because I've lived much of my adult life believing that the things I went through when I was younger didn't really count; that in the grand scheme of things, I was lucky. Hindsight tells a different story. Those early experiences made me walk through life with fear as my constant companion. That fear informed my decision-making through life. It cost me a lot of money. A big price I paid was never truly being able to live in the moment. I feel hypervigilant about personal safety, risk-averse to the point where I take no risks ever. Is it because deep down inside I've been taught that I'm to blame for the things that happened to me? That somehow I put myself in harm's way?

When the #MeToo movement came to widespread prominence, my friends told me stories of their experiences, things that they weren't sure how to define – or whether you could even call it violence. 'I had this thing happen to me . . .' they'd say in hushed tones. 'I guess you could call it a bad sexual experience.' They had also lived their whole lives carrying the full weight of something they still aren't sure 'counts'.

It dawned on me that in my limited sex education at school, no one had ever explained what sexual violence was. We'd had one lesson on consent that framed it as a one-off question before you get down to business. The moment of truth before there's no going back. Sexual violence was a thing that happened in dark alleyways, perpetrated by strangers. No one told me someone you knew could do it to you, let alone someone you liked or loved.

Looking back on my younger years, things could have been different. I think about how my life could have been if I'd learned about sexual violence and how to identify it from a young age. I didn't have the language to talk about things that were happening, but I also didn't know it was wrong.

I wonder what my relationship to sex would have been like if I'd been taught about pleasure, if someone had told me that my own wants, needs and desires mattered equally in those interactions, and that my role wasn't simply to fulfil men's needs and lie there until they were done.

Society tells us we have to be 100 per cent sure that we know what we're accusing somebody of because of the price the accused will pay. Yet we don't equip people with the knowledge that would make them sure. Talking to friends, talking to family, talking to a therapist are all things that have helped me to find words, and through words I have found validation. I have acknowledged that what I carry with me is trauma. But deep down, I wish those things had never happened. I do not see these experiences as formative, or as lessons that have brought me valuable insights.

The people who generously and bravely shared their stories with me for this book share a vision of a better future. A future where we don't live our lives weighing up the risk of whether or not we'll get harmed. That the bare minimum isn't 'well, at least he didn't rape me' but rather 'I felt safe and respected'. A future where we learn that consent is ongoing and can be withdrawn at any point. Where sexual experiences come with mutual respect and, even if you don't plan to see one another again, you at least care in the moment that the other person is OK.

Honestly though, the future is too distant a prospect. This is urgent. We need these things to be our present day. We cannot rely on laws to change or government administrations to suddenly care about this stuff. In the absence of a system that we can place our faith in, society must take responsibility for bringing about change. It's no longer enough to say 'we need to talk about this'. Four years ago, I wrote an article arguing we urgently needed to talk about the grey areas of sexual violence, but it's clear to me now that talking about it isn't enough, doesn't go far enough. We need deeds as well as words.

In acknowledging the full spectrum of harms that women and marginalised genders experience, we also need to take action to dismantle the apparatus and infrastructure that enables sexual violence. We need to tackle the myriad systems of oppression that co-exist under the patriarchy. We need to understand the ways in which these systems interact with each other, joining forces with each other to create violence. Sex isn't exempt from the issues we have in society. Misogyny doesn't wait outside the bedroom door for your temporarily non-misogynistic body to finish having sex. You don't throw off the mantle of your privilege when you strip off your clothes. When we think about the systemic power that some of us hold, we need to consider the ways in which that manifests in relationships, the way it rears its head during sex. If you're in a sexual relationship or have a sexual encounter with someone with less systemic power than you, consider the ways you can resist or subvert the power you hold.

We know that women and marginalised genders are blamed for sexual violence. We're told we were asking for it, told we dressed too slutty, told we should have said no, told that men aren't mind-readers. But the culpability lies with everyone complicit in upholding systems of power that create an environment that enables and normalises abuse.

All too often we tell people to be careful who you accuse, you'll ruin that man's career; but when a famous person is credibly accused of sexual violence, we watch them carry on in positions of power, preside over power – they are presidents of powerful nations. The message is: your story doesn't matter as much as this man's career; his clutch on power is valued higher than your life. It doesn't count. It wasn't valid.

There is deep loneliness in carrying these stories alone, in feeling they're not worthy of being shared or talked about. I hope this book shows you that you are not alone in what you carry. Though that doesn't change what happened, or the effect it's had on your life, I hope the knowledge can bring some comfort.

I wrote this book because I know how it feels to walk through life carrying something that you don't have the words to explain and that you don't believe to be a valid experience. I want to tell you that your story matters. Your experience counts.

As well as bringing comfort and reassurance, the words 'you are not alone' carry a note of sadness. The truth is, the ubiquity of these experiences is shameful. Yes, there is strength in numbers – but what if our society just accepts those numbers, however horrifyingly high they are? I want to live in a world where we don't have stories like ours. I want the legacy of violence, passed down from generation to generation like an heirloom, to die with us. I don't want our experiences of violence to be the one thing we have in common with each other.

We need change. We can't achieve that change by ourselves.

Endnotes

Chapter 1: What's in a name?

1   Angie Han, 'Aziz Ansari accused of sexual misconduct, he responds', Mashable, 14 January 2018, https://mashable.com/2018/01/14/aziz-ansari-sexual-misconduct-response/.

2   Rachel Thompson, 'It's time to stop saying "unsolicited dick pics". Here's why', Mashable, 19 July 2019, https://mashable.com/article/cyberflashing-unsolicited-dick-pics-terminology/.

3   Stephen Hiltner, 'How We Describe Sexual Assault: Times Journalists and Lawyers Respond', *The New York Times*, 31 October 2017, https://www.nytimes.com/2017/10/31/reader-center/sexual-assault-terminology.html.

4   Rachel Thompson, 'Jodi Kantor and Megan Twohey on the Harvey Weinstein investigation that ignited #MeToo', Mashable, 16 April 2020, https://mashable.com/article/jodi-kantor-megan-twohey-history-becomes-her/.

5   Rebecca Traister, 'Why Sex That's Consensual Can Still Be Bad. And Why We're Not Talking About It', The Cut, 20 October 2015,

https://www.thecut.com/2015/10/why-consensual-sex-can-still-be-bad.html.

6   Georgina Lee, 'Men are more likely to be raped than to be falsely accused of rape', Channel 4 FactCheck, 12 October 2018, https://www.channel4.com/news/factcheck/factcheck-men-are-more-likely-to-be-raped-than-be-falsely-accused-of-rape.

7   Liz Kelly, Jo Lovett and Linda Regan, *Home Office Research Study 293 A gap or chasm? Attrition in reported rape cases*, Home Office Research, Development and Statistics Directorate, February 2005, https://www.researchgate.net/publication/238713283_Home_Office_Research_Study_293_A_gap_or_a_chasm_Attrition_in_reported_rape_cases.

8   Kait Scalisi, 'This is why we should stop calling it "foreplay"', Blood + Milk, 15 May 2019, https://www.bloodandmilk.com/this-is-why-we-should-stop-calling-it-foreplay/.

9   Liz Kelly, 'The Continuum of Sexual Violence', in Jalna Hanmar and Mary Maynard, eds, *Women, Violence and Social Control*, Palgrave Macmillan, 1987, pp. 46–60, https://doi.org/10.1007/978-1-349-18592-4_4.

10   Malcolm Cowburn, 'Perceiving the continuum of sexual harm and the need for varied responses to sexual violence', *International Journal of Offender Therapy and Comparative Criminology*, 55(2), 2011, pp. 179–181, https://journals.sagepub.com/doi/pdf/10.1177/0306624X11398105.

11   Liz Kelly, *Surviving Sexual Violence* (Feminist Perspectives), Polity Press, 1989.

12   Sexual Offences Act 2003, https://www.legislation.gov.uk/ukpga/2003/42/part/1/crossheading/rape.

13   Rights of Women, *Your Rights, Your Body, Your Life – Sexual Violence and the Law: A Young Person's Guide*, Haven Paddington, 2012, https://rightsofwomen.org.uk/wp-content/uploads/2014/10/Your-rights-your-body-your-life-a-young-personss-guide-to-sexual-violence-and-the-law.pdf.

14   Ibid.

15   Ibid.

16 FPA, 'The Law on Sex', updated April 2015, https://www.fpa.org. uk/factsheets/law-on-sex#assault.

17 Law Society of Scotland, 'The vexed question of consent', *Journal*, February 2019, https://www.lawscot.org.uk/members/journal/issues/ vol-64-issue-02/the-vexed-question-of-consent.

18 Sexual Offences (Scotland) Act 2009, Section 13, https://www. legislation.gov.uk/asp/2009/9/section/13.

19 Ibid., Section 14, https://www.legislation.gov.uk/asp/2009/9/section/ 14.

20 Ibid., Section 15, https://www.legislation.gov.uk/asp/2009/9/section/ 15.

21 Paula Akpan, 'Say their names: 12 victims of state brutality in the UK', *Vice*, 25 June 2020, https://www.vice.com/en/article/qj4j8x/ remembering-police-brutality-victims-uk.

22 Alex Press, '#MeToo must avoid "carceral feminism"', Vox, 1 February 2018, https://www.vox.com/the-big-idea/2018/2/1/16952744/ me-too-larry-nassar-judge-aquilina-feminism.

23 Reality Check team, 'George Floyd death: How many black people die in police custody in England and Wales?', BBC News, 3 June 2020, https://www.bbc.co.uk/news/52890363.

24 Maya Oppenheim, 'MPs must not criminalise sex work via policing bill, say campaigners', *Independent*, 9 April 2021, https://www.independent. co.uk/news/uk/home-news/sex-work-criminalisation-policing-bill- nordic-model-b1829123.html.

25 Liv Moloney, 'Is rape the perfect crime?', Sky News, https://news. sky.com/story/99-of-rapes-reported-to-police-in-england-and- wales-do-not-result-in-legal-proceedings-why-12104130.

26 Home Office, 'Violence against women and girls and male pos- ition factsheets', Gov.uk, 7 March 2019, https://homeofficemedia. blog.gov.uk/2019/03/07/violence-against-women-and-girls-and- male-position-factsheets/.

27 Rape Crisis England and Wales, 'About sexual violence', https:// rapecrisis.org.uk/get-informed/about-sexual-violence/statistics- sexual-violence/.

28 Home Office, 'Violence against women and girls and male position factsheets'.

29 Rape Crisis England and Wales, 'About sexual violence'.

Chapter 2: Stealth

1   Robert Glatter, '"Stealthing": The disturbing new sex trends you need to know about', *Forbes*, 29 April 2017, https://www.forbes.com/sites/robertglatter/2017/04/29/stealthing-the-disturbing-new-sex-trend-you-need-to-know-about/#498a6a211b07.

2   Sophie Maullin, 'Stealthing isn't a "sex trend". It's sexual assault – and it happened to me', *The Guardian*, 22 May 2017, https://www.theguardian.com/commentisfree/2017/may/22/stealthing-sex-trend-sexual-assault-crime.

3   Lena Gunnarsson, '"Excuse me, but are you raping me now?": Discourse and experience in (the grey areas of) sexual violence', NORA 26(1), 2018, pp. 4–18, https://doi.org/10.1080/08038740.2017.1395359.

4   End Violence Against Women, *Attitudes to Sexual Consent*, December 2018, https://www.endviolenceagainstwomen.org.uk/wp-content/uploads/1-Attitudes-to-sexual-consent-Research-findings-FINAL.pdf.

5   Alexandra Brodsky, 'Rape-adjacent: Imagining legal responses to nonconsensual condom removal', *Columbia Journal of Gender and Law* 32(3), 2017, https://papers.ssrn.com/sol3/papers.cfm?abstract_id=2954726.

6   Jenavieve Hatch, 'Inside the online community of men who preach removing condoms without consent', HuffPost, 21 April 2017, https://www.huffingtonpost.co.uk/entry/inside-the-online-community-of-men-who-preach-removing-condoms-without-consent_n_58f75eb2e4b05b9d613eb997.

7   Jim Connolly, '"Stealthing" – what you need to know', BBC Newsbeat, 25 April 2017, https://www.bbc.co.uk/news/newsbeat-39705734.

8   'I remove the condom without them knowing during "stealth" sex', https://perma.cc/453V-PPQJ.

9 Georgia Aspinall, 'A man has been convicted of rape after removing a condom during sex', *Grazia*, 25 April 2019, https://graziadaily.co.uk/life/in-the-news/stealthing-conviction-rape/.

10 Nick Dent, '"Stealthing" conviction brings conditional consent out in the open', Criminal Law Blog, Kingsley Napley, 2 May 2019, https://www.kingsleynapley.co.uk/insights/blogs/criminal-law-blog/stealthing-conviction-brings-conditional-consent-out-in-the-open.

11 Crown Prosecution Services, 'Rape and Sexual Offences – Chapter 6: Consent', 19 October 2002, https://www.cps.gov.uk/legal-guidance/rape-and-sexual-offences-chapter-6-consent.

12 Matthew Robinson, 'Police officer found guilty of condom "stealthing" in landmark trial', CNN, 20 December 2018, https://edition.cnn.com/2018/12/20/health/stealthing-germany-sexual-assault-scli-intl/index.html.

13 Laura C. Wilson and Katherine E. Miller, 'Meta-Analysis of the Prevalence of Unacknowledged Rape', *Trauma, Violence & Abuse* 17(2), April 2016, pp. 149–159, https://doi.org/10.1177/1524838015576391.

14 H. L. Littleton, D. Rhatigan and D. Axsom, 'Unacknowledged rape: How much do we know about the hidden rape victim?', *Journal of Aggression, Maltreatment, and Trauma* 14(4), 2007, pp. 57–74, https://doi.org/10.1300/J146v14n04_04.

15 C. L. Muehlenhard and Z. D. Peterson, 'Distinguishing between *sex* and *gender*: History, current conceptualizations, and implications', *Sex Roles* 64 (2011), pp. 791–803, https://doi.org/10.1007/s11199-011-9932-5.

16 N. Tatiana Masters, Erin Casey, Elizabeth A. Wells and Diane M. Morrison, 'Sexual Scripts among Young Heterosexually Active Men and Women: Continuity and Change', *The Journal of Sex Research* 50(5), 2013, pp. 409–420, https://doi.org/10.1080/00224499.2012.661102.

17 FPA, 'Less than half of people think it's OK to withdraw sexual consent if they're already naked', 24 September 2018, https://www.fpa.org.uk/news/less-half-people-think-its-ok-withdraw-sexual-consent-if-theyre-already-naked

18 Heather Littleton et al., 'Unacknowledged rape and re-victimization risk: Examination of potential mediators', *Psychology of Women Quarterly* 41(4), 2017, pp. 437–450, https://doi.org/10.1177/0361684317720187.

Chapter 3: A hand around your throat

1   Alys Harte, 'A man tried to choke me without warning during sex', BBC News, 28 November 2019, https://www.bbc.co.uk/news/uk-50546184.

2   'Can we consent to harm?', Rightscast, 23 January 2020, https://anchor.fm/rightscast/episodes/R-v-Brown-Can-We-Consent-to-Harm–with-Dr-Matt-Lodder–Dr-Emily-Jones-and-Alexandra-Grolimund-eac19d.

3   Hamish Stewart, 'The limits of consent and the law of assault', *Canadian Journal of Law & Jurisprudence* 24(1), July 2015, pp. 205–223, https://doi.org/10.1017/S0841820900005129.

4   '"Dr Evil": Wolverhampton tattooist jailed for tongue-splitting', BBC News, 21 March 2019, https://www.bbc.co.uk/news/uk-england-birmingham-47658303.

5   Sexual Offences Act 2003, Section 3, https://www.legislation.gov.uk/ukpga/2003/42/section/3.

6   Christopher J. Ferguson, Richard D. Hartley, 'Pornography and sexual aggression: can meta-analysis find a link?', July 21, 2020, https://journals.sagepub.com/doi/abs/10.1177/1524838020942754?journalCode=tvaa.

7   Feona Attwood, Clare Bale and Meg Barker, 'The Sexualization Report', 2013, https://thesexualizationreport.files.wordpress.com/2013/12/thesexualizationreport.pdf.

8   Justin Hancock, 'Does Porn Harm Young People?', Bish Training, 11 May 2016, https://bishtraining.com/does-porn-harm-young-people/.

9   Sex Education Forum, 'Heads or tails? – what young people are telling us about SRE', 1 January 2016, https://www.sexeducationforum.org.uk/resources/evidence/heads-or-tails-what-young-people-are-telling-us-about-sre.

10   Anna Moore and Coco Khan, 'The fatal, hateful rise of choking during sex', *The Guardian*, 25 July 2019, https://www.theguardian.com/society/2019/jul/25/fatal-hateful-rise-of-choking-during-sex.

11   Jess Joho, '"Bonding" Season 2 is a good crash course in BDSM for curious couples', Mashable, 5 February 2021, https://mashable.com/article/bonding-season-2-review-valentines-day/.

12   Debby Herbenick et al., 'Feeling scared during sex: Findings from a UK probability sample of women and men ages 14 to 60', *Journal of Sex & Marital Therapy* 45(5), 2019, https://doi.org/10.1080/00926 23X.2018.1549634.

13   Olga Khazan, 'The startling rise of choking during sex', *The Atlantic*, 24 June 2019, https://www.theatlantic.com/health/archive/2019/06/how-porn-affecting-choking-during-sex/592375/.

14   Moore and Khan, 'The fatal, hateful rise of choking during sex'.

15   Harte, 'A man tried to choke me without warning during sex'.

Chapter 4: 'This went too far'

1   FPA, 'Less than half of people think it's OK to withdraw sexual consent if they're already naked'.

2   BBFC,Research,https://www.bbfc.co.uk/about-classification/research. https://www.mdx.ac.uk/__data/assets/pdf_file/0017/223280/Online-Pornography-and-Young-People-CYP-Version.pdfhttps://www.mdx.ac.uk/__data/assets/pdf_file/0017/223280/Online-Pornography-and-Young-People-CYP-Version.pdf.

3   Middlesex University London, 'Report reveals: damaging impact of online pornography on children', 15 June 2016, https://www.mdx.ac.uk/news/2016/06/children-desensitised-to-damaging-impact-of-online-pornography.

4   https://www.nus.org.uk/en/news/students-turn-to-porn-to-fill-the-gaps-in-their-sex-education/.

5   'Birds & Bees', *This American Life*, https://www.thisamericanlife.org/557/transcript.

6   @lalalaletmexplain, Instagram post, 29 January 2021, https://www.instagram.com/p/CKoO2nHHY7k/?utm_source=ig_web_copy_link.

7   @lalalaletmexplain, Instagram post, 3 February 2021, https://www.instagram.com/p/CK2Na12HzQA/?utm_source=ig_web_copy_link.

8   Nicole Froio, 'Whatever his kink, Armie Hammer is an abuser', Bitch Media, 20 January 2021, https://www.bitchmedia.org/article/armie-hammer-cannibal-jokes-hide-abuse-allegations.

9   Sophie Saint Thomas, 'A beginner's guide to impact play', *Allure*, 1 May 2019, https://www.allure.com/story/impact-play-spanking-sex-tips-guide.

10   Alice Little, 'Impact Play 101: Do's, don'ts, and more!', TheAliceLittle.com, https://thealicelittle.com/bdsm/impact-play-101/.

Chapter 5: The money shot

1   Statista, 'During your life, did you ever have intercourse resulting in facial ejaculation?', October 2013, https://www.statista.com/statistics/790136/youth-experience-ejaculation-facial-partner-la-france/.

2   'Making a splash: The history of the money shot', *Penthouse*, 24 August 2020, https://www.penthouse.com.au/articles/history/making-a-splash-the-history-of-the-money-shot.

3   Mary Stampoulos, 'I'm a feminist, but I like when he comes on my face', *Cosmopolitan*, 20 July 2015, https://www.cosmopolitan.com/sex-love/a43563/im-a-feminist-but-i-like-when-he-comes-on-my-face/.

4   https://twitter.com/AskDrRuth/status/101644208833695744?s=20.

5   Rebecca Reid, 'It's time to talk about facials – the kind that involve semen', *Metro*, 23 February 2018, https://metro.co.uk/2018/02/23/time-talk-facials-kind-involve-semen-7337371/.

6   Thompson, 'How the new UK porn block could put independent sex workers at risk'.

7   Beth Ashley, 'Inside the world of educational porn', Restless Network, 3 September 2020, https://www.restlessnetwork.com/inside-the-world-of-educational-porn/.

8   Nicholas Kristof, 'The children of Pornhub', *New York Times*, 4 December 2020, https://www.nytimes.com/2020/12/04/opinion/sunday/pornhub-rape-trafficking.html.

9   Pornhub, 'Our commitment to trust and safety', https://help.pornhub.com/hc/en-us/categories/360002934613-Trust-and-Safety.

10   Anna Iovine, 'Mastercard and Visa will stop processing payments to Pornhub', Mashable, 11 December 2020, https://mashable.com/article/mastercard-visa-stop-pornhub-payments/.

11   Michael Kan, 'Pornhub purges 10 million videos after losing credit card support', *PC Mag*, 14 December 2020, https://uk.pcmag.com/old-video-streaming-services/130496/pornhub-purges-10-million-videos-after-losing-credit-card-support.

12   Megha Mohan, 'I was raped at 14, and the video ended up on a porn site', BBC News, 10 February 2020, https://www.bbc.co.uk/news/stories-51391981.

13   Samantha Cole, 'Girls Do Porn employees charged with sex trafficking, potentially face life in prison', *Vice*, 11 October 2019, https://www.vice.com/en/article/qvgxvw/girls-do-porn-employees-charged-with-sex-trafficking-potentially-face-life-in-prison.

14   Samantha Cole and Emanuel Maiberg, 'Pornhub finally removes Girls Do Porn', *Vice*, 14 October 2019, https://www.vice.com/en/article/43kb5q/pornhub-finally-removes-girls-do-porn.

15   Brittany Shammas, 'Judge awards $13 million to women who say they were tricked into pornography', *Washington Post*, 3 January 2020, https://www.washingtonpost.com/business/2020/01/03/judge-awards-million-women-who-say-they-were-tricked-into-pornography/.

16   Jess Joho, 'The best alternatives to Pornhub and Xvideos', Mashable, 15 December 2020, https://mashable.com/article/pornhub-alternatives-free-porn-paid-porn/.

17   Annie Lord, 'Porn doesn't just suffer from a "piracy problem", it actively relies on it', *Vice*, 3 September 2019, https://www.

vice.com/en/article/kz4899/free-youporn-redtube-pornhub-piracy-alessa-savage-ukcutegirl.

Chapter 6: 'Lie there and let him do it'

1   Sara G. Kern and Zoë D. Peterson, 'From freewill to force: Examining types of coercion and psychological outcomes in unwanted sex', *The Journal of Sex Research* 57(5), October 2019, pp. 570–584, https://doi.org/10.1080/00224499.2019.1671302.

2   C. M. Meston and D. M. Buss, 'Why humans have sex', *Archives of Sexual Behavior* 36, July 2007, pp. 477–507, https://doi.org/10.1007/s10508-007-9175-2.

3   Lisa Fedina, Jennifer Lynne Holmes and Bethany L. Backes, 'Campus sexual assault: A systematic review of prevalence research from 2000 to 2015', *Trauma, Violence, & Abuse* 19(1), January 2018, pp. 76–93, https://doi.org/10.1177/1524838016631129.

4   'More than four in 10 women live in fear of refusing partners' sexual demands, new study finds', UN News, 10 April 2019, https://news.un.org/en/story/2019/04/1036431.

5   Laina Y. Bay-Cheng, 'Agency is everywhere, but agency is not enough: A conceptual analysis of young women's sexual agency', *The Journal of Sex Research* 56(4–5), 2019, pp. 462–474, https://doi.org/10.1080/00224499.2019.1578330.

6   Marianne Cense, 'Rethinking sexual agency: proposing a multi-component model based on young people's life stories', *Sex Education* 19(3), 2019, pp. 247–262, https://doi.org/10.1080/14681811.2018.1535968.

7   Gabrielle Jackson, *Pain and Prejudice: A Call to Arms for Women and Their Bodies*, Little, Brown, 2019, p. 123.

8   Mind, 'Dissociation and dissociative disorders', https://www.mind.org.uk/information-support/types-of-mental-health-problems/dissociation-and-dissociative-disorders/about-dissociation/.

9   u/pontmarie, 'Guy [25] buys me [f24] $350 dinner. Do I owe him sex?', Reddit post, https://www.reddit.com/r/relationships/

comments/1bk9mu/guy_25_buys_me_f24_350_dinner_do_i_
owe_him_sex/.

10 Marisa Gizzi, 'A man demanded drinks money off this Hull
    student because she didn't go home with him', The Tab, 7 June 2019,
    https://thetab.com/uk/2019/06/07/a-man-demanded-money-
    off-this-hull-student-for-drinks-after-she-didnt-go-home-with-
    him-103790.

11 Claudia Cuskelly, 'Man buys "gorgeous" student a drink then asks
    her to pay him BACK two weeks later', Express, 12 September
    2016, https://www.express.co.uk/life-style/life/709525/man-buys-
    gorgeous-student-drink-asks-her-pay-him-back-two-weeks-later-
    viper-rooms.

12 Sophie Gallagher, 'I bought your drinks, so you owe me sex – why do
    some men believe dating is a transaction?', HuffPost, 18 June 2019,
    https://www.huffingtonpost.co.uk/entry/i-bought-your-drinks-so-
    you-owe-me-sex-why-do-some-men-believe-dating-is-a-transaction_
    uk_5cf6a9cce4b0a1997b724e30.

13 Emily A. Impett and Letitia Anne Peplau, 'Why some women con-
    sent to unwanted sex with a dating partner: Insights from attach-
    ment theory', Psychology of Woman Quarterly 26(4), December 2002,
    pp. 360–370, https://doi.org/10.1111%2F1471-6402.t01-1-00075.

14 Courtney E. Ackerman, 'What is attachment theory? Bowlby's 4
    stages explained', Positive Psychology, https://positivepsychology.
    com/attachment-theory/.

15 Gurit E. Birnbaum et al., 'When sex is more than just sex: Attach-
    ment orientations, sexual experience, and relationship quality', Jour-
    nal of Personality and Social Psychology 91, pp. 929–43, 2006, https://
    doi.org/10.1037/0022–3514.91.5.929.

16 Emily Nagoski, Come As You Are: The Suprising New Science That Will
    Transform Your Sex Life, Scribe, 2015.

17 Birnbaum et al., 'When sex is more than just sex'.

18 Kern and Peterson, 'From freewill to force'.

19 Wendy Rose Gould, 'What is maintenance sex? It may help
    strengthen your marriage', Better by Today, 13 January 2019,

https://www.nbcnews.com/better/pop-culture/what-maintenance-sex-it-may-help-strengthen-your-marriage-ncna956216.

20   Jessica J. Hille, Megan K. Simmons and Stephanie A. Sanders, '"Sex" and the ace spectrum: Definitions of sex, behavioral histories, and future interest for individuals who identify as asexual, graysexual, or demisexual', *The Journal of Sex Research* 57(7), 2020, pp. 813–823, https://doi.org/10.1080/00224499.2019.1689378.

21   Justin Lehmiller, 'Unwanted sex and nonconsensual sex are not the same thing', Sex & Psychology, 15 June 2020, https://www.lehmiller.com/blog/2020/6/15/unwanted-sex-and-nonconsensual-sex-are-not-the-same-thing.

Chapter 7: All agony, no ecstasy

1   Olivia Funnell, 'Like many other women, I find sex agonising', *The Guardian*, 9 June 2016, https://www.theguardian.com/commentisfree/2016/jun/09/women-sex-agonising-vaginismus-penetrative.

2   K. R. Mitchell et al., 'Painful sex (dyspareunia) in women: Prevalence and associated factors in a British population probability survey', *BJOG* 124, 2017, pp. 1689–1697, https://doi.org/10.1111/1471-0528.14518.

3   D. Herbenick et al., 'Pain experienced during vaginal and anal intercourse with other-sex partners: Findings from a nationally representative probability study in the United States', *The Journal of Sexual Medicine* 12(4), April 2015, pp. 1040–1051, https://doi.org/10.1111/jsm.12841.

4   Suzannah Weiss, 'How one couple maintained their sex life when sex became painful', Bustle, 2 October 2017, https://www.bustle.com/p/what-is-sex-like-with-vulvodynia-how-one-couple-coped-when-intercourse-became-painful-75898.

5   Lili Loofbourow, 'The female price of male pleasure', *The Week*, 25 January 2018, https://theweek.com/articles/749978/female-price-male-pleasure.

6   Katie Way, 'I went on a date with Aziz Ansari. It turned into the worst night of my life', Babe, https://babe.net/2018/01/13/aziz-ansari-28355.

7   Sara I. McClelland, 'Intimate justice: A critical analysis of sexual satisfaction', *Social and Personality Psychology Compass* 4(9), 2010, pp. 663–680, https://doi.org/10.1111/j.1751–9004.2010.00293.x.

8   Kelly M. Hoffman et al., 'Racial bias in pain assessment and treatment recommendations, and false beliefs about biological differences between blacks and whites', *Proceedings of the National Academy of Sciences of the United States of America* 113(16), 2016, pp. 4296–4301, https://doi.org/10.1073/pnas.1516047113.

9   mbrrace-UK, *Saving Lives, Improving Mothers' Care*, November 2019, https://www.npeu.ox.ac.uk/assets/downloads/mbrrace-uk/reports/MBRRACE-UK%20Maternal%20Report%202019%20-%20WEB%20VERSION.pdf.

10   Endometriosis UK, 'Endometriosis facts and figures', https://endometriosis-uk.org/endometriosis-facts-and-figures.

11   O. Bougie et al., 'Influence of race/ethnicity on prevalence and presentation of endometriosis: A systematic review and meta-analysis', *BJOG* 126(9), 2019, pp. 1104–1115, https://doi.org/10.1111/1471–0528.15692.

12   Lucia Osborne-Crowley, 'How can we not know what causes endometriosis?', Refinery29, 7 September 2020, https://www.refinery29.com/en-gb/endometriosis-can-be-as-severe-as-cancer.

13   Weijmar Schultz et al., 'Women's sexual pain and its management', *The Journal of Sexual Medicine* 2(3), 2005, pp. 301–316, https://doi.org/10.1111/j.1743–6109.2005.20347.x.

14   Allison Carter et al., '"Fulfilling his needs, not mine": Reasons for not talking about painful sex and associations with lack of pleasure in a nationally representative sample of women in the United States', *The Journal of Sexual Medicine* 16(12), December 2019, pp. 1953–1965, https://doi.org/10.1016/j.jsxm.2019.08.016.

15   Rachel Thompson, 'Why masturbation needs to be taught in sex ed', Mashable, 26 September 2018, https://mashable.com/article/masturbation-sex-ed/.

Chapter 8: 'If you want to fuck me, fuck all of me'

1   Gina Tonic, 'How to have sex with a fat girl', *Vice*, 18 September 2019, https://www.vice.com/en_uk/article/mbm7wx/how-to-have-sex-fat-girl-guide.

2   Your Fat Friend, 'Is fat a fetish?', Medium, 21 May 2018, https://medium.com/@thefatshadow/is-fat-a-fetish-b07df64d00d.

3   @sophiehagendk, Instagram post, 2 September 2020, https://www.instagram.com/p/CEuLLllpKAA/.

4   Tonic, 'How to have sex with a fat girl'.

5   Stephanie Yeboah, 'Why dating as a plus size woman in 2019 is so traumatic', *Stylist*, https://www.stylist.co.uk/people/stephanie-yeboah-dating-trauma-instagram-body-positivity-movement/289682.

6   Laura Bogart, 'Quitting sex was the best thing I ever did for myself', BuzzFeed News, 9 July 2020, https://www.buzzfeednews.com/article/laurabogart/sex-celibate-dating-weight-body-image.

7   Jeannine A. Gailey and Ariane Prohaska, '"Knocking off a fat girl": An exploration of hogging, male sexuality, and neutralizations', *Deviant Behavior* 27(1), 2006, pp. 31–49, https://doi.org/10.1080/016396290968353.

Chapter 9: 'If I can't get a hard-on, I'll know I'm definitely racist'

1   V. M. Keith et al., 'Microaggressions, discrimination, and phenotype among African Americans: A latent class analysis of the impact of skin tone and BMI', *Sociological Inquiry* 87(2), 2017, pp. 233–255, https://doi.org/10.1111/soin.12168.

2   Greenridge, 'Why black people discriminate against ourselves'.

3   Afua Hirsch, '"As a black woman I'm always fetishized": Racism in the bedroom', *The Guardian*, 13 January 2018, https://www.theguardian.com/lifeandstyle/2018/jan/13/black-woman-always-fetishised-racism-in-bedroom.

4   Akeia A. F. Benard, 'Colonizing black female bodies within patriarchal capitalism: Feminist and human rights perspectives',

Sexualization, Media, & Society 2(4), December 2016, https://doi.org/10.1177/2374623816680622.

5   K. A. Story, 'Racing sex – Sexing race: The Invention of the Black Feminine Body', in Carol E. Henderson, ed., *Imagining the Black Female Body*, Palgrave Macmillan, 2010, pp. 23–43.

6   Deborah Gray White, *Ar'n't I a Woman?: Female Slaves in the Plantation South*, W. W. Norton, 1999, https://archive.org/details/arntiwomanfemal00whit.

7   Patricia Hill Collins, *Black Feminist Thought: Knowledge, Consciousness, and the Politics of Empowerment* 'Routledge Classics'

8   Benard, 'Colonizing black female bodies within patriarchal capitalism'.

9   Vaness Ntinu, 'Hyper-sexualisation: The realities of my black, female body', *gal-dem*, 14 January 2017, https://gal-dem.com/hypersexualisation-black-female-body/.

10   Ruby Hamad, *White Tears/Brown Scars: How White Feminism Betrays Women of Colour*, Catapult Books, 2020.

11   Hirsch, 'As a black woman I'm always fetishized'.

12   Candice Carty-Williams, *Queenie*, Orion, 19 March 2019.

13   Stephanie Yeboah, 'I don't care if you're "fascinated" by my afro, stop touching it', *Metro*, 9 September 2019, https://metro.co.uk/2019/09/09/i-dont-care-if-youre-fascinated-by-my-afro-stop-touching-it-10708877/.

14   Emma Dabiri, *Don't Touch My Hair*, Penguin, 2 May 2019.

15   Maria Thomas and Isabella Steger, 'In over 40 countries, laws against homosexuality are a lasting legacy of British rule', Quartz India, 7 September 2018, https://qz.com/india/1380947/section-377-the-former-british-colonies-with-laws-against-gay-people/.

16   john a. powell, 'Us vs. them: The sinister tactics of "Othering" and how to avoid them', *The Guardian*, 8 November 2017, https://www.theguardian.com/inequality/2017/nov/08/us-vs-them-the-sinister-techniques-of-othering-and-how-to-avoid-them.

17   Rachel Thompson, 'Instagram changes breast holding policy after #IwantToSeeNyome campaign', Mashable, 26 October 2020, https://

mashable.com/article/instagram-breast-squeezing-policy-nyome-nicholas-williams/.

18 L. L. Wall, 'The medical ethics of Dr J. Marion Sims: A fresh look at the historical record', *Journal of Medical Ethics* 32(6), 2006, pp. 346–350, https://dx.doi.org/10.1136/jme.2005.012559.

19 Emma Kasprzak, 'Why are black mothers at more risk of dying?', BBC News, 12 April 2019, https://www.bbc.co.uk/news/uk-england-47115305.

20 Tobi Oredein, 'Editor's letter: Why we need to talk about Black motherhood in 2020', Black Ballad, 6 January 2020, https://blackballad.co.uk/views-voices/editors-letter-why-we-need-to-talk-about-black-motherhood-in-2020.

21 Drew C. Pendergrass and Michelle Y. Raji, 'The bitter pill: Harvard and the dark history of birth control', *The Harvard Crimson*, 28 September 2017, https://www.thecrimson.com/article/2017/9/28/the-bitter-pill/.

22 Natasha Lennard, 'The long, disgraceful history of American attacks on Brown and Black women's reproductive systems', *The Intercept*, 17 September 2020, https://theintercept.com/2020/09/17/forced-sterilization-ice-us-history/.

23 Lut Kaelber, 'Eugenics/sexual sterilizations in North Carolina', 30 October 2014, https://www.uvm.edu/~lkaelber/eugenics/NC/NC.html.

24 Chicago Women's Liberation Union Herstory Project, '35% of Puerto Rican women sterilized', https://www.cwluherstory.org/health/35-of-puerto-rican-women-sterilized?rq=Puerto%20rico.

25 Nikita Stewart, 'Planned Parenthood in NY disavows Margaret Sanger over eugenics', *New York Times*, 21 July 2020, https://www.nytimes.com/2020/07/21/nyregion/planned-parenthood-margaret-sanger-eugenics.html.

26 Planned Parenthood, 'Opposition Claims about Margaret Sanger', Planned Parenthood Federation of America, October 2016, https://www.plannedparenthood.org/uploads/filer_public/37/fd/37fdc7b6-de5f-4d22-8c05-9568268e92d8/sanger_opposition_claims_fact_sheet_2016.pdf.

Chapter 10: 'How could you call me a racist?'

1 Nerdy POC, 'The Aladdin Discourse: Disney And Browning Up Extras', Medium, https://medium.com/@nerdypoc/the-aladdin-discourse-disney-and-browing-up-actors-92292c3af331.

2 'Brown Girls Do It Too', BBC Sounds, https://www.bbc.co.uk/sounds/brand/p08k5cp0.

3 Rae Chen, 'How to stop fetishizing my Chinese identity', *Teen Vogue*, 28 June 2018, https://www.teenvogue.com/story/how-to-stop-fetishizing-my-chinese-identity.

4 Brittany Wong, 'Dear white guys: Your Asian fetish is showing', HuffPost, 29 August 2020, https://www.huffingtonpost.co.uk/entry/asian-fetish-dating-red-flags_n_5ce6ca27e4b05c15dea89437?ri18n=true.

5 Rachel Kuo, 'How rape culture and racism combine to hurt Asian women', HuffPost, 27 May 2017, https://www.huffpost.com/entry/how-rape-culture-and-racism-combine-to-hurt-asian-women_b_592a15ade4b0a7b7b469cb22.

6 Evie Muir, 'Experiencing childhood racism makes women of colour vulnerable to abusive relationships in adulthood', *Cosmopolitan*, 27 October 2020, https://www.cosmopolitan.com/uk/reports/a34463365/racism-abusive-relationships-women-of-colour/.

7 Siobhan Neela-Stock, 'How to recognize if you're being racially gaslighted', Mashable, 26 June 2020, https://mashable.com/article/how-to-recognize-racial-gaslighting/.

8 u/shesocrafty, Reddit post, https://www.reddit.com/r/interracialdating/comments/83rvg1/my_white_husband_is_gaslighting_me_about_race/.

9 Reni Eddo-Lodge, *Why I'm No Longer Talking to White People About Race*, Bloomsbury, 2019, p. 89.

10 Muir, 'Experiencing childhood racism makes women of colour vulnerable to abusive relationships in adulthood'.

11 Yaa Gyasi, 'White people, black authors are not your medicine', *The Guardian*, 20 March 2021, https://www.theguardian.com/books/2021/mar/20/white-people-black-authors-are-not-your-medicine.

12 Gina Martin, *Be The Change: A Toolkit for the Activist in You*, Sphere, 11 June 2019.

Chapter 11: For your viewing pleasure

1   NISVS, 'An Overview of 2010 Findings of Victimization by Sexual Orientation', CDC, https://www.cdc.gov/violenceprevention/pdf/cdc_nisvs_victimization_final-a.pdf.

2   Anonymous, 'An open letter to straight men: My bisexuality is NOT a fetish', Swipe Life, 20 April 2020, https://swipelife.tinder.com/post/bisexual-women.

3   Human Rights Campaign, 'Sexual assault and the LGBTQ community', https://www.hrc.org/resources/sexual-assault-and-the-lgbt-community.

4   Lehigh University, 'Study finds higher rates of sexual violence among bisexual women', 15 November 2017, https://www.eurekalert.org/pub_releases/2017–11/lu-sfh111517.php.

5   Human Rights Campaign, 'Sexual assault and the LGBTQ community'.

6   Nicole L. Johnson and MaryBeth Grove, 'Why us?: Toward an understanding of bisexual women's vulnerability for and negative consequences of sexual violence', *Journal of Bisexuality* 17(4), 2017, pp. 435–450, https://doi.org/10.1080/15299716.2017.1364201.

7   Zachary Zane, 'Who do bi women face higher rates of sexual violence?', bi.org, 22 October 2017, https://bi.org/en/articles/why-do-bi-women-face-higher-rates-of-sexual-violence.

8   Paisley Gilmour, 'How straight people can be better to their bisexual friends', *Cosmopolitan*, 23 September 2020, https://www.cosmopolitan.com/uk/love-sex/relationships/a34110852/bisexual-friendships-straight-people/.

9   Charlotte Summers, 'Opinion: Stop sexualising queer women', *Diva*, 21 March 2019, https://divamag.co.uk/2019/03/21/opinion-stop-sexualising-queer-women/.

10 Patrick Kelleher, 'Liam Payne finally apologises for his "harmful biphobic" track Both Ways … but it's a bit meagre, to be honest', Pink News, 17 April 2020, https://www.pinknews.co.uk/2020/04/17/liam-payne-one-direction-both-ways-apology-bisexual/.

11 Christine Hannigan, 'You saw me covered in blood on a bus. But do you get outraged about all homophobia?', The Guardian, 14 June 2019, https://www.theguardian.com/commentisfree/2019/jun/14/homophobic-attack-bus-outrage-media-white.

12 Harvey Day, 'Section 28'.

13 Rachel Thompson, 'Campaigner Ruth Hunt on straightwashing and erasure of LGBTQ history', Mashable, 28 May 2020, https://mashable.com/article/ruth-hunt-history-becomes-her/.

14 Thompson, 'Why masturbation needs to be taught in sex ed'.

Chapter 12: 'Sex wasn't for people like me'

1 @thatsinglemum, Instagram post, 12 November 2020, https://www.instagram.com/p/CHfS1RJlHBx/.

2 Disability Wisdom Consulting, 'On the desexualization of Disabled women', 20 July 2018, https://www.disabilitywisdom.com/2018/07/20/on-the-desexualization-of-Disabled-women/.

3 The Asexual Visibility and Education Network, 'About asexuality', https://www.asexuality.org/?q=overview.html.

4 Alaina Leary, 'Asexual Disabled people exist, but don't make assumptions about us', Rooted in Rights, 28 June 2018, https://rootedinrights.org/asexual-Disabled-people-exist-but-dont-make-assumptions-about-us/.

5 Amy Gravino, 'Why Autism Is Sexier Than You Think It Is', TEDx Talks, 28 September 2017, https://www.youtube.com/watch?v=shgy43CxBX8.

6 Kathleen C. Basile, Matthew J. Breiding and Sharon G. Smith, 'Disability and risk of recent sexual violence in the United States', American Journal of Public Health 106, 2016, pp. 928–933, https://doi.org/10.2105/AJPH.2015.303004.

7   Office for National Statistics, 'Disability and crime UK: 2019', 2 December 2019, https://www.ons.gov.uk/peoplepopulationand community/healthandsocialcare/disability/bulletins/disability andcrimeuk/2019/.

8   National Organization for Women, 'The disability community and sexual violence', https://now.org/wp-content/uploads/2018/05/Disabled-Women-Sexual-Violence-4.pdf.

9   Joseph Shapiro, 'The sexual assault epidemic no one talks about', NPR, 8 January 2018, https://www.npr.org/2018/01/08/570224090/the-sexual-assault-epidemic-no-one-talks-about?t=1612974324470.

10   World Health Organization, *World Report on Disability 2011*, 12 December 2011, https://www.who.int/teams/noncommunicable-diseases/disability-and-rehabilitation/world-report-on-disability.

11   Office for Disability Issues, 'Disability facts and figures', Gov.uk, https://www.gov.uk/government/statistics/disability-facts-and-figures/disability-facts-and-figures.

Chapter 13: Seeking closure at closed doors

1   Human Rights Campaign, 'Sexual assault and the LGBTQ community'.

2   Jamie Windust, 'My full stop: The victim impact statement I was denied', *Gay Times*, 4 December 2020, https://www.gaytimes.co.uk/life/my-full-stop-the-victim-impact-statement-i-was-denied/.

3   GLAAD, 'Glossary of terms – Transgender', *GLAAD Media Reference Guide*, https://www.glaad.org/reference/transgender.

4   A. Hasenbush, A. R. Flores and J. L. Herman, 'Gender identity non-discrimination laws in public accommodations: A review of evidence regarding safety and privacy in public restrooms, locker rooms, and changing rooms', *Sexuality Research and Social Policy* 16, 2019, pp. 70–83, https://doi.org/10.1007/s13178-018–0335-z.

5   Stonewall and YouGov, *LGBT In Britain: Home and Communities*, https://www.stonewall.org.uk/sites/default/files/lgbt_in_britain_home_and_communities.pdf.

6   Moya Lothian-McLean, '"If they sound like a man, hang up" – how transphobia became rife in the gender-based violence sector', *gal-dem*, 1 February 2021, https://gal-dem.com/transphobia-sexual-violence-sound-like-a-man-hang-up-vawg-investigation/.

7   Stonewall, *Supporting trans women in domestic and sexual violence services*, 2018, https://www.stonewall.org.uk/system/files/stonewall_and_nfpsynergy_report.pdf.

8   Anrows, 'Crossing the line: Lived experience of sexual violence among trans women of colour from culturally and linguistically diverse backgrounds in Australia', June 2020, https://www.anrows.org.au/project/crossing-the-line-lived-experience-of-sexual-violence-among-trans-women-from-culturally-and-linguistically-diverse-backgrounds-in-australia/.

9   Lydia Feng, 'Australian study finds risk of sexual assault and violence significantly higher for trans women of colour', ABC News, 25 June 2020, https://www.abc.net.au/news/2020–06-26/study-finds-high-sexual-assault-rates-for-trans-women-of-colour/12395226.

10   Hannah Ewens, 'Inside the Great British TERF War', *Vice*, 16 June 2020, https://www.vice.com/en/article/889qe5/trans-rights-uk-debate-terfs.

11   Rachel Thompson, 'Trans woman googles every news story containing the word "transgender" in a year', Mashable, 21 August 2019, https://mashable.com/article/trans-media-coverage-fourth-estate/.

12   Shon Faye, 'Shon Faye on changing the conversation around trans rights', *Vogue*, 22 November 2018, https://www.vogue.co.uk/article/shon-faye-on-changing-the-conversation-around-trans-rights.

13   Government Equalities Office, 'Written Ministerial Statement: Response to Gender Recognition Act (2004) consultation', https://www.gov.uk/government/speeches/response-to-gender-recognition-act-2004-consultation.

14   Stonewall, 'What does the UK government announcement on the Gender Recognition Act mean?', https://www.stonewall.org.uk/what-does-uk-government-announcement-gender-recognition-act-mean.

15 Lothian-McLean, '"If they sound like a man, hang up".'

16 Paisley Gilmour, 'Your no BS guide to the Gender Recognition Act reforms', *Cosmopolitan*, 11 June 2020, https://www.cosmopolitan. com/uk/reports/a29590439/gender-recognition-act/.

17 Amy Greaves, 'These are the countries that already allow trans people to self-identify', *Gay Star News*, 16 October 2018, https://www. gaystarnews.com/article/countries-trans-self-identify/.

18 Syd Stephenson, 'How to navigate gender dysphoria during sex', *Teen Vogue*, 27 June 2019, https://www.teenvogue.com/story/how-to-navigate-gender-dysphoria-during-sex/.

19 Rachel Thompson, 'It's time to reclaim singledom as a symbol of power', Mashable, 14 February 2019, https://mashable.com/article/being-single-symbol-strength/.

20 BBC Three, 'Are trans women "real women"?', https://www.bbc. co.uk/bbcthree/clip/2237b1ff-f932-4893–9827-5917b636e96c.

Chapter 14: Unprotected

1   Sophie Gallagher, 'The government missed a crucial deadline to support victims of sexual harassment', HuffPost, 24 December 2018, https://www.huffingtonpost.co.uk/entry/this-is-why-today-matters-for-any-woman-who-has-experienced-cyberflashing_uk_5c13 bd37e4b0860b8b5d846f.

2   Thompson, 'It's time to stop saying "unsolicited dick pics". Here's why'.

3   Matthew Smith, 'Four in ten female millennials have been sent an unsolicited penis photo', YouGov, 15 January 2018, https:// yougov.co.uk/topics/politics/articles-reports/2018/02/15/four-ten-female-millennials-been-sent-dick-pic.

4   City, University of London, 'Researcher discusses "unjust burden" put on women by online harassment', 5 November 2018 (updated 9 November 2020), https://www.city.ac.uk/news/2018/october/online-abuse-and-harassment-research.

5   Law Commission, 'Greater protections for victims of online abuse proposed by Law Commission', 11 September 2020, https://www.lawcom.gov.uk/greater-protections-for-victims-of-online-abuse-proposed-by-law-commission/.

6   History Becomes Her, 'Gina Martin on the power of activism and how she made upskirting illegal', 30 April 2020, https://play.acast.com/s/historybecomesher/ginamartinonthepowerof activismandhowshemadeupskirtingillegal.

7   'One in ten people "are revenge porn victims"', The Times, 21 March 2019, https://www.thetimes.co.uk/article/one-in-ten-people-are-revenge-porn-victims-mhm2bb6fc.

8   Sophie Gallagher, '"Revenge porn" is not the right term to describe our experiences, say victims', HuffPost, 3 August 2019, https://www.huffingtonpost.co.uk/entry/why-are-we-still-calling-it-revenge-porn-victims-explain-change-in-the-laws-needed_uk_5d3594c2e4b020cd99465a99.

9   Cyber Civil Rights Initiative, 'Nonconsensual porn: A common offense', 12 June 2017, https://www.cybercivilrights.org/2017-natl-ncp-research-results/.

10 Birmingham Law School, 'More than just "revenge porn"', https://www.birmingham.ac.uk/schools/law/research/spotlights/ibsa.aspx.

11 Rachel Kraus, 'Telegram's massive revenge porn problem has made these women's lives hell', Mashable, 29 October 2020, https://mashable.com/article/nudes-revenge-porn-crime-telegram/.

12 Shanti Das, 'Broken by revenge porn, my beautiful girl killed herself', The Times, 3 August 2019, https://www.thetimes.co.uk/article/broken-by-revenge-porn-my-beautiful-girl-killed-herself-70dsff92h.

13 Cyber Civil Rights Initiative, 'End Revenge Porn', https://www.cybercivilrights.org/wp-content/uploads/2014/12/RPStatistics.pdf.

14 Refuge, The Naked Threat, July 2020, https://www.refuge.org.uk/wp-content/uploads/2020/07/The-Naked-Threat-Report.pdf.

15 Caroline Davies, 'Campaigners welcome extra protections in domestic abuse bill', *The Guardian*, 1 March 2021, https://www.theguardian.com/society/2021/mar/01/campaigners-welcome-extra-protections-in-domestic-abuse-bill.

16 Lizzie Dearden, 'Rape "decriminalised" as only 1.4% of reported attacks prosecuted in England and Wales', *Independent*, 17 October 2019, https://www.independent.co.uk/news/uk/crime/rape-prosecutions-uk-disclosure-mobile-phones-cps-a9160556.html.

17 Alexandra Topping and Caelainn Barr, 'Prosecution service under fire over record low convictions', *The Guardian*, 30 July 2020, https://www.theguardian.com/society/2020/jul/30/prosecution-service-under-fire-over-record-low-convictions.

18 Lucy Adams, 'Sex attack victims usually know attacker, says new study', BBC News, https://www.bbc.co.uk/news/uk-scotland-4312 8350.

19 Topping and Barr, 'Prosecution service under fire over record low convictions'.

20 Caelainn Barr, Owen Bowcott and Alexandra Topping, 'CPS secretly dropped "weak" rape cases, say rights groups', *The Guardian*, 30 June 2020, https://www.theguardian.com/law/2020/jun/30/cps-secretly-dropped-weak-cases-say-rights-groups.

21 Sara Haque, 'Sexts are still being used as evidence in rape trials', *Vice*, 22 March 2021, https://www.vice.com/en/article/bvx9zd/digital-messages-sexting-rape-trial-evidence.

22 Victoria Law, 'Against carceral feminism', *Jacobin*, October 2014, https://www.jacobinmag.com/2014/10/against-carceral-feminism.

23 Rachel Thompson, 'How "hatewank" videos became a tool for harassing women in the public eye', Mashable, 7 July 2020, https://mashable.com/article/hatewank-videos-harassment/.

24 Jessica Roy, 'How tech companies are fighting revenge porn – and winning', The Cut, 24 June 2015, https://www.thecut.com/2015/06/how-tech-companies-are-fighting-revenge-porn.html.

25 Kraus, 'Telegram's massive revenge porn problem has made these women's lives hell'.

26 Criminal Justice and Courts Act 2015, Section 33, https://www.legislation.gov.uk/ukpga/2015/2/section/33/enacted.

27 Law Commission, 'Taking, making and sharing intimate images without consent', https://www.lawcom.gov.uk/project/taking-making-and-sharing-intimate-images-without-consent/.

28 Department for Digital, Culture, Media and Sport, 'Consultation outcome: Online Harms White Paper', 15 December 2020, https://www.gov.uk/government/consultations/online-harms-white-paper/online-harms-white-paper.

Chapter 15: The ones who didn't get away

1 Anna North, 'She was fatally strangled. The media is making it about her sex life', Vox, 21 November 2019, https://www.vox.com/2019/11/21/20976064/grace-millane-death-new-zealand.

2 Eleanor Ainge Roy, '"She should have been safe here": How Grace Millane's murder shocked New Zealand', The Guardian, 22 November 2019, https://www.theguardian.com/world/2019/nov/22/she-should-have-been-safe-grace-millane-murder-new-zealand.

3 Sean Morrison, 'Grace Millane was member of BDSM dating sites and asked ex-partner to choke her during sex, court hears', Evening Standard, 19 November 2019, https://www.standard.co.uk/news/world/grace-millane-was-member-of-bdsm-dating-sites-and-asked-expartner-to-choke-her-during-sex-court-a4290251.html.

4 Stephen D'Antal, '"Naïve and trusting": Grace Millane gave man on BDSM site list of sex fetishes like electric shocks and being "submissive slave" court hears', The Sun, 20 November 2019, https://www.thesun.co.uk/news/10382685/grace-millane-bdsm-site-list-court/.

5 Stephen D'Antal, 'Grace Millane "encouraged date to choke her during sex and apply more force"', Mirror, 21 November 2019, https://www.mirror.co.uk/news/world-news/grace-millane-encouraged-date-choke-20926342.

6   BBC News, 'Grace Millane death: Prosecution presents first evidence', 6 November 2019, https://www.bbc.co.uk/news/world-asia-50312090.

7   BBC News, 'Grace Millane died "accidentally during sex", murder accused claims', 19 November 2019, https://www.bbc.com/news/uk-england-essex-50468890.

8   Giovanni Torre, 'Grace Millane murder suspect "choked two other women during sex"', *Telegraph*, 11 November 2019, https://www.telegraph.co.uk/news/2019/11/11/cant-way-die-grace-millane-murderer-suffocated-woman-sex-court/.

9   Press Association, 'Grace Millane murderer loses appeal against conviction and sentence', *The Guardian*, 18 December 2020, https://www.theguardian.com/world/2020/dec/18/grace-millane-murderer-loses-appeal-against-conviction-and-sentence.

10 Franki Cookney, 'The "rough sex" defence as a gross perversion of BDSM, I'm delighted it's finally been banned', *Independent*, https://www.independent.co.uk/voices/rough-sex-defence-ban-domestic-abuse-bdsm-chalk-a9570561.html.

11 Rebecca Reid, 'Grace Millane might have been a member of BDSM sites – that still doesn't explain her death', *Grazia*, 22 November 2019, https://graziadaily.co.uk/life/in-the-news/sex-game-gone-wrong-22/.

12 @BarristerSecret, Twitter thread, 1 July 2020, https://twitter.com/BarristerSecret/status/1278411385471369216.

13 Sian Norris, '"Rough sex" as a defence for murder is grotesque victim-blaming', *The Guardian*, 24 February 2020, https://www.theguardian.com/commentisfree/2020/feb/24/rough-sex-defence-murder-grace-millane.

14 'Let's end the "rough sex" defence', Change.org, https://www.change.org/p/uk-parliament-let-s-end-the-rough-sex-defence-604fb426-47ae-4d92-ad5a-75135fd020ff.

15 BBC News, '"Rough sex" defence will be banned, says justice minister', 17 June 2020, https://www.bbc.co.uk/news/uk-politics-53064086.

16 Harriet Harman, as told to Anna Silverman, 'We need to stop sexual liberation being used as a defence for men killing women', *Grazia*, 11 September 2019, https://graziadaily.co.uk/life/in-the-news/harriet-harman-we-need-to-stop-sexual-liberation-being-used-as-a-defence-for-men-killing-women/.

17 Caroline Lowbridge, 'Rough sex murder defence: Why campaigners want it banned', BBC News, 22 January 2020, https://www.bbc.co.uk/news/uk-england-51151182.

18 Sophie Gallagher, 'Rough sex defence: What will a change in law mean?', *Independent*, 7 July 2020, https://www.independent.co.uk/life-style/women/rough-sex-defence-ban-domestic-abuse-bill-government-2020-a9374386.html.

19 @BarristerSecret, Twitter thread, 1 July 2020.

20 Charlie Jones, 'Grace Millane's family welcome "rough sex" defence ban', BBC News, 18 June 2020, https://www.bbc.co.uk/news/uk-england-essex-53082345.

21 Femicide Census, https://www.womensaid.org.uk/what-we-do/campaigning-and-influencing/femicide-census/.

22 Nancy Glass et al., 'Non-fatal strangulation is an important risk factor for homicide of women', *The Journal of Emergency Medicine* 35(3), October 2008, pp. 329–335, https://doi.org/10.1016/j.jemermed.2007.02.065.

23 Helen Bichard et al., 'The neuropsychological outcomes of non-fatal strangulation in domestic and sexual violence: A review', *Neuropsychological Rehabilitation*, January 2021, https://doi.org/10.1080/09602011.2020.1868537.

24 Will Humphries, 'Abuse victim calls for law on throttling', *The Times*, 21 October 2019, https://www.thetimes.co.uk/article/abuse-victim-calls-for-law-on-non-fatal-strangulation-9mq75nj9c.

25 Sam Bonham and Natalie Ktena, 'Change in strangling law "would save lives"', BBC News, 28 October 2019, https://www.bbc.co.uk/news/uk-50185648.

26 Rajeev Syal, 'Non-fatal strangulation to carry five years in prison under reforms', *The Guardian*, 1 March 2021, https://www.theguardian.

com/society/2021/mar/01/non-fatal-strangulation-to-carry-five-years-in-prison-under-reforms.

27 BBC News, 'New non-fatal strangulation law to target domestic abusers', 1 March 2021, https://www.bbc.co.uk/news/uk-56231916.

Chapter 16: Prata om det

1   Ben Quinn, 'Sweden drops Julian Assange investigation', *The Guardian*, 19 November 2019, https://www.theguardian.com/media/2019/nov/19/sweden-drops-julian-assange-investigation.

2   Lena Gunnarsson, 'Excuse me, but are you raping me now?'

3   Rachel Thompson, 'Women over 50 see sexual harassment very differently than millennials', Mashable, 1 December 2018, https://mashable.com/2017/12/01/sexual-harassment-over-50s-millennials/.

4   Matthew Smith, 'Sexual harassment: How the genders and generations see the issue differently', YouGov, 1 November 2017, https://yougov.co.uk/topics/lifestyle/articles-reports/2017/11/01/sexual-harassment-how-genders-and-generations-see-.

5   Rachel Thompson, '97% of young women have been harassed, study finds', Mashable, 10 March 2021, https://mashable.com/article/sexual-harassment-un-women-uk/.

6   Rachel Thompson, 'Hey Aziz Ansari defenders, saying "no" is more complex than you think', Mashable, 15 January 2018, https://mashable.com/2018/01/15/aziz-ansari-consent-saying-no/.

7   @benshapiro, Twitter post, 16 November 2020, https://twitter.com/benshapiro/status/1328342542287589381?s=20.

8   Allie Malloy, 'Trump unleashes on Kavanaugh accuser', CNN Politics, 22 September 2018, https://edition.cnn.com/2018/09/21/politics/donald-trump-brett-kavanaugh-accuser-tweets/index.html.

9   AJ Willingham and Christina Maxouris, 'These tweets show why people don't report sexual assaults', CNN Health, 21 September 2018, https://edition.cnn.com/2018/09/21/health/why-i-didnt-report-tweets-trnd/index.html.

Chapter 17: The new sex scene

1   *Normal People*, (2020), BBC Three, 26 April 2020.

2   Terrence Higgins Trust, 'Relationships and Sex Education (RSE)', https://www.tht.org.uk/our-work/our-campaigns/relationships-and-sex-education-rse.

3   Rita Seabrook et al., 'Girl power or powerless girl? Television, sexual scripts, and sexual agency in sexually active young women', *Psychology of Women Quarterly* 41(2), 2017, pp. 240–253, https://doi.org/10.1177/0361684316677028.

4   *I May Destroy You*, (2020), BBC One / HBO, 7 June – 14 July 2020.

5   Sophie Wilkinson, '"I felt a joy of vindication": How "I May Destroy You" has helped stealthing victims', *Vogue*, 16 July 2020, https://www.vogue.co.uk/arts-and-lifestyle/article/what-is-stealthing.

6   Chelsea Hale and Meghan Matt, 'The intersection of race and rape viewed through the prism of a modern-day Emmett Till', American Bar, 16 July 2019, https://www.americanbar.org/groups/litigation/committees/diversity-inclusion/articles/2019/summer2019-intersection-of-race-and-rape/.

7   Caroline Framke, '"I May Destroy You" star Weruche Opia reflects on the "trippy" finale and setting her own boundaries on set', *Variety*, 24 August 2020, https://variety.com/2020/tv/news/i-may-destroy-you-finale-weruche-opia-michaela-coel-1234739086/.

8   *Sex Education*, (2020), Netflix, 17 January 2020.

9   Rachel Thompson, '"Sex Education" star Aimee Lou Wood on getting through lockdown and how sex in TV is changing', Mashable, 10 July 2020, https://mashable.com/article/aimee-lou-wood-sex-education/.

10   Rachel Thompson, 'The powerful story behind Aimee's "Sex Education" storyline', Mashable, 31 January 2020, https://mashable.com/article/sex-education-aimee-assault-storyline/.

11   @louisa_compton, Twitter post, 22 August 2018, https://twitter.com/louisa_compton/status/1032322276501454851.

12   Rachel Thompson, 'Meet the educator behind the chlamydia out-break in "Sex Education"', Mashable, 11 February 2020, https://mashable.com/article/alix-fox-sex-education-script-consultant/.

13   Annie Lord, 'Why Normal People gets rough sex wrong', *Independent*, 13 May 2020, https://www.independent.co.uk/arts-entertainment/tv/features/normal-people-bdsm-rough-sex-wrong-fifty-shades-of-grey-a9511856.html.

14   Adrienne Westenfeld, 'Sally Rooney is more than "the great millennial novelist"', *Esquire*, 18 April 2019, https://www.esquire.com/entertainment/books/a27194707/sally-rooney-interview-normal-people/.

Chapter 18: How do we change our sexual culture?

1   Kayla Chadwick, 'I don't know how to explain to you that you should care about other people', HuffPost, 26 June 2017, https://www.huffpost.com/entry/i-dont-know-how-to-explain-to-you-that-you-should_b_59519811e4b0f078efd98440.

2   Jaclyn Friedman, 'Sex & consent: It's time to go beyond the rules', Refinery29, 6 September 2018, https://www.refinery29.com/en-us/sex-consent-laws-yes-means-yes-jaclyn-friedman.

3   Rachel Thompson, 'Please, I beg of you, stop suggesting consent apps', Mashable, 19 March 2021, https://mashable.com/article/consent-apps-not-the-solution/.

4   Kate Julian, 'Why are young people having so little sex?', *The Atlantic*, December 2018, https://www.theatlantic.com/magazine/archive/2018/12/the-sex-recession/573949/.

5   Ben Hurst, 'Boys will be boys', TEDx Talk, https://www.ted.com/talks/ben_hurst_boys_won_t_be_boys_boys_will_be_what_we_teach_them_to_be/transcript?language=en.

6   Tony Porter, 'A call to men', TED Talk, 2010, https://www.ted.com/talks/tony_porter_a_call_to_men/transcript?language=en.

7   Rachel Thompson, 'How to talk to the men in your life about toxic masculinity', Mashable, 14 September 2019, https://mashable.com/article/liz-plank-toxic-masculinity-conversation/.

8   BBC News, 'Jordan Peterson on the "backlash against masculinity"', 6 August 2018, https://www.bbc.co.uk/news/av/world-us-canada-45084954.

9   Veronica M. Lamarche and Laurie James-Hawkins, 'It happened to a friend of mine: The influence of perspective-taking on the acknowledgment of sexual assault following ambiguous sexual encounters', *Journal of Interpersonal Violence*, September 2020, https://journals.sagepub.com/doi/full/10.1177/0886260520957678.

10   Rachel Hills, 'The Sex Myth: The Gap Between Our Fantasies and Reality', 4 August 2015, Simon & Schuster.

11   Leni Morris, 'Six ways to be an ally to asexual people', Stonewall, 6 April 2021, https://www.stonewall.org.uk/about-us/news/six-ways-be-ally-asexual-people#:~:text=Ace%20people%20have%20intimacy%20issues,broken%20or%20having%20a%20disorder.

12   Rachel Thompson, 'How to set boundaries in the early stages of dating', Mashable, 16 September 2020, https://mashable.com/article/setting-boundaries-dating-relationship/.

13   Erin Taylor, 'How to make (and maintain) healthy sexual boundaries', *Allure*, 29 November 2019, https://www.allure.com/story/how-to-make-sexual-boundaries.

14   Bessel van der Kolk, *The Body Keeps the Score: Mind, Brain and Body in the Transformation of Trauma*, Penguin; 1st edition (24 Sept. 2015).

Acknowledgements

To my wonderful, beloved agent, Florence Rees: I truly couldn't have done this without your support, guidance, and kindness. Thank you for believing in this book and for holding this very anxious author's hand throughout this entire process, for sending me emails that made me breathe deep sighs of relief, and for being a friend to me. I feel very lucky that you're my agent.

To my brilliant editor, Mireille Harper: from that very first Zoom meeting in Lockdown 1, I knew you saw the vision for this book and believed in its value. I am so grateful to you for having faith in me and this project. From the moment I nervously handed in my manuscript, I felt I was in safe hands, and your edits were smart, sensitive, and insightful. It's been a dream come true to work with you. To Maxine Sibihwana – thank you for the sensitive edit notes, I so loved working with you on this book. To Gemma Wain – your copy-edits were so thorough and I'm so thankful for your time and attention to detail.

I am indebted to everyone who generously shared their experiences with me for this book. Talking about trauma is far from easy and I am honoured that you trusted me with your stories. Strength and solidarity to each of you. Gratitude to the experts whose insights were invaluable to me during the research phase. Talking to you was fascinating and I learned so much from each of you.

I'm so thankful to the team at AM Heath – to Prema Raj and the Rights team. Thank you to Zoe King for bringing me into the AMH family and for shaping *Rough* in its nascent stage. Thank you to everyone on the Square Peg and Vintage team who worked on this book. Huge thanks to Alison Davies and Kate Neilan – you're both a joy to work with. Thank you to Kate MacDonald, Stella Newing and the audiobook team.

I owe a debt of gratitude to the people who mentored me in the early stages of my career, who developed me as a writer and journalist, and provided me with opportunities that changed my life. My eternal thanks go to Preston Witts, Jon Stock, Sameer Rahim, Blathnaid Healy, Laura Silverman, Liz Thompson, and Danny Evans. Thank you to Fiona Rose for reading very early drafts of this book and for chatting to me during those early, nerve-wracking stages.

To my dear friends, I don't know what I'd have done without you. Writing a book over the course of three national lockdowns was challenging to say the very least, but your friendship made me feel loved and supported even at the darkest and loneliest points. Thank you Lizzie Isherwood for listening to my daily 20 minute voice notes (which are basically podcast episodes tbh) and being one of the kindest, most understanding people I know. To Elisha Hartwig and Amber Fahrner for showing up on my doorstep with flowers, sausage rolls, and coffee on the day I finished writing! Elisha, your friendship means the world to me, and you've been a confidante to me every step of the way with this book. I love you and I know you're probably crying right now so I'll stop now. But thank you. To Liza Hearon, the first human to pre-order *Rough*, thank you for reading my book proposal chapters and giving me thoughtful notes on the early drafts. (Thank you also for Deliverooing margaritas to my front door the moment I finished writing my manuscript!) To Maya Robert, my guardian angel, thank you for the pep talks when my fretting got the better of me, thank you for being in my corner no matter what. Vicky Leta, my sweet friend, thank you for the enormous bouquet you sent to me when I finished editing my manuscript. Even when there's an ocean separating us, you are there for me, and it is so appreciated. Thank you to my dearest friend Shannon Kephart, your friendship has been one of the most important of my life. Ever since we bonded over cheap red wine and Neko Case in France, you've had my back. Thank you to all my kind-hearted friends who sent me gifts and cards in the final stretch and who kept me sane with Zooms and socially distanced walks – thank you Michelle Morton, Gianluca Mezzofiore, Theresa Morgan,

Gabi Doyle, Evan Kaplan, Stephen Rooney, and Alice Cross-Watson.

Gratitude to my therapist, Zara, for helping me through the most difficult and triggering parts of writing this book.

There aren't enough words in the English language to thank my lovely family for the never-ending love and support they have given me throughout the writing process (and during my lifetime). To the McArthurs, Lisa, Alan, Ellen and Freya, you are some of my favourite people on this planet. To the Carvill women, your strength is an inspiration to me and I am in total admiration of all of you.

Darling Jamie, thank you for being the best brother in the world. Thank you for a lifetime of understanding and patience. You were the first person I called when I got a book deal and you've been there throughout all the stress, tears, and self-doubt. Thank you also for all the prezzies along the way. You're a good egg.

Most of all, I want to thank my wonderful parents, Nancy and Gary. You both nurtured a love of storytelling in me from a young age that had a profound impact on my life. Mum, from sitting around the dining room table teaching me to write my name, to reading my little stories and encouraging me to write more, you have been my biggest supporter my whole life. I will never forget you proofreading my entire manuscript while recovering from surgery. Thank you for being the comforting voice on the end of the telephone when I was writing this book alone in lockdown. Dad, thank you for always believing in me and for standing by your very headstrong daughter who wanted to do nothing else in life but write. This might not be a Bertie Story, but I hope it makes you proud. Thank you for being my most trusted financial advice-giver and contract-reader-in-chief. You both made it possible for me to become a writer and I feel really blessed to be your daughter.